Memphis and the Delta Blues Trail

The ducks at the Peabody Hotel, Memphis

A COMPLETE GUIDE

1ST EDITION

MEMPHIS AND THE DELTA BLUES TRAIL

Melissa Gage &
Justin Gage

The Countryman Press
Woodstock, Vermont

Frontispiece: Credit: Courtesy Memphis Convention & Visitors Bureau

ISBN 978-1-58157-101-1

Cover photo courtesy of Memphis Convention & Visitors Bureau
Interior photographs by Melissa Gage unless otherwise specified
Maps by Mapping Specialists Ltd., Madison, WI, © The Countryman Press
Book design by Bodenweber Design
Composition by PerfecType, Nashville, TN

Published by The Countryman Press, P.O. Box 748, Woodstock, VT 05091

Distributed by W. W. Norton & Company, Inc., 500 Fifth Avenue, New York, NY 10110

Printed in the United States of America

10 9 8 7 6 5 4 3 2 1

GREAT DESTINATIONS TRAVEL GUIDEBOOK SERIES

Recommended by *National Geographic Traveler* and *Travel + Leisure* magazines

A CRISP AND CRITICAL APPROACH, FOR TRAVELERS WHO WANT TO LIVE LIKE LOCALS.
—*USA Today*

Great Destinations™ guidebooks are known for their comprehensive, critical coverage of regions of extraordinary cultural interest and natural beauty. Each title in this series is continuously updated with each printing to ensure accurate and timely information. All the books contain more than one hundred photographs and maps.

Current titles available:

THE ADIRONDACK BOOK

THE ALASKA PANHANDLE

ATLANTA

AUSTIN, SAN ANTONIO
  & THE TEXAS HILL COUNTRY

THE BERKSHIRE BOOK

BIG SUR, MONTEREY BAY
  & GOLD COAST WINE COUNTRY

CAPE CANAVERAL, COCOA BEACH
  & FLORIDA'S SPACE COAST

THE CHARLESTON, SAVANNAH
  & COASTAL ISLANDS BOOK

THE CHESAPEAKE BAY BOOK

THE COAST OF MAINE BOOK

COLORADO'S CLASSIC MOUNTAIN TOWNS

COSTA RICA: GREAT DESTINATIONS
  CENTRAL AMERICA

DOMINICAN REPUBLIC

THE FINGER LAKES BOOK

THE FOUR CORNERS REGION

GALVESTON, SOUTH PADRE ISLAND
  & THE TEXAS GULF COAST

GUATEMALA: GREAT DESTINATIONS
  CENTRAL AMERICA

THE HAMPTONS BOOK

HAWAII'S BIG ISLAND: GREAT DESTINATIONS
  HAWAII

HONOLULU & OAHU: GREAT DESTINATIONS
  HAWAII

THE JERSEY SHORE: ATLANTIC CITY TO CAPE MAY

KAUAI: GREAT DESTINATIONS HAWAII

LAKE TAHOE & RENO

LAS VEGAS

LOS CABOS & BAJA CALIFORNIA SUR:
  GREAT DESTINATIONS MEXICO

MAUI: GREAT DESTINATIONS HAWAII

MEMPHIS AND THE DELTA BLUES TRAIL

MICHIGAN'S UPPER PENINSULA

MONTREAL & QUEBEC CITY:
  GREAT DESTINATIONS CANADA

THE NANTUCKET BOOK

THE NAPA & SONOMA BOOK

NORTH CAROLINA'S OUTER BANKS
  & THE CRYSTAL COAST

NOVA SCOTIA & PRINCE EDWARD ISLAND

OAXACA: GREAT DESTINATIONS MEXICO

PALM BEACH, FORT LAUDERDALE, MIAMI
  & THE FLORIDA KEYS

PALM SPRINGS & DESERT RESORTS

PHILADELPHIA, BRANDYWINE VALLEY
  & BUCKS COUNTY

PHOENIX, SCOTTSDALE, SEDONA
  & CENTRAL ARIZONA

PLAYA DEL CARMEN, TULUM & THE RIVIERA MAYA:
  GREAT DESTINATIONS MEXICO

SALT LAKE CITY, PARK CITY, PROVO
  & UTAH'S HIGH COUNTRY RESORTS

SAN DIEGO & TIJUANA

SAN JUAN, VIEQUES & CULEBRA:
  GREAT DESTINATIONS PUERTO RICO

SAN MIGUEL DE ALLENDE & GUANAJUATO:
  GREAT DESTINATIONS MEXICO

THE SANTA FE & TAOS BOOK

THE SARASOTA, SANIBEL ISLAND & NAPLES BOOK

THE SEATTLE & VANCOUVER BOOK

THE SHENANDOAH VALLEY BOOK

TOURING EAST COAST WINE COUNTRY

TUCSON

VIRGINIA BEACH, RICHMOND
  & TIDEWATER VIRGINIA

WASHINGTON, D.C., AND NORTHERN VIRGINIA

YELLOWSTONE & GRAND TETON NATIONAL PARKS
  & JACKSON HOLE

YOSEMITE & THE SOUTHERN SIERRA NEVADA

The authors in this series are professional travel writers who have lived for many years in the regions they describe. Honest and painstakingly critical, full of information only a local can provide, Great Destinations guidebooks give you all the practical knowledge you need to enjoy the best of each region. Why not own them all?

CONTENTS

Acknowledgments

We would like to thank the following people for their assistance during the writing of this book: Kappi Allen, Luther Brown, Michael Curran, Jim O'Neal, Jackie Reed, Richard Stolle, and all of the friendly Memphians and people of the Mississippi Delta who offered their endless advice, opinions, and guidance. We would also like to thank all of our friends and family who have encouraged and supported us throughout this process.

Introduction

There is a rhythm in the air around Memphis, there always has been. I don't know what it is, but it's magic.
—Carl Perkins

The Delta's rich musical heritage runs deeper than the rolling waters of the Mississippi River. Long before a young Elvis Presley ever stepped foot inside Sun Studio, the cotton fields south of Memphis were alive with haunting lyrics of love, loss, and sorrow. Out of the flat, fertile fields of the Mississippi Delta, the blues were born. Blues music, with its syrupy lyrics and infectious rhythm, connects this region at its roots. From the ramshackle juke joints along Highway 61 to Memphis's famed barbecue shops, timeless melodies transport visitors back to another era.

While Memphis has long celebrated her musical heritage, historical landmarks throughout the Delta have been difficult to find and, at times, nearly forgotten. Thankfully, that's all starting to change. Founded in 2004, the Mississippi Blues Commission is working to create the Mississippi Blues Trail, which at its estimated completion in 2011 will be comprised of about 150 historical markers and interpretive sites around the state. As of press time, around 60 markers have been erected throughout the Delta and beyond, but more are going up every month. (For more information about the Blues Trail, visit www.msblues
trail.org.)

If the Mississippi Delta is the birthplace of the blues, Memphis gets credit for the conception of rock 'n' roll. Visitors flock to the city to tour legendary recording studios, listen to live music on Beale Street, and gawk at Graceland. An impressive number of museums pay homage to Memphis's musical heritage, while cultural attractions like the National Civil Rights Museum, located at the site of Martin Luther King Jr.'s assassination, are reminders of a long history of social unrest.

Located on a bluff overlooking the mighty Mississippi, Memphis has experienced a wave of development since the turn of the 21st century. Downtown's landscape has changed dramatically with the addition of Peabody Place entertainment complex (1999), AutoZone Park (2000), and the FedEx Forum (2004). The more recent rejuvenation of the historic South Main Arts District is a sign of continued city improvements, giving travelers even more reasons to visit.

To truly experience the birthplace of the blues, a stint in Memphis must be followed by an adventure down into the Delta, which is sparsely populated, often impoverished, and most definitely rural. If you're looking for cushy luxury and poolside cocktails, you'd best continue south to the casinos on Mississippi's Gulf Coast. But if you want to sleep at the hotel where Bessie Smith took her final breath, stand at the crossroads where Robert Johnson (allegedly) sold his soul to the devil, and sip a cold beer while listening to a living legend at one of the few remaining juke joints, the Blues Trail is a dream destination. The air may be thick as molasses and the pace slow, but the music will seep into your very pores. From fried catfish and friendly locals to endless cotton fields and jumpin' jukes, this is travel at its most authentic.

THE WAY THIS BOOK WORKS

This book will be useful whether you read it before your trip or peruse various listings as you travel from town to town. Within the Memphis chapter, lodging, restaurants, nightlife, and part of the shopping section are arranged by neighborhood, then alphabetically, while the other sections are simply arranged alphabetically. The Delta portion of the book begins with Clarksdale, as it's the best hub for a Mississippi blues excursion. Beyond Clarksdale, the book is arranged roughly from north to south, including the chapters and the towns within them. Highway 61, often referred to as the Blues Highway, is the main route through the Delta, but several places of interest are also located off US 82 and 49, as well as many smaller highways; planning your route is part of the fun of visiting the Delta. If your time is limited, be sure to see the If Time Is Short section of chapter 8 for our favorite picks in both Memphis and the Delta.

We've done our best to ensure that all of the information is as up-to-date as possible, but things change constantly, so always call ahead. In the Delta, businesses—especially juke joints—open and close at a rapid clip, so ask around before you go.

Prices at restaurants and accommodations have been indicated using the ranges below. Lodging prices are based on a per-room rate, double occupancy. Restaurant prices include an appetizer, entrée, dessert, tax, and tip, but not alcoholic beverages.

Price Codes

	Lodging	Dining
Inexpensive	Up to $90	Up to $15
Moderate	$90–130	$15–30
Expensive	$130–225	$30–65
Very Expensive	More than $225	More than $65

The following abbreviations are used for restaurants to identify what meals are served:

B—Breakfast
L—Lunch
D—Dinner
SB—Sunday brunch

Bronze Elvis statue at the end of Beale Street, Memphis

1

HISTORY

From King Cotton to the King of Rock 'n' Roll

delta \'del-t \n: an alluvial deposit at the mouth of a river

One can see a hundred years of history in twenty years in the Delta.

—*Shelby Foote*

The oval-shaped region known as the Mississippi Delta has often been described as beginning in the lobby of Memphis, Tennessee's, Peabody Hotel and ending on Catfish Row in Vicksburg, Mississippi. While this loose approximation rings fairly true, the region, forged by thousands of years of constant flooding, in reality encompasses parts of Tennessee, Mississippi, and Arkansas.

Like the country at large, the Delta's history has been heavily shaped by wars, the mechanization of agriculture, and social change. The fertile soil from the flood plain seems to have influenced every facet of life in the Delta from the ground up. From art and music to commerce and culture, the Delta's everlasting influence can be felt around the world.

NATIVE AMERICANS

Long before blues music ever made its way up the Mississippi, the Delta was settled by people thought to have originated from Siberia, who crossed into present-day Alaska via the Bering Straight land bridge during the Upper Paleolithic Ice Age. Migrating south nearly twelve thousand years ago, these Native Americans traveled in search of hospitable living conditions, which ultimately led them to settle in the Delta. With its temperate climate and abundant natural resources, the area made for an ideal home, flush with rich soil, easy access to fishing, and plenty of game for hunting.

The three major tribes that dominated the region were the Chickasaw, Natchez, and Choctaw. The word *Mississippi* is derived from Choctaw, translating to "father of the waters." These autonomous, self-governing tribes of the Mississippi River Valley were known as mound-building societies, and the mounds they built served various purposes, from burial sites and ceremonial rituals to village centers. Expert agriculturists, the Delta's Native Americans farmed the land for much of their sustenance and also hunted quail, deer, bear, and wild turkey.

By the time European explorers reached the New World, these tribes had relatively complex systems and subsystems in place for most aspects of everyday life. It was Spanish explorer Hernando de Soto who first encountered regional tribes in 1540, a meeting that led to the Chickasaw's attack on his camp, which nearly crushed the Spaniard's expedition. As more European explorers arrived over the next century, relations between the Natives and the newcomers improved with trade. But as the presence of the Euro-Americans continued to increase, relations with the Native Americans grew uneasy. By the mid-1800s, the U.S. government's Indian-removal process was in place, and Native tribes were moved to reservations west of the Mississippi. This trend forever changed the cultural landscape of the Delta, as well as that of the country at large.

EUROPEAN SETTLEMENT TO THE CIVIL WAR

Not long after Native Americans relinquished their land to the U.S. government, the city on the bluff became known as Memphis, a nod to the ancient Egyptian capital that also sat upon a powerful river: the Nile. The first settlers were European immigrants of primarily Irish and German descent, who were the first to erect churches, businesses, neighborhoods, and establish a local government. They were also the first to create commerce in a city whose rich delta soil would prove to be an invaluable agricultural resource for generations to come.

The antebellum South's power and influence strengthened with the proliferation of cotton as a cash crop, as did that of the Delta, thanks to this rich soil. Buoyed by the Mississippi River, upon whose bluffs she sits (hence the nickname Bluff City), Memphis soon became an important hub for transportation, distribution, and general North/South trade—all of which would place the city in the dubious position of being exceedingly important to both the Union and Confederate armies during America's Civil War.

As the unofficial capital of the Delta, and a natural port city, Memphis was a major player in the slave trade as well as a key hub in the Underground Railroad movement. Just as the river served in the transportation of slaves, it conversely aided some of the enslaved to escape to freedom. With the help of the Underground Railroad, runaway slaves were secretly stowed away upon boats traveling north.

As frictions between the North and South escalated, Tennessee seceded from the United States, joining the Confederate States of America (the Confederacy) in 1861. With its position on the river, Memphis's direct involvement in Civil War combat was inevitable. In June 1862, the First Battle of Memphis was fought between Union and Confederate troops on the Mississippi River. Strategically, the river—and who had control of it—was all important, and it led to an eventual turning point in the war. While the two naval forces were equally matched in terms of vessels, the Union far exceeded the Confederates in terms of weaponry, strategy, and overall experience. With this upper hand, the Union army disseminated the opposing Confederate fleet to gain control of the city and occupy Memphis throughout the duration of the war.

Of all the Civil War battles that took place in and around the Delta, none compared to the Vicksburg Campaign in Mississippi. Known as "The Gibraltar of the Confederacy," Vicksburg, like Memphis, was a strategic stronghold for the Southern army. Situated on a bluff, the city's natural defenses made it an ideal outpost—difficult to attack from the river, and easy to defend against approaching naval fleets. One of the key turning points in the Civil War, the Vicksburg Campaign included a series of battles and initiatives that culminated in Grant's Operations Against Vicksburg that lasted from March until July of 1863.

During the long siege, Confederate forces led by Lt. Gen. John C. Pemberton grew exhausted, diseased, and starved, finally surrendering to Grant on July 4, 1863.

THE YELLOW FEVER AND BEYOND

Following the Civil War, the Union's occupation ended, leaving Memphis largely unscathed compared to other Confederate states. By the 1870s, however, deaths linked to yellow fever began to plague the city. For more than a decade, yellow fever was transferred via the ever-present Delta mosquito, ravaging Memphis and killing thousands. Many Memphians fled the city for fear of death, eventually leaving less than twenty thousand residents remaining in the city, a fourth of whom fell victim to the epidemic. By the mid-1880s, the disease finally subsided, yet it its wake lay an economically devastated city.

Keeping an eye firmly planted on the future, Memphis began to see prosperity again in the early 20th century. The city's new status as the world's largest spot cotton market boosted the economy to new heights. Another contributing factor to the resurgence of Memphis business and commerce was the hardwood market. With a significant number of lumber mills in close proximity to the city, Memphis capitalized on the country's increased demand for timber. The city's convenient access to both the Mississippi River and the railroad system supported the growth of these cornerstone industries.

By the 1950s, the Bluff City had become the capital of the mid-South and one of the largest urban centers in the southern United States. Part of the city's success can be attributed to famed Memphis politician E. H. "Boss" Crump. In 1910, Crump's election as mayor ushered in a new era of Memphis reforms designed to clean up the city. Crump built a political machine whose legacy and influence would be felt in Memphis for decades. In his relatively short time as mayor (he was ousted from office in 1916), Crump focused on abolishing establishments like brothels and gambling houses, and he created parks and public works throughout the city. After his stint as mayor, Crump became no less of a political force, holding various elected offices, including that of congressman.

THE GREAT MIGRATION FROM THE MISSISSIPPI DELTA

From the time of the First World War to the 1970s, nearly a million African Americans left the Mississippi Delta in search of social equality, job opportunities, and a better overall quality of life. Northern cities were generally the destination, and Chicago was especially popular as the city was easily accessible by train. The first wave of migration can be attributed, in large part, to poverty, poor educational opportunities, oppressive sharecropper conditions, and Jim Crow laws. The availability of industrial jobs in northern cities like Chicago was also a major factor in the decision of many to leave their Southern homes for a seemingly better life up north. During the World Wars, labor jobs were especially plentiful as the immigrant labor force dwindled and American workers were called to military service.

The devastating Great Flood of 1927 also contributed to the historic migration. Excessive rainfall and rising waters led to hundreds of broken levies that resulted in flooding over 27,000 square miles, including major Delta cities like Greenville and Vicksburg. The flood lasted several months, resulting in more than 200 deaths and the displacement of 700,000 people, many of them Mississippi natives. Many of those displaced from the

Delta lost everything in the flood, and they stayed put in their new homes up North, where they rebuilt their lives.

Into the 1930s and beyond, the mechanization of agriculture also had a dramatic affect on life in the Delta, leaving many rural laborers without jobs. Machines replaced farm workers, and many moved north in search of job opportunities. As the people of the Mississippi Delta established new homes, they brought the region's culture with them. The most notable influence, of course, was the blues, which exploded onto the Chicago music scene, where it evolved from the acoustic blues that grew from the fields of the Mississippi Delta.

THE CIVIL RIGHTS MOVEMENT

We hold these truths to be self-evident, that all men are created equal, that they are endowed by their Creator with certain unalienable rights, that among these are life, liberty, and the pursuit of happiness.
—Thomas Jefferson, 1776

Jim Crow: Between 1876 and 1965 various states (primarily in the South) set up ordinances, known as Jim Crow laws, that required all public works to be segregated under the guise of "separate but equal." Eventually, the Supreme Court overruled these laws under the Civil Rights Act of 1964 and the Voting Rights Act of 1965.

In many ways, the Delta, and especially Memphis, can be viewed as a microcosm of what was happening throughout America during the civil rights movement. Following the Emancipation Proclamation, the Civil War, and the Reconstruction period, many states—especially in the South—treated African Americans like second-class citizens. Mandatory segregation of the two races affected everything from public drinking fountains and restrooms to schools and, perhaps most famously, seating on public transportation. In 1955, a black woman in Montgomery, Alabama, named Rosa Parks refused to give up her seat to a white passenger, which instigated the Montgomery Bus Boycott. The same year, a 14-year-old African American boy visiting the Delta from Chicago was brutally murdered for wolf-whistling at a white woman. Emmett Till was killed just north of Greenwood in Money, Mississippi, his body later recovered from the Tallahatchie River. Both of these events helped spark a movement that laid the groundwork for a nonviolent social revolution.

In the 1960s, two tragic assassinations in the region fueled racial tensions and spurred the civil rights movement. Medgar Evers, an African American civil rights activist, was an outspoken supporter of desegregation. A field secretary for the NAACP, Evers was involved in Emmett Till's murder investigation and played a key role in forcing the University of Mississippi to enroll an African American student, James Meredith. On June 12, 1963, a member of the Ku Klux Klan shot Medgar Evers in the back, killing him in his driveway in Jackson, Mississippi. Evers was carrying a box of NAACP T-shirts with the motto JIM CROW MUST GO.

By the end of the decade, tensions came to a boiling point. In 1968, Memphis's black sanitation workers went on strike after a malfunctioning truck fatally crushed two Memphis garbage collectors. The Reverend Martin Luther King Jr. came to the city in support of the strike, addressing a group of black city elders and civil rights activists, and encouraging others to join the strike in a citywide work stoppage. In his March 18th address, King praised the striking sanitation workers for "demonstrating that we can stick together. You are demonstrating that we are all tied in a single garment of destiny, and that if one black person suffers, if one black person is down, we are all down."

A few days later, King led a demonstration that quickly (and unintentionally) turned chaotic as looting and violence erupted. One teenage boy was shot and killed, and the police resorted to using billy clubs and tear gas. City officials declared martial law, bringing in four thousand National Guard troops to restore the peace. On April 3, King again returned to Memphis to address a group of sanitation workers with a speech that would foreshadow his death: "Like anybody, I would like to live a long life. Longevity has its place. But I'm not concerned about that now . . . I've seen the Promised Land. I may not get there with you. But I want you to know tonight that we, as a people, will get to the Promised Land." The following evening, King was shot and killed on the balcony of the Lorraine Motel. Life in Memphis, and throughout the United States, would never be the same.

MEMPHIS AND THE DELTA SINCE THE 1970S

After the King assassination, Memphis entered the 1970s in what would turn out to be a decade of decay and stagnation. Much of downtown was crumbling, and the once-vibrant Beale Street was virtually dead, as was the multiracial music-hit factory, Stax Records. Neither ducks nor guests stayed at the famed Peabody Hotel, and its doors stayed closed for nearly a decade. In a final blow, Memphis's most famous ambassador, Elvis Presley, died at age 42 in 1977. As the decade came to an end, city leaders and developers began to formulate a plan of revitalization.

In 1981, the Peabody Hotel reopened under new ownership after multimillion-dollar renovations. Restored to its former glory, the icon ushered in a new wave of downtown revitalization. Around the same time (though several years after Congress officially declared the street "The Home of The Blues"), Beale Street finally began to reclaim its former glory. The city purchased all of the properties covering the three main blocks of Beale, and new shops and clubs gradually revitalized the strip. Along with the rebirth of Beale as a popular destination for music tourism, the city saw the opening of Graceland in 1982 and Sun Studio in 1987. Around this same time, Mud Island River Park opened, and the monthlong Memphis In May festival (founded in 1977) picked up steam. Tourism wasn't the only Memphis industry booming in the '80s: In 1983, the Memphis-based shipping company Federal Express became the first U.S. company to reach revenues of $1 billion within 10 years of startup without merger or acquisition.

Progress in Memphis slowed in the 1990s as the city battled a recession, but the 21st century brought new business, industry, and opportunities. The millennium saw the opening of the AutoZone ballpark in downtown Memphis, home of the Redbirds, and arguably one of the nicest AAA parks in the country. In 2004, the NBA Grizzlies were granted a new home with the construction of the FedEx Forum, which anchors the Beale Street Entertainment District and shares real estate with the Rock 'n' Soul Museum (new in 2000). In 2001, the National Civil Rights Museum, partially housed in the Lorraine Motel, expanded to include the building across the street from which James Earl Ray fired upon Martin Luther King Jr. In addition to downtown's 21st-century attractions and ever-expanding amenities, historic neighborhoods like the South Main Arts District are actively being restored, with roots firmly planted in the past.

Progress in the rural, sparsely populated Delta has been significantly slower than that of its northern neighbor. The population never quite recovered from the great migration of the 20th century, and though agriculture has remained essential to the region's economy, constantly evolving new technologies make the need for human labor minimal. Likewise, the decreased importance of the Mississippi River as a transportation and trade hub has led to the decline of many riverside towns. One fairly recent development, however, has led to an economic upturn in some Delta cities. The legalization of gambling in Mississippi has benefited the economy of cities like Vicksburg, Greenville, and most notably, Tunica. Once the poorest county in the country, the Tunica area is now booming, thanks in large part to revenues from its many gaming venues.

It has only been within the past decade or so that the Mississippi Delta has truly begun to embrace, preserve, and promote the area's incredibly rich musical heritage. As more Blues Trail markers are erected and historic landmarks are restored, new blues festivals continue to pop up, and the old standbys continue to grow and expand. While a great number of European tourists have been visiting the Delta in search of blues history for years, many Americans are finally starting to catch on. Still, as historic sites are increasingly recognized, juke joints continue to struggle, and many of the original bluesmen are creeping up into their 90s. The Delta's greatest hope may just be a new wave of blues-based tourism, which not only would help preserve the region's heritage, but perhaps inspire a new generation to carry on the musical traditions of the Mississippi Delta.

Shaping Musical History

The Delta, and more acutely, Memphis, is responsible for shaping the musical genres that would become known as blues, soul, R&B, and rock 'n' roll. But it was the blues that started it all. Originally developed in the fields of Delta plantations, the blues took shape from spirituals and work songs, including field hollers, call and response, and oral traditions that originated in Africa. American composer and musician W. C. Handy, known as the "Father of the Blues," is given credit for popularizing the regional style of music after a chance encounter at a Tutwiler train depot with a bluesman who was scraping the blade of his knife against a guitar, singing "goin' where the Southern crosses the Dog." Handy was so taken with what he heard that he spent the rest of his life's work emulating the sound, contributing greatly to the evolution of the blues from its Delta roots. The popularity of blues music extended to Memphis and beyond, spurring various subgenres like big band blues, jump blues, boogie woogie, and, of course, the electric Chicago blues. Individually, and collectively, these distinct styles would influence the future of music well beyond the blues genre.

In addition to the blues, Memphis was a hotbed for soul, R&B, country, and rock 'n' roll. The list of labels and recording studios that sprung from the Memphis soil reads like a "who's who" of half a century of popular music. Sun Studio, Stax Records, Hi Records, and Ardent Studio all started in Memphis. Some of the many artists who emerged from these institutions include B. B. King, Ike Turner, Rufus Thomas, Elvis Presley, Johnny Cash, Al Green, Otis Redding, the Staple Singers, Wilson Pickett, Booker T. and the MGs, Sam & Dave, Isaac Hayes, and Big Star.

In the 1960s, the "Memphis sound" was often imitated, never replicated, but the King assassination forever changed the city's music scene. Before the tragedy, black and white artists easily worked together for the greater good of the music, but after King's assassination on April 4, 1968, there was an uneasiness in Memphis that permeated the music. By the early 70s, the boomtown era of hit after hit came to an end, and in 1976, the great Memphis musical beacon, Stax Records, filed for bankruptcy. While the local music scene may not have returned to the heyday of decades past, Memphis today is home to all manner of blues, soul, R&B, and rock 'n' roll acts, including a healthy independent local music scene that includes artists like Lucero and Harltan T. Bobo, independent record stores Goner and Shangri-La Records, and venues including the Hi-Tone and Young Avenue Deli.

2

TRANSPORTATION

Cruising the Blues Highway

The Mississippi Delta is a rural, sparsely populated, impossibly flat region that hasn't changed much since the blues were born here. Perhaps the biggest change came after World War II and into the 1970s, when a staggering number of African Americans living in the Delta traveled north for better jobs and a higher quality of life. As agriculture jobs tightened up and the mechanized cotton picker was introduced, many African Americans (including quite a few bluesmen) hopped on a train or a Greyhound bus to better their lives in Chicago and elsewhere.

Today, the Greyhound still runs through the Delta, but train travel is extremely limited. To truly experience the Delta, visitors will need a car. There's no better way to travel between the region's tiny towns, and driving through the endless cotton fields is part of the experience. A car is also indispensible in Memphis, as many of the city's attractions are beyond downtown's limits, and the public transportation system isn't always the most convenient option. The exception is downtown's trolley system, which follows the Main Street route once traveled by the trolley's mule-drawn predecessor. Riding the trolley is like taking a step back in time: Restored vintage cars feature period details like brass accents, hand-carved mahogany corbels, and antique lighting fixtures.

GETTING TO MEMPHIS AND THE DELTA

By Plane

Several major airlines fly into the midsize **Memphis International Airport**, including AirTran, American Airlines, Continental Airlines, Delta Airlines, KLM, Northwest Airlines, United Airlines, and US Airways. Located in a somewhat undesirable area 11 miles south of downtown Memphis, the airport is a quick 20-minute drive into downtown. Expect it to take at least twice that long during rush hour. Taxis and shuttles are available outside baggage claim at Terminal B on the airport's ground level. A one-way taxi ride downtown will cost around $27. Check with your hotel before catching a cab, as quite a few downtown accommodations offer complimentary shuttles.

Memphis is the best jumping-off point for exploring the Blues Trail. Whether or not you're planning on driving to Memphis, you'll need a car to venture down into the Delta. Starting in New Orleans is another option, although expect it to take a little longer to hit the heart of the Blues Trail, which is located in the northern half of Mississippi. Situated

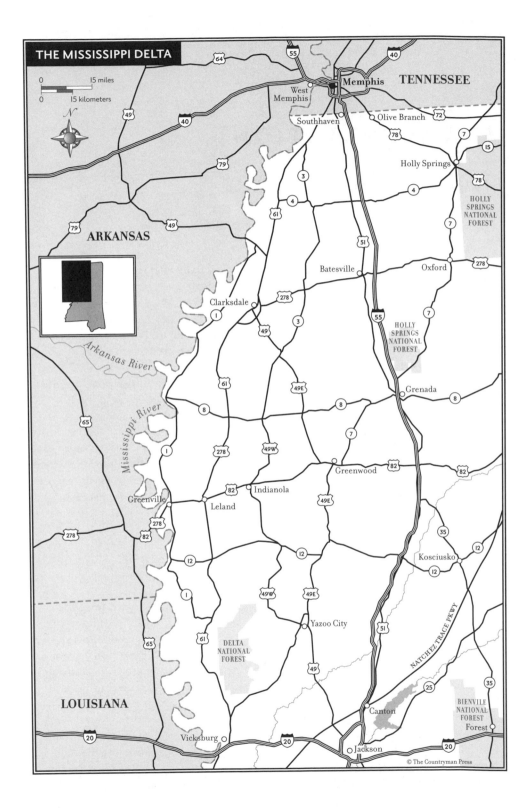

THE MISSISSIPPI DELTA

between New Orleans and Memphis—east of Highway 61—Jackson, Mississippi's, smaller airport offers a third option for arrival by air; the drive from Jackson to Memphis takes just under three and a half hours. Finally, tiny regional airports are also located in Tupelo, Greenville, and Meridian, Mississippi. No matter where you arrive by air, your first order of business should be to rent a car.

By Car

Memphis can be accessed via two major highways: I-40 from the east and west, and I-55 from the north and south. The two interstates converge in Arkansas just west of Memphis before splitting once again to cross the Mississippi River and enter downtown Memphis from two different bridges—the iconic Hernando de Soto Bridge (aka the M Bridge) north via I-40, and the older, cantilevered Memphis–Arkansas Bridge to the south via I-55. Within the city limits, the I-240 loop circles the city and connects downtown to the surrounding suburbs.

To get to the Delta from Memphis, head south on Highway 61, aka the Blues Highway, straight into Clarksdale. If you're driving to the Delta from New Orleans, hop on I-55 and head north to Jackson. From there, you can head west on I-20 toward Vicksburg, then drive north on Highway 61. If you're entering the Delta from the east or west (south of Memphis), take I-20 east from Dallas, or I-20 west from Birmingham, then head north from Vicksburg or Jackson.

By Bus

Serving 2,400 locations around the country, **Greyhound** buses offer access to both Memphis and the Delta from all over the country. Memphis's Greyhound bus station is

Memphis's iconic Hernando de Soto Bridge connects downtown Memphis to West Memphis, Arkansas. Courtesy Memphis Convention & Visitors Bureau

The infamous crossroads of Blues Highway 61 and US 49, Clarksdale

located downtown near AutoZone Park at 203 Union Avenue (901-523-9253). In the Delta, the bus line serves **Clarksdale** (662-627-7893), **Cleveland** (662-846-5112), **Greenville** (662-335-2633), **Indianola** (662-887-2716), **Jackson** (601-353-6342), **Rolling Fork** (662-873-2866; tickets are not sold at this location), **Vicksburg** (601-638-8389), and **Yazoo City** (662-746-3155). There are also bus stops, but not full stations, in Belzoni and Tunica. For information on rates and schedules, go to www.greyhound.com or call 1-800-231-2222.

By Train

AMTRAK's City of New Orleans route travels between Chicago and New Orleans, with stops in Memphis, Greenwood, Yazoo City, and Jackson. The train pays homage to New Orleans by serving cuisine like shrimp rémoulade, red beans and rice, and jambalaya. The Memphis AMTRAK station is located on the downtown trolley line at 545 South Main Street. For information on rates and schedules, visit www.amtrak.com or call 1-800-872-7245.

By Boat

For a unique experience, consider boarding a paddle-wheeler for a cruise down the Mississippi River. **Mississippi River Cruises** (1-800-510-4002; www.mississippi rivercruises.com) offers steamboat travel on historic boats and period reproductions. Ports of departure include Memphis and New Orleans, and a variety of trips are available.

GETTING AROUND MEMPHIS

By Rental Car

Unless you're planning on sticking to downtown attractions, you'll need a car to explore Memphis. Sites like Graceland, the Stax Museum, and Sun Studio are beyond downtown's limit, so unless you opt for a guided tour or a hotel package (some of which include transportation), plan on having your own vehicle. Several companies offer car rental at the airport, including: **Alamo** (901-345-0070), **Avis** (901-346-6129), **Budget** (901-398-8888), **Dollar** (1-866-434-2226), **Enterprise** (901-396-3736), **Hertz** (901-345-5680), **National** (901-345-0070), and **Thrifty** (901 345-0170). Contact any of these companies at the airport's telephone bank in baggage claim; all rental companies provide courtesy shuttles to their lots, located outside the terminal.

Memphis's main roads are conveniently set on a grid system, with Union and Poplar avenues connecting downtown to Midtown on an east–west access. From Midtown, Poplar Avenue runs east into the heart of East Memphis. Getting to East Memphis from downtown, drivers may choose between surface streets like Poplar, or the I-240 loop. Not surprisingly, the surface streets can be slightly faster during rush hour; otherwise, the highway is the quickest way to go.

Parking around Memphis is generally free and plentiful, with the exception of downtown, where you'll find metered parking and pay garages. Metered spaces cost 50 cents per hour and are free weekdays after 6 PM, and all day Saturday and Sunday (special events are often the exception). Garages offer plenty of parking, and though they vary in price, the maximum you'll pay is $1 per half hour, with a $12 all-day maximum. Several garages offer early-bird and late-bird rates and shopping validation. Special-event parking is often

Crime-Proofing Your Rental Car

Theft from motor vehicles is a serious problem in Memphis, but there are a few steps you can take to avoid a broken window, or worse. First, always park in well-lit places, and in garages with security rather than on the street, when possible. Second, don't leave anything valuable in your car—and we're not just talking about the obvious, like laptops and luggage. Always keep small items like CDs, change, cell phones, sunglasses, and even clothing items out of sight. Lastly, when you're walking to your car at night, it's a good idea to have your keys at the ready, rather than having to dig around for them when you get to your vehicle.

inflated.

By Bus

The **Memphis Area Transit Authority (MATA)** offers public bus transportation around Memphis and the surrounding suburbs. Call 901-274-MATA, or visit www.matatransit .com for route information. While it's not the easiest or most convenient way for tourists to get around, traveling by bus is inexpensive. The base fare is $1.50, and exact change is required. Transfers are 10 cents, and discounts are offered for students, seniors, and individuals with disabilities. You can pick up a route map and ask for directions at downtown's North End Terminal, located at 444 North Main Street.

By Trolley

Also operated by MATA, downtown's **1920s-style trolleys** (both vintage and reproductions) shuttle individuals around downtown via a track that runs down Main Street, then loops around on Riverside Drive. An additional track goes east on Madison Avenue to Cleveland Street. The Main Street and Riverfront lines run every 10 minutes from 6 AM to 11 PM Monday through Thursday, 6 AM–1 AM on Friday, 9:30 AM–1 AM on Saturday, and 10 AM–6 PM on Sunday. The base fare is $1 (50 cents for seniors and the disabled), and exact change is required. From 11 AM to 1:30 PM, a special lunch fare is offered for 50 cents. Visitors who plan to get around downtown via trolley for a day or two should consider buying a discounted trolley pass from the North End Terminal at 444 North Main Street, where you can also pick up a trolley map. Passes include two trips for $1.50, an all-day pass for $3.50, and a three-day pass for $8.

By Taxi

Don't expect to be able to hail a cab on the streets of Memphis. Unlike cities like San Francisco and New York, taxis are few and far between in Memphis. The easiest solution is to call for a cab—or have your hotel call for you. Keep the numbers of a couple different companies with you for easy pickup. Note that Memphis cabs aren't always the most reliable when it comes to arriving on time, so if you're on a schedule, or heading to the airport, allow extra time, and always order a cab before you're ready to go. Two companies to try are **Yellow Cab/Checker Cab** (901-577-7777) or **Metro Cab** (901-323-3333). Fares are $3.80 for the first mile, $1.80 for each additional mile, and $1 for each additional passenger. The fare from the airport to downtown Memphis is around $27.

Memphis trolleys stop near most major downtown attractions.

On Foot

Downtown is the only truly walkable area in Memphis, other than individual neighborhoods like Midtown's Cooper-Young area. Combined with the trolley, you can get to most of downtown's attractions fairly easily. A word of warning: Walking downtown (or anywhere in Memphis) alone at night is never advisable, and even if you're in a pair or a small group, always avoid walking through less-populated areas of the city. If you're out somewhere like Beale Street until the wee hours, it's always advisable to call a cab to take you back to your hotel.

GETTING AROUND THE DELTA

By Rental Car

While Greyhound buses travel between many Delta towns (see the By Bus section), the best way to get around the Delta is undoubtedly by car. For a list of rental car companies at the Memphis airport, see the By Rental Car section. If you're flying into New Orleans, rental companies include: **Alamo** (504-469-0532), **Avis** (504-464-9511), **Budget** (504-467-1296), **Dollar** (504-467-2286), **Enterprise** (504-468-3018), **Hertz** (504-468-3675), **National** (504-469-0532), and **Thrifty** (504-463-0800).

As far as getting around the Delta, I-55 may be the quickest route from New Orleans to Memphis, but US 61 (the Blues Highway) is the heart of the Blues Trail. US 49 snakes through several towns of interest after veering off from 61, and the stretch of US 82 that connects Greenville and Greenwood passes through key stops like the town of Indianola. Don't miss the chance to drive a stint on MS 1, otherwise known as the Great River Road, which hugs the Mississippi River and goes through tiny towns like Rosedale.

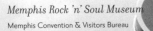

Memphis Rock 'n' Soul Museum
Memphis Convention & Visitors Bureau

3

Memphis

Birthplace of Rock 'n' Roll

Memphis is proud of its musical heritage, and it should be. An American gem, the city shaped the course of popular music not only within this country, but throughout the world—not bad for a medium-size metropolis of well under a million people. Of course, the city's most notable contribution to music is the introduction of rock 'n' roll. While Elvis often gets credit for creating this revolutionary new style of music, the first real rock 'n' roll record was actually "Rocket 88," recorded in 1951 by Jackie Brenston and his Delta Cats (led by Ike Turner) at Sun Studio. Today, everyone from casual music fans to hard-core Elvis enthusiasts flock to Memphis to tour Sun Studio and Graceland, where rock 'n' roll was born, and Beale Street, where the blues continue to flourish. Of course, Memphis also has plenty of soul, as visitors to the hit factory Stax Records and the Rock 'n' Soul Museum are sure to discover.

Memphis is a city of many monikers. In addition to being the Home of the Blues and Birthplace of Rock 'n' Roll, this is also the Bluff City or River City, thanks to a prime location on the banks of the mighty Mississippi River. And let's not forget that Memphis is the Pork Barbecue Capital of the World. Leaving the city without experiencing her unbeatable 'cue would be like traveling to Paris and skipping the Eiffel Tower. While music sites and attractions tend to be the city's main draw, there's much more to Memphis than Beale Street and Graceland. Beyond making its mark on music history, Memphis played a crucial role in the civil rights movement, a heritage that's preserved at the National Civil Rights Museum in downtown's Lorraine Motel, where Martin Luther King Jr. was assassinated on April 4, 1968. Like the majority of the city's attractions, the museum is located downtown, an area that has experienced a monumental transformation over the past decade. As new restaurants and attractions have exploded on the scene, crumbling historic areas have been given a much-needed face-lift. The city's trendiest new neighborhood is downtown's historic South Main Arts District, where galleries and boutiques share space with lofts and longtime favorites like Ernestine & Hazel's bar and the Arcade Restaurant. Antique trolleys are an easy and unique way to explore all that downtown Memphis has to offer.

Beyond downtown, Memphis is home to several areas worth exploring—namely, Midtown. In addition to being the location of Sun Studio, primarily residential Midtown (just east of the city) is also home to gems like the hip Cooper-Young area, which features a slew of restaurants, shops, and trendy nightlife. Just around the corner, the Central Avenue Antiques District offers endless shops stocked with antique treasures. There's also

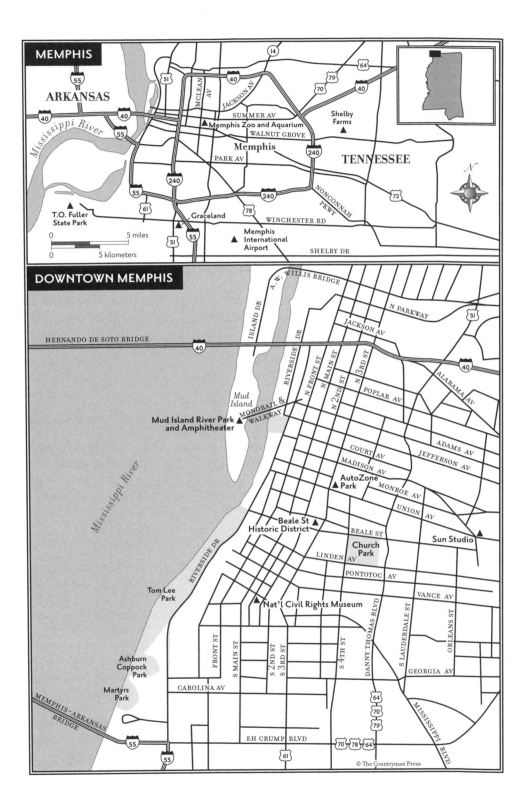

Made in Memphis

Rock 'n' roll isn't the only American institution born in Memphis. The city spawned the modern, self-serve supermarket in 1916 when Clarence Saunders opened the first Piggly Wiggly store. You can stroll through a life-size replica of the first Piggly Wiggly, which is tiny in comparison to today's megamarkets, at the Pink Palace Museum—housed in Clarence Saunders's mansion. Then, in 1952, a family road trip inspired Kemmons Wilson to open an affordable, quality hotel in Memphis called the Holiday Inn. Less than a decade later, more than a hundred Holiday Inns were spread across America. The Bluff City is also home to worldwide shipping giant FedEx. Although the company formerly known as Federal Express was founded in Little Rock, Arkansas, in 1971, operations moved to Memphis in 1973, and that's exactly where company headquarters have remained ever since.

Overton Park, Midtown's historic green space where the Memphis Zoo and Brooks Museum of Art are located. Funky Midtown is also home to several legendary dive bars and the city's best indie music venues, including the Hi-Tone and Young Avenue Deli. As the bumper stickers around town declare: Midtown is Memphis.

As fellow blues travelers are sure to tell you, some of the city's best spots are off the beaten path. While Beale Street is an obvious place to seek out live music, blues enthusiasts will argue that a more authentic experience can be found at juke joints like Wild Bill's, tucked away in a lesser-known corner of the city. Graceland and the Stax Museum are located on the south side of town, an area that's both rough around the edges and home to legendary spots like the Four Way Restaurant and Al Green's church. For a true taste of Memphis, start at the city's many well-trodden attractions, and then venture off the tourist track to experience the true heart and soul of the city.

LODGING

The majority of Memphis tourist hotels are located downtown, close to endless dining options and top attractions like Beale Street. Of course, downtown is also where hotel rates tend to be the highest. If you don't have a car or have limited time to visit, staying downtown is worth the extra cash. You'll still have to find your way to attractions like Graceland and Sun Studio (try the latter's free shuttle), but you'll be in the heart of the action and can easily walk or ride the trolley to get around downtown.

If you do have a car (which is recommended), you can save money by staying in Midtown or East Memphis. While Midtown's properties are limited, downtown is only a few minutes away, and you'll be close to Cooper-Young and Overton Park. As much as East Memphis is known for sprawling suburbs, endless strip malls, and office buildings, the area is also home to fantastic restaurants, upscale shopping, tony neighborhoods, and a wide range of accommodations. While East Memphis is located a good 20 minutes from downtown (more in traffic), the rates are often significantly lower than comparable accommodations downtown. Families sometimes prefer the safety, comfort, and amenities of the East Memphis suburbs. Midtown is fairly close by, and attractions like the Botanic Gardens and Dixon Gallery are just minutes away.

Finally, if Graceland is your primary destination, the most convenient place to stay is either at the Heartbreak Hotel or

Days Inn Graceland, both just steps away from the mansion. Heartbreak Hotel also offers a free downtown shuttle. If you're on a budget, you'll find plenty of inexpensive motels on Elvis Presley Boulevard, surrounding the airport, and even across the bridge from downtown in West Memphis, Arkansas.

Lodging Price Codes

Inexpensive	Up to $90
Moderate	$90–130
Expensive	$130–225
Very Expensive	More than $225

Downtown

Comfort Inn Downtown

901-526-0583
www.choicehotels.com
100 N. Front St., Memphis, TN 38103
One block east of Riverside Dr.
Price: Expensive
Credit Cards: Yes
Handicap Access: Yes

From the outside, the 15-floor Comfort Inn may not look like much, but the reliable property offers clean, basic rooms and a central downtown location for rates significantly lower than many other downtown hotels. Located across from Mud Island, the hotel is less than a block from downtown's Main Street trolley line. From the upper floors, rooms boast views of the Pyramid, Mud Island, and the Mississippi River. Accommodations are simple and tasteful, with a minifridge, microwave, safe, work desk, and Internet access. For a little extra space, ask for a corner king or book one of the property's suites. A free continental breakfast is served each morning, and guests pay a minimal fee ($5 per day) for on-site parking. Bus parking is also available, so don't be surprised to see busloads of tourists. Additional amenities include business and fitness centers, and, most impressively, a rooftop pool with fantastic views of the river and the iconic Hernando de Soto Bridge.

A rooftop pool with river views is a nice bonus at the value-minded Comfort Inn Downtown.

Crowne Plaza Hotel Memphis

901-525-1800
www.cpmemphis.net
300 N. Second St., Memphis, TN 38105
Two blocks from Cook Convention Center
Price: Expensive
Credit Cards: Yes
Handicap Access: Yes
Special Features: Free wireless

This upscale property was completely renovated before reopening in 2008. Located on the Pyramid side of downtown near the convention center, the swanky property features stylish decor, from the marble lobby to sleek, modern guest rooms. Quiet, eye-catching accommodations feature a seating nook with an armchair, ottoman, and cubelike side table, and a contemporary work space. Comforts and little luxuries include 32-inch flat-screen TVs, a pulsing showerhead in the marble-tiled bathroom, and the Crowne Plaza's "Sleep Advantage" bedding, which goes beyond cushy linens to include a sleep CD, eye mask, earplugs, and lavender aromatherapy spray. Rooms on the Executive Club level feature a few additional in-room amenities, plus access to the 11th-floor concierge lounge. There are also three well-equipped two- and three-room suites. Dining includes American cuisine at the Garden Cafe and lite bites and cocktails in the Lobby Lounge. Guests have access to a fitness center and a very nice seasonal outdoor pool area. Ample meeting space and proximity to the convention center makes this a popular choice for business meetings and events. The downtown trolley is also within easy walking distance.

Doubletree Hotel Memphis Downtown

901-528-1800
www.memphisdoubletree.com
185 Union Ave., Memphis, TN 38103
Across from AutoZone Park
Price: Expensive
Credit Cards: Yes
Handicap Access: Yes
Special Features: Free wireless; on-site T.G.I. Friday's

Located directly across from AutoZone Park, home of the Memphis Redbirds baseball team, this 10-floor property offers contemporary style and comfort. Inside, the dimly lit lobby sets the tone, stretching six stories in height with three glass elevators overlooking a sleek, cushy living area. The lobby's centerpiece, however, is the building's original brick facade, which lends a dramatic design element to the common area. Behind the facade, guests will find a T.G.I. Friday's in the corner of the property. Spacious, upscale accommodations are both comfortable and stylish, with cushy beds featuring plush-top mattresses and down comforters, a contemporary armchair with a leather ottoman, and modern design elements throughout. For more space, suites with separate living areas are also available. Well-appointed bathrooms feature tile showers and spacious granite countertops. Decor within the accommodations and throughout the property gives a nod to Memphis's musical heritage, featuring W. C. Handy posters, sheet music for "Great Balls of Fire," and modern, music-themed artwork. Guests have access to a fitness center and rooftop pool on the property's second floor. The bustling hotel is just steps from both Beale Street and Peabody Place.

Hampton Inn & Suites Memphis—Beale Street

901-260-4000
www.bealestreetsuites.hamptoninn.com
175 Peabody Pl., Memphis, TN 38103
Steps from Beale St.
Price: Expensive–Very Expensive
Credit Cards: Yes
Handicap Access: Yes

Special Features: Free wireless in lobby; high-speed Internet in rooms

You can't get any closer to Beale Street than the downtown Hampton Inn, which literally overlooks the action from its prime corner perch. There's an extra charge for rooms with balconies, but you really can't beat the view, which includes W. C. Handy Park, where seasonal concerts and prime people-watching provide hours of entertainment. Light sleepers take note: Ask for a room on the quiet side of the building, or request earplugs from the front desk. The FedEx Forum is only a block away, and hotel guests have direct access to Peabody Place via a skywalk. The property is home to nearly 144 upscale rooms, including 30 suites. Tastefully decorated accommodations feature nice extras like 32-inch flat-screen HDTVs and lap desks for working from the comfort of your bed. Roomy suites boast well-equipped kitchens and separate living rooms that may feature a sofa bed or recliner. Guests have access to a fitness center, a small indoor pool, and a business center. In the morning, a complimentary breakfast is served off a well-decorated lobby that's stocked with comfy couches, breakfast tables, and a TV; breakfast includes hot items like eggs, sausage, and French toast sticks.

Holiday Inn Select Downtown Memphis
901-525-5491, 1-888-300-5491
www.hisdowntownmemphis.com
160 Union Ave., Memphis, TN 38103
Across from the Peabody and next door to AutoZone Park
Price: Expensive—Very Expensive
Credit Cards: Yes
Handicap Access: Yes

This 192-room property is situated in the heart of downtown Memphis. Beale Street and the FedEx Forum are just a few blocks away, and the landmark Rendezvous restaurant is in an alley adjacent to the property—

hence the smell that's been making your mouth water. Amenities include a fourth-floor terrace pool, fitness room, and business center. Rooms feature traditional decor, free wireless Internet access, and standard amenities. For a little more space, opt for a corner Executive room with extras like a microwave, minifridge, sofa bed, and robe. On-site dining options are a definite bonus. The Russwood Park Sports Bar and Grill is a popular spot before and after nearby Redbirds games, featuring eight flat-screen TVs and live music on the weekends. The Holiday Inn Select is also home to the popular Sekisui sushi restaurant.

The Inn at Hunt Phelan
901-525-8225
www.huntphelan.com
533 Beale St., Memphis, TN 38103
Two blocks east of Beale Street Entertainment District
Price: Very Expensive
Credit Cards: Yes
Handicap Access: Limited
Special Features: Wireless Internet; valet parking

Steeped in Old South luxury, this gorgeously restored antebellum mansion offers visitors an authentic step back in time. The address may be on Beale Street, but this genteel oasis is tucked away on the quiet end of the street, two blocks away from the raucous blues clubs. Designed by famed architect Robert Mills, who is also responsible for D.C.'s Washington Monument and the U.S. Treasury Building, the house dates back to the late 1820s. In the Civil War years, Ulysses S. Grant set up his headquarters in the home's library. Later, Hunt Phelan hosted President Jefferson Davis and many other distinguished guests.

Beyond the home's iconic white columns, four downstairs rooms serve as dining rooms for the inn's four-star restaurant. Down the hallway, the more casual Veranda Grill features a cozy bar area, exposed brick walls, and outdoor seating that spills into the property's fountain courtyard and gardens—site of many a Memphis wedding. Upstairs, the bed & breakfast's five elegant rooms feature graceful antique furniture, lavish period decor, and plenty of modern comforts like king or queen beds, cable TV, and wireless Internet. Each room features distinct design elements like stunning hand-painted ceilings, ornate curtains, vibrant wall coverings, four-poster beds, and fireplaces. The sprawling Chef's Suite is equipped with a separate living room and private staircase. Next door, six new condo-style rooms featuring spacious floor plans and modern furnishings are also available. Continental breakfast is served in the Veranda Grill.

Lauderdale Courts

901-523-8662
www.lauderdalecourts.com
252 N. Lauderdale, Memphis, TN 38103
North of Poplar Ave.
Price: Very Expensive
Credit Cards: Yes
Handicap Access: No
Special Features: Free wireless Internet

Welcome to Lauderdale Courts, the *second-most* famous home of Elvis. From September 1949 to January 1953, the Presley family resided here at 185 Winchester, Apartment 328, in the Lauderdale Courts public housing projects. Rent was $35 per month. It was here in the Courts that a young Elvis began his love affair with the guitar, practicing both in his room and in the communal laundry room in the basement. Saved from demolition in the late 1990s, the site was added to the National Register of Historic Places, and it was restored and reopened in 2004. Since staying at Graceland is not an option, fans looking to

catch some Z's under the same roof as the King can now book a night in the Elvis Suite. In accordance with the Memphis Heritage Society, every effort has been made to furnish the apartment as it would have looked while the Presleys were in residence. The two-bedroom suite features period details like a 1951 Frigidaire and freestanding sinks, plus modern comforts like a flat-screen HDTV and plenty of Elvis movies to watch on it. Aside from the Elvis Suite, the property is actually the Uptown Square apartment complex. Guests have access to the gated property's amenities, which include a swimming pool, fitness center, billiard room, business center, and media room.

Madison Hotel

901-333-1200
www.madisonhotelmemphis.com
79 Madison Ave., Memphis, TN 38103
Five blocks north of Beale St.
Price: Very Expensive
Credit Cards: Yes
Handicap Access: Yes
Special Features: Free wireless Internet, 24-hour room service

Opened in 2002, this luxury boutique hotel offers contemporary European-style accommodations with a splash of Southern hospitality. Housed in the stately Tennessee Trust Bank building that dates back to 1904, the property is located on a quiet block just off the trolley line. Inside, modern furnishings and bold splashes of violet offset artsy touches that pay tribute to the city's musical heritage. A mezzanine-level sitting area is stocked with music-themed books and portraits of local blues legends. Just off the lobby, the upscale Grill 83 serves steaks and New American entrées. Perhaps the property's most dramatic feature, the rooftop terrace boasts some of the city's best river views. On Thursday evenings from spring through summer, locals flock here for sunset cocktails, live music, and hors d'oeuvres

The Madison Hotel's rooftop offers one of the city's best river views.

overlooking the mighty Mississippi. The property's unique features continue below ground with a subterranean lap pool and an adjacent gym area that's housed in the bank's ancient vault.

One hundred and ten guest rooms include 44 spacious suites with sitting areas, wet bars, and roomy bathrooms, many of which are equipped with jetted tubs. In keeping with the Madison's bold decor, rooms feature contemporary furnishings like high-backed couches, sky-high headboards, and vibrant music-themed prints. Round-the-clock room service, well-stocked minibars, and free wireless Internet are nice touches, while cushy bedding and high-end bath products are appropriate for the price tag. Free continental breakfast is served in Grill 83, but expect to be billed if you order off the menu.

Memphis Marriott Downtown

901-527-7300
www.marriott.com

250 N. Main St., Memphis, TN 38103
Two blocks southeast of the Pyramid
Price: Expensive
Credit Cards: Yes
Handicap Access: Yes
Special Features: Blues City Tours packages include Graceland, National Civil Rights Museum, Beale St., and Music Tour options

Located on the north end of the Main Street trolley line, this sprawling convention hotel is the city's largest. Connected to the Cook Convention Center, the 19-floor property is home to 600 rooms and suites, 47 meeting rooms, the Trolley Stop Bar, and Magnolia Grille restaurant and Fidalgo Bay Gift and Coffee Shop. Several stories in height, the expansive atrium lobby features sparkling white marble floors, a trickling fountain, and plenty of loungy seating areas. Ample amenities include an indoor pool, whirlpool, sauna, fitness room, game room, laundry facilities, and business center. Comfortable, well-appointed guest rooms feature plush bedding with down comforters, Internet access, work desks, and the usual standard amenities. Corner kings offer extra space with a seating area and sofa bed. Three concierge levels on the upper floors offer a few extra bells and whistles (like robes) and access to the concierge lounge, featuring complimentary continental breakfast and hors d'oeuvres. Suites boast views of the Mississippi River.

The Peabody

901-529-4000
www.peabodymemphis.com
149 Union Ave., Memphis, TN 38103
Three blocks north of Beale St.
Price: Very Expensive
Credit Cards: Yes
Handicap Access: Yes

It's been said that the Delta starts in the lobby of the Peabody hotel. Steeped in Southern tradition and genteel luxury, downtown's Italian Renaissance–style grand dame has been a Memphis landmark since 1925. Inside, the gracious, two-story lobby sets a sophisticated tone with its glittering chandeliers, elaborate floral arrangements, hand-painted glass ceiling, and massive marble pillars. Anchored by a popular bar area, the lobby's real draw is the iconic ducks that waddle down the red carpet to the fountain every morning at 11. At 5 PM, the formally clad Duckmaster leads the five mallards back up to a rooftop "palace" where they sleep. For a fountainside table, get there as early as 4 PM, or overlook the action from the mezzanine level.

The hotel's 13 stories include 449 rooms and 15 well-appointed suites furnished with everything from spiral staircases and fireplaces to expansive parlors. Standard accommodations feature khaki walls with white trim, rich woods, floral curtains, and cushy beds. A host of amenities include a salon, day spa, and indoor pool with mosaic floors and Grecian columns. Among the lobby shops, Lansky's is famed as the one-time clothier of Elvis Presley. Ample dining options include French cuisine at Chez Philippe, steaks and pasta at Capriccio Grill, and a deli for light bites and decadent desserts. The Corner Bar is a loungy spot for martinis, small bites, and music on the weekends. Traditional Sunday brunch is served on the Peabody's top floor. Not to be missed is the hotel's rooftop terrace—site of many a marriage proposal—where guests and visitors can sip cocktails and listen to live music while taking in spectacular downtown views (Thursday, April through August.)

Residence Inn Memphis Downtown

901-578-3700
www.marriott.com/memri
110 Monroe Ave., Memphis, TN 38103
Between Madison and Union aves.
Price: Expensive–Very Expensive
Credit Cards: Yes
Handicap Access: Yes
Special Features: Complimentary breakfast buffet, weekday social hour, Internet access; Graceland packages

This historic all-suite property in the heart of downtown offers spacious accommodations, ample amenities, and plenty of character. Originally built as the William Len Hotel in 1930, the building later housed apartments before being converted back to a hotel. Inside, the two-story art deco lobby is a stunner, with original details that include marble floors, light fixtures, marble columns, elevators, and chandeliers. A second-floor terrace overlooking the grand lobby leads to a more traditional mezzanine area with a double-faced fireplace, flat-screen TVs, and ample comfy seating spaces. A hot breakfast buffet is served on the mezzanine in the mornings, and evening wine, beer, and light dinner are offered during a weekday social hour. Guests have access to a small billiards room, well-stocked business center, library with books and DVDs, a small food shop, and a fitness center. Twelve floors up, the amazing rooftop terrace offers fantastic river and downtown views that guests can soak up from the raised hot tub. When it's not too hot out, the inn treats guests to a weekly rooftop cookout. Apartment-like suites are plenty spacious, with full kitchens, living areas, and work space spread out over around 600 square feet. Decor is traditional and understated, with neutral hues, dark wood furnishings, and historic black-and-white photos adorning the walls. Extended-stay guests will appreciate the hotel's laundry facilities and complimentary grocery-shopping service.

River Inn of Harbor Town

901-260-3333
www.riverinnmemphis.com
50 Harbor Town Sq., Memphis, TN 38103
Mud Island, less than a mile from downtown Memphis
Price: Very Expensive
Credit Cards: Yes
Handicap Access: Yes
Special Features: On-site fine dining; complimentary breakfast; wireless Internet

New in 2007, this luxurious boutique hotel in Mud Island's charming, upscale Harbor Town neighborhood may just be the nicest place to stay in Memphis. Perched near the Mississippi River and less than five minutes from downtown Memphis, the inti-mate River Inn offers fantastic personal service. The utterly romantic four-story property is accented by gas-lit lanterns, flowerbox windows, and a rooftop terrace with stunning river views. Twenty-eight posh rooms and suites feature traditional European decor with warm Southern accents like walnut furniture, four-poster beds, and super cushy bedding with Frette linens and piles of pillows. Upscale extras include 32-inch flat-screen TVs, CD players with iPod docs, and Gilchrist & Soames bath products. Six types of rooms, most with river views, range from well-appointed standards to a penthouse suite with a spacious sitting room, fireplace, wet bar, garden tub, and separate shower. Guests are pampered with a glass of champagne upon arrival, full breakfast at the inn's upscale restaurant, and port and truffles at turndown.

Gracious common areas include cozy library nooks on each floor, and a gorgeous candlelit lobby featuring a wood-burning fireplace with an antique mantel, Oriental rugs, oil paintings, fresh-cut flowers, and a crystal chandelier. Just off the lobby, Currents restaurant offers fantastic fine dining with an indulgent dinner menu including entrées like rack of lamb, duck breast, and pan-seared sea bass. Want to learn how to cook like chef David Schrier? The River Inn offers hands-on culinary instruction that includes an overnight stay. For more casual comfort food like burgers and sandwiches, Tug's restaurant is just

The Peabody Ducks

A prime example of Memphis eccentric, the ducks in the lobby of the famed Peabody hotel are as ingrained in the city's folklore as the cotton that used to be traded off the banks of the Mississippi. The story goes back to 1933, when the hotel's general manager, Frank Schutt, returned to Memphis empty-handed after a weekend hunting trip across the river in Arkansas. Tipsy, Schutt and his hunting buddy decided to unleash their (live) duck decoys in the fountain of the hotel lobby. In the morning, not only were the ducks still there, the guests were wild about them. Hence, a tradition was born.

across the street. The inn's cozy Little Bar is a fine spot to sip cocktails before dinner, but for the ultimate sunset cocktails, head to the rooftop terrace that overlooks the Mississippi River.

Sleep Inn at Court Square

901-522-9700
www.sleepinn.com
40 N. Front St., Memphis, TN 38103
Downtown's Court Square
Price: Moderate–Expensive
Credit Cards: Yes
Handicap Access: Yes
Special Features: Free wireless Internet

Located on historic Court Square on the Main Street trolley line, this quiet, centrally located property offers a great value and easy access to downtown attractions. Rooms and suites tend to fill up quickly, as this is one of few moderately priced hotels in the heart of downtown. Rooms are simple and adequate, and some are equipped with microwaves and minifridges. In addition to standard accommodations, there are also a few suites. Guests are treated to complimentary continental breakfast and a fitness room. The trolley passes right behind the property, so guests can easily hop on or walk to nearby restaurants and attractions on Main Street.

Memphis Downtown Springhill Suites

901-522-2100
www.springhillsuites.com
21 N. Main St., Memphis, TN 38103
Downtown's Court Square
Price: Expensive–Very Expensive
Credit Cards: Yes
Handicap Access: Yes
Special Features: Historic Kress Conference Center; free wireless

Located on the Main Street trolley line overlooking Court Square, this downtown hotel is connected to the historic Kress building, now home to several additional suites and conference space. The four-story Kress building once housed a five-and-dime store dating back to 1927, and it still features the original blue, green, and gold facade—an ornate terra cotta affair with designs that include cornucopias, fruit, flowers, and eagle and lion heads. Within the historic building, a stylish foyer with a floor-to-ceiling art deco mural leads to a ballroom. Additional meeting space is located on the building's lower level and third floor, along with a well-appointed hospitality suite. The Kress building's crown jewel, however, is the two-level penthouse that opens onto a roof deck with views of both Court Square and the Mississippi River.

Suites in the main property feature a separate living area, work space, sofa bed, minifridge, microwave, and wet bar. Traditional decor is clean and simple, with neutral tones and dark woods. The best rooms are those facing leafy Court Square, where guests can linger on their wrought-iron balconies and watch the Main Street trolley chug by below. Accommodations in the historic Kress building are slightly larger (500 square feet compared to 400 square feet) and feature lofted ceilings, granite countertops, and flat-screen TVs. Guests have access to a fitness center, heated outdoor pool, and complimentary continental breakfast.

Talbot Heirs

901-527-9772, 1-800-955-3956
www.talbothouse.com
99 S. Second St., Memphis, TN 38103
One block south of the Peabody
Price: Moderate–Expensive
Credit Cards: Yes
Handicap Access: None

Downtown's most uncommon lodging option offers eight artsy apartment-style rooms just a block and a half from Beale Street. Distinctly decorated digs on the property's second floor are located off a narrow hallway adorned with vibrant local folk art. Spacious suites offer plenty of room to spread out and get comfortable, with full kitchens, queen beds, CD players, cable TV with HBO, and Internet access. Most rooms feature roomy separate living areas, while all boast distinct style and decor. Guests can opt for funky lavender walls with a black-and-white checkered floor; more subdued accommodations with hardwood floors, a four-poster bed, and private patio; or a beachy suite with coral walls, blond hardwoods, and crisp white furniture. Rooms may also feature Tennessee marble floors, a desk, kitchen table, or even a baby grand piano. No matter where you choose to rest your head, your kitchen will be stocked with milk, yogurt, water, cereal, coffee, and snacks. A few in-room exercise machines are also available. The friendly innkeepers are happy to offer advice and recommendations, or even stock your fridge if you provide a grocery list ahead of time. They also keep a DVD library and stash of CDs featuring local blues musicians. Weekly and monthly rates are available.

The Westin Memphis Beale Street

901-334-5900
www.westin.com/bealestreet
170 Lt. George W. Lee Ave., Memphis, TN 38103
Beale and Second sts.
Price: Expensive
Credit Cards: Yes
Handicap Access: Yes

New in 2007, this luxury property offers an upscale oasis just off frenetic Beale Street. Surrounded by the FedEx Forum (home of the NBA's Memphis Grizzlies), Gibson Guitar Factory, Memphis Rock 'n' Soul Museum, and the Ground Zero Blues Club (new in 2008), its downtown location is hard to beat. After games and concerts at the FedEx Forum, the sleek lobby lounge is a popular spot for a nightcap. The elegant marble- and glass-filled lobby also connects to Sole Restaurant & Raw Bar. The more than two hundred spacious rooms and suites are modern and comfortable, with contemporary style, soothing earth tones, and the Westin's superplush Heavenly Beds. Accommodations feature work desks, HD flat-screen TVs, iPod docking stations, and coffeemakers with Starbucks coffee. Luxurious bathrooms are equipped with slate floors, glass showers with dual showerheads, and granite vanities with plenty of counter space. Visiting NBA teams are treated to a special floor designed with extra-tall ceilings, doors, and showerheads. One word of caution: If you're planning on turning in early, request a room that's not on the Beale Street side of the property.

Downtown Budget Lodging

Kings Court Motel

901-527-4305
265 Union Ave., Memphis, TN 38103

Popular with European backpackers who arrive in town on the bus (the station is just steps away), this inexpensive, basic property boasts a central downtown location within easy walking distance of AutoZone Park, the Peabody, and Beale Street.

Super 8 Memphis

901-948-9005
www.super8.com
340 W. Illinois St., Memphis, TN 38106

For budget-minded travelers who don't mind a few rough edges—and a somewhat unsavory location south of downtown by the river—this property offers budget rates, a pool, and quick access to downtown attractions for those with a car.

Budget Lodging across the Bridge

Just across the Hernando de Soto Bridge on
I-40, where it meets up with I-55, the
unexciting town of West Memphis (which is
actually in Arkansas) offers basic, no-frills
accommodations at bargain rates—and it's
only around 10 minutes from downtown
Memphis. The majority of these properties
are just off the highway, so traffic noise may
be an issue at some spots.

Best Western West Memphis Inn

870-735-7185
www.bestwestern.com
3401 Service Loop Rd., West Memphis, AR
72301

Days Inn West Memphis

870-735-8600
www.daysinn.com
1100 Ingram Blvd., West Memphis, AR
72301

Econo Lodge West Memphis

870-732-2830
www.econolodge.com
2315 S. Service Rd., West Memphis, AR
72301

Howard Johnson

870-735-3232
www.hojo.com
210 W. Service Rd., West Memphis, AR
72301

Motel 6

870-735-0100
www.motel6.com
2501 S. Service Rd., West Memphis, AR
72301

Quality Inn

870-702-9000
www.qualityinn.com
1009 S. Service Rd., West Memphis, AR
72301

Relax Inn

870-735-0425
2407 S. Service Rd., West Memphis, AR
72301

Midtown

Gen X Inn

901-692-9136
www.genxinnhotel.com
1177 Madison Ave., Memphis, TN 38104
West side of I-240 loop
Price: Moderate
Credit Cards: Yes
Handicap Access: Yes
Special Features: Free Internet access

Located on a quiet stretch near Victorian
Village on the Madison Avenue trolley line,
this trendy, Euro-style hotel opened in
2006. Geared toward younger, style-
conscious travelers, the five-story property
is a step above chain motels in both style and
amenities. The contemporary lobby sets the
tone, with vibrant orange walls, a white
suede seating area, and four small tables
where guests can sip coffee and nibble on
pastries in the morning while watching the
plasma TV. Located off deep blue hallways
with faux blond hardwoods, the 32 spacious
guest rooms feature contemporary, IKEA-
minded decor, including modern desk
chairs, floor lamps that glow blue, futuristic
telephones, and cushy blue suede armchairs.
While not exactly luxurious, the accommodations have a few bells and whistles,
including plasma TVs with DVD players, a
minifridge, and oversize showerheads. All
nonsmoking, guest rooms feature one king
or two queen beds.

Holiday Inn Express Memphis Medical Center Midtown

901-276-1175
www.hiexpress.com
1180 Union Ave., Memphis, TN 38104
Next to the medical center
Price: Moderate

Credit Cards: Yes
Handicap Access: Yes
Special Features: Free wireless

Located just inside the I-240 loop, around
five minutes from both downtown and
Midtown attractions, this former Hampton
Inn lives up to the Holiday Inn Express
promise of reliable accommodations at
value-minded rates. While many guests
stay here for the close proximity to the
Methodist University Hospital, the property
is a solid option for travelers who want to
be close to downtown attractions without
paying for the prime real estate. Midtown
attractions are also nearby, including some
good eats—Tops Bar-B-Q and the Cupboard
are just a couple of blocks east on Union.
Rooms are simple, comfortable, and more
than adequate, with traditional decor like
hunter green carpeting, dark wood furnishings, and hunting-themed prints. Guests
have access to a fitness center, a sunny
breakfast area with a flat-screen TV, and an
outdoor pool with a spacious patio.
Complimentary breakfast includes hot
items like scrambled eggs, bacon, and biscuits and gravy, plus the Holiday Inn's signature cinnamon rolls.

Holiday Inn University of Memphis
901-678-8200
ichotelsgroup.com
3700 Central Ave., Memphis, TN 38111
University of Memphis campus
Price: Expensive
Credit Cards: Yes
Handicap Access: Yes
Special Features: Free wireless

This hidden gem tucked away on the leafy
University of Memphis campus features
comfortable, all-suite accommodations just
east of Midtown and less than five minutes
from the Botanic Gardens and Dixon
Gallery. The property is affiliated with the
university's Kemmons Wilson School of
Hospitality & Resort Management, and no,
it's not run by students. Inside, the property's four floors overlook a spacious atrium
lobby area with seating areas, ample greenery, and plenty of sunshine. Eighty-two spacious suites decorated in dark woods and
neutral tones offer separate living areas with
sofa beds, and wet bars with a minifridge,
microwave, and coffeemaker. Guests have
access to a business center and on-site fitness room, and they may use the university's gym for a $5 fee. Just off the lobby,
Medallion Restaurant serves Continental
fare and a popular Sunday brunch, while the
lobby's more casual Central Grill offers salads, sandwiches, and burgers. Don't miss
the second-floor gallery dedicated to
Holiday Inn founder Kemmons Wilson.
Four large, museum-quality display cases at
the top of the lobby escalator feature photos,
awards, inspirational quotes, and retro
Holiday Inn artifacts.

Midtown Budget Lodging

Motel 6
901-528-0650
www.motel6.com
210 S. Pauline St., Memphis, TN 38104

A good budget bet for clean, simple rooms
in a good location less than a mile from
downtown; you can also get Wi-Fi for
around three bucks a day.

Red Roof Inn
901-526-1050
www.redroof.com
42 S. Camilla St., Memphis, TN 38104

While the area immediately surrounding
the hotel is a little rough around the edges,
this basic budget accommodation offers
clean rooms and a pool close to both downtown and Midtown.

Graceland Area

Days Inn at Graceland
901-346-5500, 1-800-329-7466

www.daysinn.com
3839 Elvis Presley Blvd., Memphis, TN
38116
Across from Graceland
Price: Moderate
Credit Cards: Yes
Handicap Access: Yes
Special Features: Free airport shuttle,
Internet

A favorite of Elvis fans, this reliable, value-minded motel is located across the street from Graceland. One step in the lobby, and it becomes clear that you're in Elvis country: Walls are plastered with framed gold records, photos, and even a life-size Elvis strumming his guitar. The atrium-style breakfast area just off the lobby is nice and sunny, and guests are treated to a continental breakfast that includes muffins and waffles in the mornings. Rooms go beyond basic Days Inn offerings with walls covered in framed photos and posters featuring the King, and an all-Elvis channel on the 27-inch flat-screen TV. The two-story motel wraps around what is perhaps the property's most impressive feature: a spacious, guitar-shaped swimming pool.

Elvis Presley's Heartbreak Hotel at Graceland
901-332-1000, 1-877-777-0606
www.elvis.com/epheartbreakhotel
3677 Elvis Presley Blvd., Memphis, TN
38116
Adjacent to Graceland parking lot
Price: Moderate–Very Expensive
Credit Cards: Yes
Handicap Access: Yes
Special Features: Free downtown and airport shuttles, parking; Graceland packages

You can't stay any closer to Elvis's place than the Heartbreak Hotel, which is located across the street from Graceland. Safely tucked away behind a security gate, the property looks oddly institutional thanks to a lack of windows. Inside the lobby, the retro vibe is in full effect, with plenty of purple, yellow, and red velvet decor, plus a 1950s-era living room setup, complete with an antique television showing Elvis films. Beyond the lobby and gift shop, there's the small Jungle Room lounge, and a much larger breakfast area that leads to the pool patio. The heart-shaped pool (complete with a break down the middle) is a nice place to beat the heat. Within the accommodations, black-and-white framed photos of Elvis spruce up otherwise simple rooms with blond wood furnishings. Kitchenettes and complimentary in-room Elvis movies are nice extras, while roomy suites are equipped with separate living rooms. All guests have access to an on-site fitness center and are treated to a continental breakfast with waffles. The hotel's four themed suites are considerably more elaborate than the standard accommodations: Hard-core Elvis fans can choose from the Graceland Suite, decorated like the King's place; the art deco Hollywood Suite, celebrating Elvis's film career; the Gold & Platinum Suite, honoring his hits; or the romantic Burning Love Suite. All four suites boast more than 1,000 square feet, with a pair of bedrooms, bathrooms, and living areas.

Airport Area
While the Memphis airport isn't in the most ideal part of town, it is close to Graceland, and area accommodations are around 15 to 20 minutes south of downtown. There are also some good budget options down here, and rates tend to be quite a bit lower than downtown properties.

Clarion Hotel Airport/Graceland Area
901-332-3500
www.clarionmemphis.com
1471 E. Brooks Rd., Memphis, TN 38116

Located around a mile from Graceland (toward the airport), this property features traditional decor, an outdoor pool, restaurant, and clubby lounge.

Courtyard by Marriott Memphis Airport

901-396-3600
www.ichotelsgroup.com
1780 Nonconnah Blvd., Memphis, TN 38132

Located just off the south side of the I-240 loop, this comfortable, tucked-away spot features a nice outdoor pool area, an indoor atrium hot tub, and more.

Holiday Inn Select Memphis Airport

901-332-1130
www.selectmemphis.com
2240 Democrat Rd., Memphis, TN 38132

Popular for business meetings and events, this expansive property features 374 guest rooms, more than 33,000 square feet of conference space, and a spacious atrium-style lobby with a fountain and a lounge area.

Homestead Studio Suites

901-344-0010
www.extendedstayhotels.com
2541 Corporate Ave. E., Memphis, TN 38132

Surrounded by office parks set amid lush greenery, this pleasant oasis offers plenty of room to spread out; suites feature full kitchens, a work area, and wireless Internet.

Quality Inn Airport/Graceland Area

901-345-3344
www.qualityinn.com
1581 E. Brooks Rd., Memphis, TN 38116

Positioned between the airport and Elvis Presley Boulevard, this consistent, budget-minded property features extras like a weekday newspaper and an outdoor pool.

Radisson Hotel Memphis Airport

901-332-2370
www.radisson.com/memphistn_airport
2411 Winchester Rd., Memphis, TN 38116

You can't get closer to the airport than the Radisson, located adjacent to the FedEx runway. Amenities include an outdoor pool and on-site restaurant and bar.

East Memphis (Central)

The following accommodations are all within easy access to the I-240 loop—on, or just off Poplar Avenue in the heart of East Memphis's business district. The good news for leisure travelers is that rates generally fall significantly on the weekends, when the business set clears out. Most of these properties fall in the moderate price range during weekends, and some bump up to the expensive category for midweek stays.

Courtyard by Marriott—Park Avenue

901-761-0330
www.marriott.com
6015 Park Ave., Memphis, TN 38119

Traditional decor, standard amenities, an on-site lounge, and an outdoor pool area all come at a reasonable rate near the I-240 loop and the Lichterman Nature Center.

Doubletree Hotel Memphis

901-767-6666
www.memphis.doubletree.com
5069 Sanderlin Ave., Memphis, TN 38117

Located inside the I-240 loop, this well-situated property offers an indoor-outdoor pool, ample business amenities, and Cal's Championship Steakhouse—named for University of Memphis basketball coach John Calipari.

Embassy Suites Memphis

901-684-1777
www.memphis.embassysuites.com
1022 S. Shady Grove Rd., Memphis, TN 38120

Home of the popular Frank Grisanti's Italian restaurant, this all-suite property features roomy accommodations and a tropical lobby atrium with lush foliage and waterfalls, plus an indoor pool and arcade for the kids.

Extended Stay America—Quail Hollow
901-685-7575
www.extendedstayamerica.com
6325 Quail Hollow Rd., Memphis, TN 38120

Full-size kitchens and separate sleeping, living, and work areas make for a comfortable visit whether you're staying for a couple of days or several weeks.

Hampton Inn—Poplar
901-683-8500
www.hamptoninn.com
5320 Poplar Ave., Memphis, TN 38119

This standard, relatively small Hampton Inn just west of the I-240 loop may not have all the bells and whistles of the Shady Grove location, but the price is right, and Corky's BBQ is just across the street.

Hampton Inn & Suites Memphis—Shady Grove
901-762-0056
www.hamptoninn.com
962 S. Shady Grove Rd., Memphis, TN 38120

Located next to the Embassy Suites behind the Regalia shopping center (home of Owen Brennan's restaurant), this quiet property offers 76 rooms and suites, plus nice extras like a free hot breakfast and lap desks for comfortable work on the computer.

Hilton Memphis
901-684-6664
www.memphis.hilton.com
939 Ridge Lake Blvd., Memphis, TN 38120

A striking glass cylinder rising 27 floors above East Memphis's business district, this hotel features more than four hundred upscale guest rooms with contemporary style, 30,000 square feet of meeting space, on-site dining, and a large outdoor pool and hot tub.

Holiday Inn Select
901-682-7881
ichotelsgroup.com
5795 Poplar Ave., Memphis, TN 38119

Located adjacent to Homewood Suites and Park Place Hotel just off I-240, this expansive property features an atrium lobby, on-site restaurant, and an indoor pool and hot tub.

Homewood Suites by Hilton
901-763-0500
www.memphispoplar.homewoodsuites.com
5811 Poplar Ave., Memphis, TN 38119

Comfortable, apartment-style living in amenity-rich one- and two-bedroom suites that surround a spacious pool area and basketball court.

Hyatt Place
901-680-9700
www.memphisprimacyparkway.place.hyatt.com
1220 Primacy Pkwy., Memphis, TN 38119

Extra comforts at this contemporary property come in the form of stylish rooms with 42-inch flat-screen HDTVs, cushy bedding, a sleeper sofa, and a slew of modern amenities.

La Quinta Inn & Suites
901-374-0330
www.lq.com
1236 Primacy Pkwy., Memphis, TN 38119

This reliable, value-minded property offers rooms and suites with contemporary decor, plus an outdoor pool and hot tub, and free wireless.

Park Place Hotel

901-767-6300
www.parkplacehotelmemphis.com
5877 Poplar Ave., Memphis, TN 38119

A good value just off the interstate, this
five-floor, 126-room, locally owned property features a stylish marble lobby, spacious workout room, and an outdoor pool.

Residence Inn—Memphis East

901-685-9595
www.marriott.com
6141 Old Poplar Pike, Memphis, TN 38119

Connected to an ear clinic, this extended-
stay property offers spacious rooms in a
series of apartment-style brick buildings,
plus complimentary grocery shopping services, a breakfast buffet, and weekday social
hour.

Staybridge Suites

901-682-1722
www.ichotelsgroup.com
1070 Ridge Lake Blvd., Memphis, TN 38120

Located in the shadow of the towering
Hilton, this quiet, lush oasis off busy Poplar
Avenue offers comfy suites, an outdoor
pool, and plenty more. It's also an easy walk
to the Malco movie theater.

East Memphis (South)

The following East Memphis properties are
located just south of the I-240 loop, which
makes them a little closer to Graceland and
the airport. They're also slightly less expensive than the more centrally located East
Memphis properties listed above—generally
falling within, or very close to, the moderate
price range on both weekdays and weekends.

Comfort Suites I-240 East—Airport

901-365-2575
www.comfortsuites.com
2575 Thousand Oaks Cove, Memphis, TN
38118

Fairfield Inn & Suites Memphis—I-240 & Perkins

901-795-1900
www.marriott.com
4760 Showcase Blvd., Memphis, TN 38118

Hampton Inn Memphis—I-240 at Thousand Oaks

901-367-1234
www.hamptoninn.com
2700 Perkins Rd. S., Memphis, TN 38118

Memphis Marriott—East

901-362-6200
www.marriott.com/memtn
2625 Thousand Oaks Blvd., Memphis, TN
38118

Ramada Plaza—Mt. Moriah Rd. & I-240

901-362-8010
2490 Mt. Moriah Rd., Memphis, TN 38115

Sleep Inn—American Way

901-363-4800
www.sleepinn.com
5119 American Way, Memphis, TN 38115

Camping

Agricenter International

901-355-1977
7777 Walnut Grove Rd., Memphis, TN 38120

Tucked away on quiet Walnut Grove Road in
East Memphis, this RV campground features 300 sites, including 96 with sewer
access, plus a dump station, bathhouse, and
laundry facilities.

Memphis-Graceland RV Park and Campground

901-396-7125
www.elvis.com/rvpark
3691 Elvis Presley Blvd., Memphis, TN
38116

Located within walking distance of
Graceland, this 19-acre campground

behind Elvis Presley's Heartbreak Hotel offers RV hookups, tent spaces, and cabins, plus a pool, store, and free wireless throughout.

Mississippi River RV Park
901-946-1993
870 Cotton Gin Pl., Memphis, TN 38106

Located on the south side of downtown Memphis near I-55 and the Memphis–Arkansas Bridge, this site offers RV hookups and tent camping, plus laundry facilities and a bathhouse.

T. O. Fuller State Park
901-543-7581
www.stateparks.com/fuller.html
1500 Mitchell Rd., Memphis , TN 38109

Located on the southern edge of Memphis, this 1,138-acre park offers 45 campsites for RVs and tents, plus a picnic area, playground, bathhouse, laundry, and pool.

Tom Sawyer's Mississippi River RV Park
870-735-9770
1286 S. Eighth St., West Memphis, AR 72301

Located across the Mississippi River from downtown Memphis in West Memphis, Arkansas, this verdant riverside site offers ample RV and tent sites, plus a store, laundry facilities, a bathhouse, and trails.

CULTURE

Guided Tours

American Dream Safari
901-527-8870
www.americandreamsafari.com
P.O. Box 3129, Memphis, TN 38173

Even in the 21st century, it doesn't get much more American than riding around Memphis and the Delta in a restored 1955 Cadillac. Tad Pierson, owner/driver of American Dream Safari, agrees. Since 1989, Pierson and his Cadillac have been giving personalized tours of the real South—the nuanced nooks and crannies that you won't find just by pulling off the interstate. A world away from a by-the-book bus tour, American Dream Safari specializes in providing a glimpse into the Memphis music scene, both past and present. Whether you're looking for an all-day excursion to the Delta, an afternoon cruise in the Caddy around Memphis, or a night packed with blues clubs and bar-hopping, Pierson is your man.

Backbeat Tours
1-866-392-2328
www.backbeattours.com
140 Beale St., Memphis, TN 38103

How many sightseeing companies encourage their guests to bring along their guitars for impromptu jam sessions? Exactly. Score one for Backbeat Tours. Elvis nuts will want to hop aboard the Backbeat Bus (circa 1950, naturally) and check out the three-hour Hound Dog tour that traces Presley's life from Lauderdale Courts to lesser-known Elvis locales. Got a hankering for a little Memphis history with a side of soul, rock, and blues? If so, the

Mojo tour is your ticket. This tour, the company's most popular, incorporates the liberal use of tambourines, bongos, and shakers—all played by you, the passenger, along with your guides. If a walking tour is more your speed, you may want to explore their Historic Memphis tour, or for those feeling a bit more daring, the spooky Haunted Memphis tour.

Blues City Tours
901-522-9229
www.bluescitytours.com
325 Union Ave., Memphis, TN 38103

Since 1988, Blues City Tours has been providing charter tours covering both the Tunica gaming district as well as Memphis sites and history. Interested in Graceland, Sun Studio, Beale Street, or the Victorian Village? They've got you covered. More in the mood for the casinos down in the Delta? The tour outfit will take you there as well. Those looking for a little Memphis nightlife action will want to enquire about the Memphis After Dark package that gives sightseers a taste of Memphis blues, booze, and club life—all in three hours for under 60 bucks.

Memphis Riverboat Tours
1-800-221-6197
www.memphisriverboats.net
45 S. Riverboat Dr., Memphis, TN 38103

Those looking to truly experience the city's past as a Mississippi River port city need look no further than a riverboat tour. Whether you want to hop aboard for a sightseeing trip or

In service since 1979, the Memphis Queen III *features three decks and classic Victorian riverboat style.*
Memphis Convention & Visitors Bureau

enjoy a relaxing dinner on the Mississippi, you'll come away with an expanded sense of Memphis and her relationship to the river. With a number of paddle-wheelers in its fleet, Memphis Riverboat Tours offers varied packages based on patrons' needs and interest. Call for rates, packages, and reservations, or book online.

Mike's Memphis Tours

901-481-3877
www.memphisexplorations.com
494 Garland St., Memphis, TN 38104

Led by Mike Freeman, the four-hour Memphis tour ($60) focuses on everything Elvis, from Memphis to the Delta. Additionally, Mike also offers a Tupelo tour ($95) that highlights Elvis's early years prior to his move to Memphis.

Shangri-La Projects Ultimate Rock 'n Roll Tours

901-359-3102
www.shangrilaprojects.com
P.O. Box 40106, Memphis, TN 38174

An offshoot of Shangri-La Records (see the Shopping section), Shangri-La Projects Ultimate Rock 'n Roll Tours is led by local Memphis music historian Sherman Willmott. With a near encyclopedic knowledge of Memphis history (music and otherwise), Willmott can tailor tours to your interests. Looking for a broad, general tour of the town and a history of its music? No problem. More interested in delving into the minutiae of Soulsville and the high school programs that produced such talent? Willmott is more than happy to go there as well. In addition to the tours, Shangri-La Projects also writes, prints, and distributes the essential miniguide to Memphis nightlife and beyond: *Kreature Comforts Low-Life Guide to Memphis.* Be sure to pick one up as soon as you hit town.

Historic Buildings and Sites

Beale Street

Downtown Memphis

Originally known as Beale Avenue, Beale Street was founded in 1841 and runs just shy of 2 miles in length, stretching from the Mississippi River to Manassas Street in downtown Memphis. By the early 20th century, the properties on Beale were primarily owned and operated by African Americans, fostering a sense of community pride long before the civil rights movement. It was during this time that, in 1916, W. C. Handy penned the now famous "Beale Street Blues," increasing the street's visibility well beyond the South. From the roaring '20s through the 1940s, Beale Street became known as one of *the* premiere destinations for jazz and blues, drawing such luminaries as Louis Armstrong, B. B. King, Muddy Waters, Duke Ellington, Albert King, Memphis Minnie, and Rufus Thomas, to name just a few. By the 1960s, much of the street fell into disrepair, with many of the storefronts empty due to business closure and/or relocation. Until the late 1970s, Beale remained run down in urban decay until the city purchased all of the properties covering the three blocks of Beale now known as the historic district. Beginning in 1983, the area began to slowly revitalize, with new shops and clubs opening one by one as the area gradually regained

Beale Street is home to more than 25 bars, restaurants, and shops.

momentum. Now Beale Street is both Memphis's and the state of Tennessee's number-one attraction, drawing 6 million visitors annually from all around the world.

Elmwood Cemetery

901-774-3212
www.elmwoodcemetery.org
824 S. Dudley St., Memphis, TN 38104

Established in 1852, Elmwood Cemetery is comprised of 80 beautiful acres adorned with winding roads and paths, dogwood and magnolia trees, rolling lawns, and nearly every manner of memorial, mausoleum, and monument imaginable. The cemetery is the final resting place of more than 75,000 inhabitants, from politicians to blues singers, and includes a cross section of those who shaped the city's rich history from before the Civil War. Notables buried here include author Shelby Foote, musician Jimmie Lunceford, Robert Church (the South's first black millionaire), and influential Memphis politician E. H. Crump. Elmwood is also the final resting place of slaves, Civil War generals, and an infamous madam. Visitors should begin at the Victorian Carpenter Gothic Cottage, which offers maps to grave sites of interest, plus audio tours, picnic tables, and restrooms.

Victorian Village Historic District

198–680 Adams Ave., Memphis, TN 38105

In the mid-1800s, during what was a very prosperous and profitable time in the city's history, a group of wealthy Memphians built grand, three- and four-story Victorian mansions along Adams Avenue, which became known as Millionaire's Row. Residents included everyone from cotton moguls to riverboat tycoons. Listed on the National Register of Historic Places, Victorian Village is located on the eastern edge of downtown and primarily consists of the Woodruff-Fontaine House, the Magevney House, and the Mallory-Neely House. While most of the homes are only open for private events and occasional special home tours, the Woodruff-Fontaine House may be toured year-round.

Woodruff-Fontaine House
901-526-1469
www.woodruff-fontaine.com
680 Adams Ave., Memphis, TN 38105
Open: Wed.–Sun.
Admission: Adults $10; students $8
Special Feature: Free parking available at the lot on the corner of Orleans and Washington aves.

Built in 1870, the Woodruff Fontaine House, located among the magnolias on Millionaire's Row in Victorian Village, harkens back to a time of Memphis wealth and prosperity. Immaculately restored with period furnishings, the elegant 16-room home, now a museum, provides a glimpse into the lives of those who once called 680 Adams home. The three-story Victorian mansion was owned by two prominent Memphis families (built by the Woodruffs, then owned by the Fontaines) before it was deeded to the city in 1936. In addition to the museum's collection of furniture, 19th-century portraits, art, and antiques, it is said that the house also has a resident—the ghost of Miss Molly Woodruff Henning, daughter of the original owner. Individual and group tours are available on the half hour; allot approximately 30–40 minutes for the full tour.

Museums

Art Museum of the University of Memphis
901-678-2224
www.amum.org
CFA Room 142, 3750 Norriswood Ave., Memphis, TN 38152-3200
Admission: Free

Renovated in 2008, the Art Museum of the University of Memphis, located on the university's campus, features both touring exhibits as well as an impressive home collection. The most remarkable part of the permanent collection is the museum's ancient Egypt display, showcasing various antiquities like the two-thousand-year-old sarcophagus belonging to the mummy of Iret-Iruw. A nod to the original city of Memphis, the Egyptian exhibit is an excellent primer for those who are interested in the history of Memphis, Egypt. Visitors interested in West African artifacts will also appreciate the museum's impressive collection of African art and embellished masks.

Belz Museum of Asian & Judaic Art
901-523-ARTS
www.belzmuseum.org
119 S. Main St., Memphis, TN 38103
Open: Tues.–Sun.
Admission: Adults $6; seniors $5; students $4

Located in the heart of downtown Memphis on the Main Street trolley line, this unique collection of Asian and Judaic artwork is, quite simply, dazzling. Located within the basement level of the Pembroke Square Building (the former home of a Goldsmith's Department Store), the extensive collection includes hundreds of stunning pieces of Asian art, ranging from gorgeous antique furnishings from the Qing Dynasty to impossibly intricate carvings in jade, ivory, and red coral. Carvings include everything from small, delicate statuettes to a giant, jaw-dropping dragon boat in jade and a 6-foot pagoda in ivory. Visitors will marvel at a parade of sizeable mosaic animal statuettes that include pairs of tiger-eye horses, malachite elephants, and jade camels, among many more. A separate display room contains several finely detailed carvings on enormous ancient woolly mammoth tusks, and a nearly life-size jade horse and carriage. A separate spacious gallery is home to the Judaic art collection, which includes ceremonial objects like Passover plates, a Torah scroll encased in silver, and intricate menorahs. There are also illuminated parchments and modern bronze relief panels depicting biblical stories.

The Children's Museum of Memphis
901-458-2678
www.cmom.com
2525 Central Ave., Memphis, TN 38104
Open: Daily
Admission: $9

This pint-size fantasy land offers a world of fun for kids, with a healthy dose of education they won't even notice. Through impressive hands-on exhibits, kids can crack a safe, boogie down in a disco room, "shop" in a mini Kroger, play doctor with a plastic model, and even sit in the cockpit of a real Boeing 747. Does junior have a thing for flashing lights and sirens? The City Friends exhibit allows kids to don a fireman outfit and climb aboard a fire truck, a sheriff car, or a police motorcycle. Got a future Picasso on your hands? Young artists can perfect their self-portrait in the Art Smart space. There's even a mini Mississippi River with running water where youngsters can "fish" or operate bridges and dams. There's something for kids of all ages in this sprawling space, from a tot-size play area to a skyscraper maze that will keep the older kids occupied.

The Cotton Museum at the Memphis Cotton Exchange
901-531-7826
www.memphiscottonmuseum.org
65 Union Ave., Memphis, TN 38103
Open: Daily
Admission: Adults $5; seniors $4.50; students $4; children (6–12) $3

Located in the historic Memphis Cotton Exchange building on the corner of Front and Union, this one-room museum offers a fascinating look into the world of King Cotton. Start in the lobby, where the Cotton Hall of Fame is on display. You may recognize the opulent bronze-and-marble lobby from a scene in *The Firm,* the movie starring Tom Cruise based on the John Grisham best-seller. The main exhibits are located in a lofty room that served as the cotton exchange from 1925 until the dawn of computers, which forever changed the business. An enormous chalkboard where cotton quotes were updated throughout the day is the centerpiece, and it's easy to imagine the exchange floor below bustling with traders. After an introductory video, a self-guided tour takes visitors back to the days when the exchange was an exclusive boys' club. Display cases throughout the room detail the history of cotton and the sheer influence it had on Southern culture and society. Original details in the historic space include the revolving door, a Western Union station, and several phone booths that now house touch screens that link to various oral histories. In addition to everything cotton, several display cases are also dedicated to the blues, and how the genre's history is intertwined with that of King Cotton.

The Dixon Gallery and Gardens
901-761-5250
www.dixon.org
4339 Park Ave., Memphis, TN 38117
Open: Tues.–Sun.
Admission: Adults $7; seniors and students (18 and older with ID) $5; children 7–17 $3; children 6 and under free
Special Features: Free admission Sat. 10–noon

Located across from the Memphis Botanical Garden, this gorgeous oasis perched on 17 acres of landscaped gardens and woodlands is home to an impressive collection of more than two thousand impressionist and post-impressionist paintings. Former home to cotton mogul Hugo Dixon, the estate's rooms now house French works by the likes of Paul Cezanne, Claude Monet, and Henri Matisse. The permanent collection also includes American paintings and a collection of 18th-century porcelain, while changing exhibits feature modern installations, sculpture, and more. Beyond the mansion walls, visitors can stroll pathways through formal gardens, lush greenery, fountained courtyards, and secluded nooks and crannies with sculpture and benches.

Fire Museum of Memphis
901-320-5650
www.firemuseum.com
118 Adams Ave., Memphis, TN 38103
Admission: Adults: $6; children (3–12) $5; seniors (60 and over) $4
Open: Mon.–Sat.
Special Features: Two admissions for the price of one on Tues.

An interactive experience, the Fire Museum of Memphis is housed in a turn-of-the-20th-century fire engine house in downtown Memphis. Perfect for children (or the big kid in you), the museum earns points for hands-on exhibits that should appeal to even the shortest of attention spans. A fleet of old fire trucks (from the horse-drawn era!), a firefighters' pole, simulated house fires, and a maze are only a few of the museum's numerous exhibits. You'll also learn about some of the city's worst fires through photo histories and film exhibits. And you never know—with a heavy emphasis on fire safety and prevention education, a visit to the museum might just save your life one day.

Gibson Guitar Factory
901-544-7998
www.gibson.com
146 Lt. George W. Lee Ave., Memphis, TN 38103

See what goes into making a guitar like B. B. King's Lucille *on the Gibson Guitar factory tour.* Memphis Convention & Visitors Bureau

Open: Daily
Admission: $10; must be age 5 and over
Special Features: Group rate is $8 per person for 15 or more people. For a group reservation, e-mail groupsales.memphis@gibson.com or call 901-544-7998, ext. 4075.

Embrace your inner guitar god at Gibson Guitar's Memphis showroom and factory, located off Beale Street across from the FedEx Forum. The 45-minute walking tour of the factory is about as up close and personal as most will ever get to a Gibson masterpiece—without shelling out several thousand dollars. While the official tour begins outside of Gibson's retail space, guitar aficionados and casual fans alike will want to spend some time perusing the final product, buffed to a high sheen for display in the showroom. Depending upon when you visit, your tour group could range from one other person to 25. Those looking to capture Gibson luthiers in action should bring their cameras, as photography is allowed on the tour. No fenced-in dog-and-pony show, the Gibson tour gives visitors an up-close look at the real nitty-gritty on the factory floor, sawdust and all. Watch as a block of wood is cut, sculpted, sanded, painted, glossed, and fine-tuned before it faces the stringent quality-control inspection.

Graceland

1-800-238-2000
www.elvis.com/graceland
3734 Elvis Presley Blvd., Memphis, TN 38186
Open: Daily; closed Tues. Dec.–Feb.
Admission: Adults $28–69; seniors/youth/students $25.20–69; children 7–12 $12–69; children 6 and under free

Elvis purchased Graceland in 1957 for $102,000. Used by permission, Elvis Presley Enterprises, Inc.

Special Features: Closed Thanksgiving Day, Christmas Day, and sometimes on New Year's Day; free walk-up admission to Meditation Garden (Elvis's grave site) daily 7:30–8:30 AM except Tues. 7:30 AM–4:00 PM Dec.–Feb.

Approximately 12 miles south of Memphis, in the seen-better-days suburb of Whitehaven, sits Graceland, the home Elvis Presley purchased in 1957 and lived in until his death in 1977. Since the King's death, Graceland's stature has evolved into a near-mythical destination for Elvis fans around the globe. Now in its third decade as a museum, the 13-acre estate sees as many as six hundred thousand visitors per year and is the second most visited private residence behind the White House.

The Graceland "mansion tour" is a self-guided audio tour focusing on the downstairs and basement of the Presley home (the upstairs is off-limits to guests). Highlights include the whiter-than-white living room; Elvis's downstairs media room (complete with a row of three televisions programmed to different channels); the notorious, beyond kitschy "jungle room"; the bachelor-style pool room; a high-end (but now retro) kitchen; and Elvis's parents' bedroom. Behind the main house is Elvis's business office, racquetball court, and what is now a trophy building housing Elvis artifacts and mementos including photos, career curios, personal effects, mementos, and stage wear.

In addition to the mansion tour, one may (for an additional fee) visit the Elvis car museum, tour his private jets, and peruse the "Sincerely Elvis" museum, which features 56 of Elvis's stage outfits, from their humble beginnings to the over-the-top karate-inspired Vegas jumpsuits. There's also the Private Presley exhibit, featuring mementos and fatigues from Elvis's army days. While these additional museums have some merit, for the casual fan they may come across as an excuse for another gift shop.

Beyond the mansion tour, Graceland visitors can pay extra to see a collection of Elvis's jumpsuits at the Sincerely Elvis exhibit.

Memphis Brooks Museum of Art
901-544-6200
www.brooksmuseum.org
1934 Poplar Ave., Memphis, TN 38104
Open: Wed.–Sun.
Admission: Adults $7; seniors $6; youth and students $3; children under 6 free
Special Features: On Wed., visitors pay what they can, from a penny up

Tennessee's oldest and largest fine-arts museum is tucked away in the heart of Midtown's Overton Park. Surrounded by endless lawns and lush greenery, the striking Beaux-Arts-style museum offers an ideal setting for everything from impressionist paintings by Renoir to an ancient Greco-Roman marble sculpture of the Torso of Pan. The well-rounded collection includes a global array of works from the 13th through 20th centuries. A maze of nearly 30 galleries spread throughout three levels takes visitors through African art and antiquities upstairs; Baroque, British, and contemporary collections on the main level; and special exhibits on the lower floor that have included everything from psychedelic rock 'n' roll posters to Andy Warhol prints. Audio tours of the museum's permanent collections are available for a few extra dollars. In addition to the lobby store and the Holly Court garden, the Brooks is home to the celebrated Brushmark Restaurant. With floor-to-ceiling windows and a sweeping terrace offering panoramic views of Overton Park, the Brushmark offers a picturesque setting for an upscale lunch and the occasionally offered tapas dinner.

Memphis Rock 'n' Soul Museum

901-205-2533
www.memphisrocknsoul.org
191 Beale St., Memphis, TN 38103
Open: Daily
Admission: Adults $10; children (5–17) $7

Located off the historic Blues Highway, Highway 61 (Third Street), within downtown's FedEx Forum sports and entertainment complex, this Smithsonian Institute museum provides an all-encompassing overview of the Bluff City's unique musical history, from its roots in big cotton to Memphis music legend Alex Chilton's band, Big Star. After a brief introductory video, plug in your headphones and allow the self-guided tour to take you back to the rural outskirts of Memphis as gospel spirituals come to life in the Delta cotton fields. As you progress through the museum's seven galleries, the history and social impact of Memphis's musical heritage unfolds through archived audio recordings, candid photographs, video displays, and an impressive collection of restored equipment—ever wonder what the first jukebox looked like? Special attention is given to the history of Beale Street as well as groundbreaking Memphis labels Sun, Stax, and Hi Records. A few of the museum's many highlights include a collection of Elvis's stage costumes, the podium from *American Bandstand,* B. B. King's guitar, and Al Green's flashy '70s-era leisure suit. You can also jam along to more than a hundred decade-spanning songs programmed into your audio set. Essential.

Mississippi River Museum at Mud Island River Park

901-576-7241, 1-800-507-6507
www.mudisland.com/museum.asp

After touring the Memphis Brooks Museum of Art, visitors can stroll through lovely Overton Park or lunch at the museum's Brushmark Restaurant. Memphis Convention & Visitors Bureau

Ardent Studios

Leaf through your record collection, and chances are you're more familiar with the work of Ardent Studios (901-725-0855; www.ardentstudios.com; 2000 Madison Ave., Memphis, TN 38104) than you may have realized. Artists who share the common bond of having recorded here include, but are not limited to, Led Zeppelin, the Staples Singers, R.E.M., Big Star, the White Stripes, the Allman Brothers, B. B. King, ZZ Top, Cat Power, and many, many more. Kick-started in the '60s, the studio still books year-round.

125 N. Front St., Memphis, TN 38103
Open: Tues.–Sun. Apr.–Oct.
Admission: Adults $8; seniors $6; children 5–11 $5; children under 5 free
Special Features: Admission includes round-trip monorail ride, full park access, museum entry, and a guided Riverwalk tour

Located within Mud Island River Park, a scenic monorail ride from downtown Memphis, this 18-gallery museum tells the story of the mighty Mississippi River. The self-guided audio tour takes around 45 minutes and traces the river's history from the days of prehistoric Indians and explorers through the Civil War years and steamboat culture. Sometimes (unintentionally) humorous voices from the past tell their point-of-view stories at each exhibit from individual audio recorders. Displays range from period artifacts and Civil War regalia to a full-size walk-on steamboat replica, and the front end of a Civil War Union ironclad gunboat where visitors can witness a gun battle. Several galleries are also dedicated to blues music, jazz, rock 'n' roll, and legendary locals like W. C. Handy and Elvis Presley. Music exhibits feature antique instruments, a re-created juke joint, and a retro recording studio. Just outside the museum, the impressive Riverwalk includes a five-block-long working scale model of the Mississippi River. The park is also home to picnic areas, a deli, the Mud Island Amphitheater, and outdoor activities including canoe, kayak, and bike rentals. (See the Recreation section for more information.)

National Civil Rights Museum

901-521-9699
www.civilrightsmuseum.org
450 Mulberry St., Memphis, TN 38103
Open: Daily
Admission: Adults $12; seniors and students $10; children (4–17) $8.50
Special Features: Free admission Mon. 3–5 PM (until 6 in summer); closed Tues. in summer

Transforming tragedy into triumph, the National Civil Rights Museum is housed, in part, in the structure formerly occupied by the Lorraine Motel, site of Dr. Martin Luther King Jr's assassination in 1968. Boasting a comprehensive overview of the American civil rights movement, the museum tells the story of African American struggles beginning with slavery under British rule in the 1600s. Continuing through the Emancipation Proclamation, Jim Crow laws, Rosa Parks, desegregation, MLK's nonviolent protests, Malcolm X, and the ultimate triumph of nondiscriminatory equality, the self-guided tour takes approximately an hour and 15 minutes at a casual pace, and audio tours are available. Standout exhibits include re-creations of critical touchstones in the civil rights movement, including Little Rock's desegregated Central High School, the bus where Rosa Parks made her stand in Montgomery, and the Woolworth's lunch counter sit-in in Greensboro, North Carolina. Every year in January, the National Civil Rights Museum celebrates Dr. Martin Luther King Jr.'s birthday over the national-holiday weekend with educational programs and events. In April, the museum hosts an annual event to commemorate King's tragic death in 1968.

National Ornamental Metal Museum

1-877-881-2326
www.metalmuseum.org
374 Metal Museum Dr., Memphis, TN 38106
Open: Tues.–Sun.
Admission: Adults $5; seniors $4; students and children (5–18) $3
Special Feature: Group tours available

Located just south of downtown Memphis near the cantilevered Memphis–Arkansas Bridge on the banks of the Mississippi River, the Metal Museum preserves and celebrates feats in the art of contemporary metalwork. With an in-house collection of more than three thousand pieces, the museum provides an expansive look at various styles of metalwork and also plays host to national traveling exhibitions. Items on display include jewelry, contemporary sculpture, custom-made knives, and gothic European lockboxes. For those looking for a more hands-on experience, the museum offers a series of ongoing classes and metal workshops. Visitors can also watch the artists in action in the working blacksmith shop. All metal aside, the 3-acre, tree-lined setting on a quiet bluff overlooking the Mississippi River is a draw in itself, and visitors are encouraged to stroll through the museum's sculpture garden and take advantage of the riverside picnic area.

The Pink Palace

901-320-6320
www.memphismuseums.org
3050 Central Ave., Memphis, TN 38111
Open: Daily
Admission: Adults $8.75; seniors $8.25; children (3–12) $6.25
Special Features: Combination tickets for museum, IMAX, and planetarium are available

Built by Piggly Wiggly founder Clarence Saunders in the 1920s, this 36,500-square-foot mansion constructed of pink marble houses Tennessee's most visited museum. Unfortunately, Saunders never saw his dream home completed, and after he declared bankruptcy in 1923, the Pink Palace was donated to the city of Memphis. Today, most of the museum's collections are housed in exhibit space located behind the main mansion, where the CTI IMAX Theater and Sharpe Planetarium are also located. Collections focus on Memphis history, natural science, and social history, with display items that range from Civil War artifacts to dinosaur models. Favorite exhibits include the full-scale replica of the first Piggly Wiggly store from 1916 and Clyde Parke's fascinating hand-carved miniature circus. Inside the gorgeous mansion, popular exhibits from the past include a creepy shrunken head from South America. Memphis-centric artifacts include Elvis Presley's Army uniform, W. C. Handy's trumpet, and costumes and memorabilia from the Cotton

The Pink Palace family of museums includes the CTI IMAX Theater, Sharpe Planetarium, and Lichterman Nature Center. Memphis Convention & Visitors Bureau

Carnival and Cotton Makers' Jubilee. After touring the museum, visitors can catch a film on the four-story IMAX theater screen, immerse themselves in far-off galaxies in the Sharpe Planetarium, or grab a bite at the on-site café.

Slave Haven Burkle Estate Museum

901-527-3427
826 N. Second Ave., Memphis, TN 38107
Open: Mon.–Sat.
Admission: Adults $6; students $4

Built by German immigrant Jacob Burkle in 1849, the Burkle Estate played a key role in the Underground Railroad during the days of American slavery. The small white clapboard house is dressed with 19th-century furnishings, setting the scene for an insightful and heart-wrenching look into America's disturbing past. The tour focuses on the plight of African American slaves, from their brutal capture and transatlantic journey aboard slave ships to life on plantations. The tour includes a trip down to the cellar, through what was once a trap door, where runaway slaves were kept in hiding before moving north. Allow around 45 minutes for the guided tour. A small gift shop inside the museum sells DVDs, books, T-shirts, and other related literature.

Stax Museum of American Soul Music

901-946-2535
www.staxmuseum.com
926 E. McLemore Ave., Memphis, TN 38106

Open: Tues.–Sun.

Admission: Adults $12; seniors, active military, and students $11; children 9–12 $9; children 8 and under free

Special Features: Group rates available; 15 percent discount for AAA members

Located in the South Memphis neighborhood known as Soulsville, USA, Stax Records is famed for releasing hit records by Otis Redding, Rufus Thomas, Booker T. & the MGs, and the Staple Singers. In the label's 1960s heyday, the in-house studio band created an instantly recognizable "Stax Sound" that would be imitated for decades to come. Today the legendary studio serves as an outstanding museum that pays tribute not only to Stax history, but that of soul music's roots dating back to gospel, jazz, and jump blues.

After a 20-minute introductory video, visitors are free to explore the colorful museum on a self-guided tour. Highlights range from a carefully reconstructed, century-old Delta church to Isaac Hayes's peacock blue '72 Superfly Cadillac El Dorado outfitted with white fur, gold trim, and a refrigerator. Visitors can step inside the re-created Studio A and marvel at the sheer volume of hits that the label turned out during its prime. Other fantastic curios include a wall display of nearly a thousand vinyl records and Tina Turner's (tiny) gold-sequined stage dress. Allow around an hour and a half for a leisurely tour—longer if you plan to peruse the gift shop or strut your stuff on the museum's "Soul Train" dance floor. Next door, the Stax Music Academy provides music education for inner-city kids—one of whom may just turn out to be the next Isaac Hayes. The museum shop is a fantastic place to stock up on music, DVDs, posters, and just about anything stamped with the cool Stax logo.

Home of Stax Records since 1959, the old Capitol Theater now houses the Stax Museum of American Soul Music. Memphis Convention & Visitors Bureau

Popular performers like U2, Bonnie Raitt, and Beck still flock to Sun Studio to try to re-create musical magic.
Memphis Convention & Visitors Bureau

Sun Studio
901-521-0664, 1-800-441-6249
www.sunstudio.com
706 Union Ave., Memphis, TN 38103
Open: Daily
Admission: Adults $12; children 5–11 free; children 4 and under not permitted

This unassuming, two-room studio achieved legendary status when a young Elvis Presley recorded his hip-shaking version of "That's All Right" here in 1954. Widely regarded as the birthplace of rock 'n' roll, the studio was deemed a National Historic Landmark in 2003. Thirty-minute guided tours given throughout the day on the half hour allow visitors to stand within the hallowed walls of the tiny, no-frills space—maintained exactly as it was in the '50s—and listen to original recordings by Sun veterans like Jerry Lee Lewis, Johnny Cash, Roy Orbison, and, of course, Elvis. Black-and-white photos of the greats look down from the walls as visitors line up behind Elvis's original microphone for photo ops. Adjacent to the museum, classic rock 'n' roll enthusiasts, and milk shake lovers alike, will not want to miss Sun's retro soda fountain and gift shop, boasting an impressive collection of music, souvenirs, CDs, and apparel. Bonus for visitors without transportation: Sun operates a free shuttle all day long between the studio, downtown's Rock 'n' Soul Museum, the Heartbreak Hotel, and Graceland. There's an hour-long stop at Sun, during which you're encouraged to tour the studio.

W. C. Handy House Museum
901-527-3427
352 Beale St. at Fourth Ave., Memphis, TN

Open: Tues.–Sat.
Admission: $3

This modest shotgun shack was once the home of the Father of the Blues—one W. C. Handy. While in residence, Handy composed songs that would later become standards, including "St. Louis Blues," "Memphis Blues," and, of course, "Beale Street Blues." Now a museum dedicated to the artist's life and work, the short tour (allot approximately 15 to 20 minutes) pays tribute to the Memphis legend via an in-house collection of rare photographs and memorabilia that tell Handy's story, including his rise to notoriety and everlasting impact on the blues, and beyond. The museum is also home to a small blues-themed gift shop. Hours of operation can be unpredictable, so be sure to call ahead before paying a visit.

Music

Gibson Lounge
901-544-7998
www.gibson.com
145 Lt. George W. Lee Ave., Memphis, TN, 38103

Located (naturally) inside the Gibson guitar factory and retail store, the Gibson Lounge is an intimate venue that can be rented out for private events and occasionally plays host to nationally touring acts. Call ahead for a schedule of public events.

Mud Island Amphitheater
901-576-7241
www.mudisland.com/concerts.asp
125 N. Front St., Memphis, TN 38103

This five-thousand-seat open-air amphitheater within Mud Island River Park offers an ideal setting for live music. Concertgoers can get to the amphitheater via the monorail (for

---

Memphis in the Movies

With its rich cultural history and incomparable atmosphere, Memphis is regularly sought after to pose as both a backdrop, and a central character, in a wide array of films. The city has long served as an artistic muse, most recently in the works of Memphis filmmaker Craig Brewer (*Hustle & Flow, Black Snake Moan*), who lives and works out of Memphis. Not since Jim Jarmusch's 1989 film *Mystery Train* has a filmmaker so expertly captured the overt and subliminal nuances of life in the capital of the mid-South. The city also hosts the Memphis International Film Festival (held in the spring) and Indie Memphis: Soul of Southern Film Festival (held in October).

Notable Films Shot in Memphis include:

Mystery Train, 1989	*21 Grams*, 2003
Great Balls of Fire, 1989	*Elizabethtown*, 2005
The Firm, 1993	*Forty Shades of Blue*, 2005
The Client, 1994	*Hustle & Flow*, 2005
The People vs. Larry Flynt, 1996	*Walk the Line*, 2005
The Rainmaker, 1997	*Black Snake Moan*, 2006
Cast Away, 2000	*My Blueberry Nights*, 2008

In addition to the concert series, Mud Island Amphitheater hosts music festivals and special events.

a fee) or on the pedestrian bridge from downtown's Front Street. Views from the venue are simply stunning, with a stage backed by the downtown Memphis skyline rising up from the banks of the Mississippi. Stars twinkle in the skies above, and although downtown is just across the water, the amphitheater feels secluded and intimate. The venue brings in national touring acts like Willie Nelson, Norah Jones, Kid Rock, and the Black Crowes.

New Daisy Theatre
901-525-8979
www.newdaisy.com
330 Beale St., Memphis, TN 38103

Located across the street from the original Daisy Theater on the east end of Beale, the New Daisy is a one-thousand-capacity room that books everything from rock and pop to jazz and blues. A converted movie theater, the venue has a balcony in addition to the floor, allowing patrons the option of choosing between the up-close-and-personal concert experience or a loftier vantage point.

Theater

The Cannon Center for Performing Arts
901-576-1269
www.thecannoncenter.com
255 N. Main St., Memphis, TN 38103

Though primarily known as the home of the Memphis Symphony Orchestra, the Cannon Center for Performing Arts also hosts national pop acts, the opera, ballet, touring theatrical productions, children's theater, and more. Opened in 2003, the 2,100-seat space is considered to be one of the mid-South's premiere multipurpose rooms. See the Web site for upcoming event listings. Tickets may be purchased via Ticketmaster or at the Cannon Center ticket office. Tickets for Memphis Symphony Orchestra performances can be purchased via the Memphis Symphony Orchestra box office (901-537-2525) or through Ticketmaster.

The Orpheum Theatre

901-525-7800
www.orpheum-memphis.com
203 S. Main St., Memphis, TN 38103

Billed as "Where Broadway Meets Beale," the Orpheum Theatre was originally called the Grand Opera House before changing its name in 1907. Primarily known as a vaudeville theater, the Orpheum burned to the ground in 1923 and was rebuilt at the same location in 1928. As movies became popular, the Orpheum embraced the new medium and was heralded as one of the South's premiere movie theaters. These days, the elegant theater hosts visiting Broadway productions, performances by local art groups Ballet Memphis and Opera Memphis, national touring musicians, and comedians. Those fascinated by the paranormal will be interested to know that one of Memphis's most famous ghosts is said to reside in the Orpheum. The entity, known as Mary, is said to be the spirit of a little girl who died in the early 1920s in an automobile accident near the theater on Beale Street. Her presence can allegedly can be found in or around seat C-5.

Tickets for performances at the Orpheum Theatre can be purchased at the box office, Davis-Kidd Booksellers, or through Ticketmaster. Memphis Convention & Visitors Bureau

Playhouse on the Square/The Circuit Playhouse
901-726-4656
www.playhouseonthesquare.org
51 S. Cooper St., Memphis, TN 38104

Known as the only professional equity theater company in Memphis, these sister theaters host both Broadway and off-Broadway productions. Circuit Playhouse, located at 1705 Poplar Avenue, was founded in 1969, with Playhouse on the Square opening nearly a decade later. Since that time, more than 720 shows have been performed between the two theaters. A forward-thinking group, the playhouses host "pay what you can" nights where patrons do just that (limit of four tickets per person). Tickets may by purchased through the box office.

Other Cultural Sites

Al Green's Full Gospel Tabernacle
901-396-9192
www.algreenmusic.com/fullgospeltabernacle.html
787 Hale Rd., Memphis, TN 38116

In 1976, a spiritually renewed Al Green founded the Full Gospel Tabernacle in South Memphis, about five minutes from Graceland. As adept at stirring up a congregation as he was an auditorium full of soul music enthusiasts, Green's church took off and has since dominated his life the past 30-plus years. With its welcoming open-door policy, the church is often frequented by out-of-town guests. Located in a residential neighborhood, it is housed in a somewhat modest church whose pews seat a good amount of churchgoers— not that you'll be sitting much. The music, if not Green's message, is sure to get you on your feet. When the Reverend Green preaches "there ain't no party like a Holy Ghost party," backed by a full band and choir, you can't help but believe him, no matter your denomination. The man's faith is as intoxicating as his music. While the Reverend Green isn't guaranteed to preach every Sunday, it's an experience not to be missed, no matter who's behind the pulpit. Expect Southern hospitality; a sermon that stretches up to two or three hours; plenty of hand clapping, humor, brow wiping, hallelujahs, palms reached towards the sky, and pastor-to-audience calls and responses; and an instinctive house band that's quick to embellish the reverend's sermon with drum and organ fills. The church depends on contributions from the congregation, so remember to bring some money for the offering. Arrive late if you must, but whatever you do, don't leave early—or expect to get called out by the reverend.

Center for Southern Folklore
901-525-3655
www.southernfolklore.com
119 S. Main St., Memphis, TN 38103
Open: Mon.–Sat.

Funky folk art rules at this downtown treasure trove of regional culture. Part performance hall, art gallery, retail space, and café, the nonprofit Center for Southern Folklore wears a multitude of hats, all focused on its vision "to preserve, defend, and promote the music, culture, arts, and rhythms of the South." When visiting the Folklore store, plan to spend a

The Center for Southern Folklore puts on the Memphis Music & Heritage Festival every Labor Day weekend.

good amount of time (and possibly money) perusing their carefully curated collection of paintings, photography, books, music, and much more. A veritable sensory overload, the shop also includes a café serving Southern specialties like homemade cobbler and hot water corn bread, and a small live music stage that caters to both bluesmen and folkies alike. The Folklore Hall, a larger performance space behind the store in the Pembroke Square Building at Peabody Place, can pack in more than two hundred for larger live music shows and private events. Tours, cultural excursions, and educational seminars are also available for groups. Check the center's Web site, or call ahead, to inquire about upcoming exhibitions, performances, and general seasonal happenings. Every Labor Day weekend the center puts on the Memphis Music and Heritage Festival with live music, a cooking stage, and much more.

SEASONAL EVENTS

January
Elvis Presley Birthday Celebration
Graceland
1-800-238-2000
www.elvis.com/graceland
3734 Elvis Presley Blvd., Memphis, TN 38186

Not surprisingly, in Memphis, the days leading up to the King's birthday are nothing short of an all-out, free-for-all celebration. A condensed version of Elvis Week in August, fans descend upon Memphis from all over the world to partake in pan-Elvis activities. The event is officially presented by Graceland, and you'll find plenty of activities on the mansion grounds and beyond. Expect casual fan meet-ups (at Marlowe's or Magnolia Restaurant), concerts (like the Memphis Symphony Orchestra performing Elvis tunes), Elvis Fan Club insider-only events, scavenger hunts, Elvis impersonators, gospel tributes, and much more.

February

Beale Street Zydeco Festival

www.southernculturalalliance.com
Beale St., Memphis, TN 38103

While Beale Street may be best known for the blues, this annual fest brings top zydeco talent to Memphis, drawing a fresh crowd to downtown's historic street. The weekend event celebrates Creole culture and zydeco music, with live music and dancing at clubs up and down the Beale Street strip. Wristbands are sold for the weekend, giving visitors admission to all of the clubs that take part in the festivities.

International Blues Challenge

901-527-2583
www.blues.org/ibc

Now in its third decade, the annual International Blues Challenge assembles the winners of 160 regional competitions from around the world in search of the best in unsigned blues bands and artists. Presented by the Blues Foundation, the Challenge is held in various clubs on Beale Street, with the finals taking place at the nearby Orpheum.

April

Africa in April Cultural Awareness Festival

901-947-2133
www.africainapril.org
Robert R. Church Park, Beale and Fourth sts.

This four-day downtown festival celebrates African culture through music, food, theater, dance, arts, crafts, and more. Every year, a different African country is showcased, and African dignitaries and ambassadors are welcomed to Memphis. In addition to watching traditional dances, live music, and a variety of performances, visitors can shop for jewelry, clothing, and more from various vendors at the festival's marketplace. Africa in April has been going strong since 1986.

May

Blues Music Awards

901-527-2583, ext. 12
www.blues.org/bluesmusicawards

Held annually in May, the Blues Music Awards (formerly known as the W. C. Handy Awards) was founded in 1979. Presented by the Blues Foundation, the awards are known worldwide as the highest form of recognition within the genre. The night brings together blues musicians and enthusiasts to commemorate excellence in blues recordings and performances from the previous year. Generally held at downtown's Cook Convention Center, the event features appearances and performances by a variety of blues artists and usually sells out.

Memphis In May

www.memphisinmay.org

Held every spring, this monthlong, citywide celebration features the Beale Street Music Festival, the World Championship Barbecue Cooking Contest, and the Sunset Symphony. The festival celebrates a different country each year through music, arts, lectures, and a variety of events presented to increase foreign cultural awareness. Founded in 1977, Memphis In May has grown into one of the South's premiere festivals, with a reputation for outstanding, genre-spanning music, art, and food.

The Beale Street Music Festival kicks off the event the first weekend of May in downtown's riverside Tom Lee Park. For three days, more than 60 artists representing a variety of genres

Hundreds of teams compete for $90,000 in prizes and ultimate bragging rights at Memphis In May's World Championship Barbecue Cooking Contest. Memphis Convention & Visitors Bureau

play on four stages, and tickets generally sell out. Past performers include Aretha Franklin, Lou Reed, Van Morrison, Bob Dylan, the Black Crowes, and Sheryl Crow. The festival's barbecue contest is also a huge draw, with connoisseurs traveling far and wide to both compete in and watch one of the world's best barbecue competitions. Capping off the festivities is the Sunset Symphony, which takes place the final weekend of May in Tom Lee Park. The Sunset Symphony marks the single largest performance of the Memphis Symphony Orchestra, with works ranging from classical standards to music from the country being honored that year.

July

Blues On The Bluff

901-528-0560
www.wevl.org/bob
374 Metal Museum Dr., Memphis, TN 38106

Each summer for more than 20 years, the Bluff City's WEVL (radio 89.9 FM) has hosted the appropriately titled Blues On The Bluff. Held on the picturesque grounds of the Metal

Museum, overlooking the Mississippi River, the day-long event features some of the best blues talent going, providing a fun environment for both adults and kids. While no pets or outside food or beverages are allowed on the premises, both alcoholic and nonalcoholic beverages are sold on-site, along with some of Memphis's award-winning barbecue.

August

Elvis Week
Graceland
1-800-238-2000
www.elvisweek.com
3734 Elvis Presley Blvd., Memphis, TN 38186

Every August, thousands of the Elvis faithful gather in Memphis to take part in a candle-light procession to Presley's final resting place: his grave site at Graceland. This caps off a week of Elvis-related events that commemorate the anniversary of the King's death on August 16, 1977. The annual pilgrimage to Memphis-Mecca draws fans from around the world with at least one thing in common: a devotion to Presley that goes beyond simple fandom. Expect Elvis impersonators from every corner of the globe, tribute acts, every sort of Elvis merchandise imaginable, and, of course, Elvis tunes piping out of every car, restaurant, store, and speaker around.

Thousands of Elvis fans flock to the King's final resting place at Graceland every August during Elvis Week.

September

Memphis Music & Heritage Festival

901-525-3655
www.southernfolklore.com
Main St., Memphis, TN 38103

Presented by the Center for Southern Folklore over Labor Day weekend, the two-day Memphis Music & Heritage Festival takes place in the center of downtown Memphis from Peabody Place to Gayoso Avenue on Main Street. With five indoor and outdoor stages, the free festival highlights live blues, jazz, gospel, R&B, rockabilly, and soul music. In addition to live music, the fest features songwriting workshops, storytellers, quilt makers, and a cooking stage featuring all manner of mouthwatering cuisine.

NIGHTLIFE

While most visitors flock to Beale Street in search of the blues, purists will tell you that you have to venture off the beaten path to find the real deal. That's finally starting to change, thanks to the opening of downtown's Ground Zero Blues Club (a sister to the popular Clarksdale club). Don't get us wrong; you'll hear plenty of live blues on Beale Street, some of it pretty darn good, but you'll also hear a lot of cover bands of the "Mustang Sally" variety. The city's favorite real-deal juke joint is in a neighborhood that is anything but touristy. Beyond the blues, Midtown is home to some fine neighborhood bars, from hip scenes to some of the city's best dives.

Every Wednesday night in spring and summer is Bike Night on Beale.

Downtown: Beale Street

Alfred's on Beale

901-525-3711
www.alfredsonbeale.com
197 Beale St., Memphis, TN 38103

Perched on prime Beale Street real estate on the corner of Third, Alfred's wears several hats: restaurant, bar, live music venue, and above all, late-night dance club. DJ's get the party started on the patio, while bands crank it up on the indoor stage next to the expansive dance floor. Bands tend to be of the rock and cover band variety, but you'll also catch the occasional blues act on the patio. In fact, Alfred's patio may just be the bar's best feature. The street-level covered patio is fine, but the best seats in the house are on the second-floor patio overlooking the bustle below. You won't find better people-watching on Beale Street.

B. B. King's Blues Club

901-524-5464
http://memphis.bbkingclubs.com
143 Beale St., Memphis, TN 38103

One of Beale Street's most popular clubs, this bi-level venue tends to draw tourists and a slightly older local crowd who don't mind shelling out for the cover charge. From the house band to big-name traveling acts (including B. B. himself, at least once a year), the music is some of the best on Beale, with a solid lineup seven days a week. Downstairs, couples flock to the checkered dance floor in front of the stage or watch the action from folksy, hand-painted tables. If you're not in the mood to cut a rug, the split-level second floor offers an unbeatable bird's-eye view of the stage and dance floor. B. B.'s also serves Southern soul food, from gumbo and ribs to fried catfish po' boys. The venue encourages folks to exit through the gift shop, but don't think you'll be contributing to B. B.'s empire—he doesn't actually own the club.

Beale Street Tap Room

901-576-2220
168 Beale St., Memphis, TN 38103

If you happen to find yourself on Beale Street and don't feel like fighting the tourist crowd, this favorite watering hole is an ideal destination. The divey oasis caters to a local crowd primarily interested in beer . . . and a variety of it, with upwards of 30 brews on tap and more than 135 bottle selections to choose from. With well-worn wooden tables and exposed brick walls, the narrow bar exudes a friendly, neighborhood vibe and plays host to everyone from college-aged Baggo enthusiasts to sports fans catching various games on the TVs. Behind the bar you'll find an impressive collection of personalized beer steins that belong to a loose membership of longtime local patrons, who get discounted refills in their personal mugs. If you show up with a taste for something beyond beer, the Tap Room provides a full liquor bar and standard bar menu for noshing. Bands generally play on Friday and Saturday nights, and there's sometimes a cover.

Blues City Café
901-526-3637
www.bluescitycafe.com
138 Beale St., Memphis, TN 38103

Barbecue lovers who happen to find themselves on Beale Street around dinnertime, take note: Blues City Café is arguably the most reliable barbecue joint on the strip. Not the best in town, mind you, but sometimes you have to work with what ya got. Look for ribs, tamales, and sausage and cheese plates. Truth be told, the café is most well known for the bar and blues venue in the adjacent room. In fact, the spot's motto is D.Y.M.O.: Dance Your Meal Off! With live music every night of the week, Blues City Café is a nonstop party that caters primarily to the tourist crowd, which usually includes conventioneers, blues travelers, and weekend warriors from the mid-South and beyond.

EP's Restaurant and Bar
901-527-1444
www.epdeltakitchen.com
126 Beale St., Memphis, TN 38103

Anchoring the western end of the Beale Street strip since 2006, this sprawling spot offers food, live music, multiple bars, and a roomy dance floor beneath a giant chandelier. When a band's not on stage, the main area's centerpiece is a 185-inch screen used to project sports games, karaoke lyrics, and movies. A handful of cozy dining areas decorated with Elvis photos and art are just off the main bar area. On the menu, you'll find dressed-up regional cuisine with a heavy Creole influence. On the second level, Hoops bar is a more casual watering hole, complete with beer pong and a retro dive bar atmosphere. Upstairs, you can also snag a table overlooking the dance floor below or settle in on the spacious patio bar with fantastic views of the Orpheum Theatre.

King's Palace Café
901-521-1851
www.kingspalacecafe.com
162 Beale St., Memphis, TN 38103

A Beale Street mainstay since the turn of the last century, King's Palace Café exudes a healthy sense of history without getting lost in its own past. Patrons can drink and dine on King's classic New Orleans–style fare in the main dining room, then take the party outside to the side patio area. There's live jazz and blues in the room adjacent to the main dining area as well as outside. The patio tends to draw a younger set, while the inside area caters to a more mature crowd.

Rum Boogie Café
901-528-0150
www.rumboogie.com
182 Beale St., Memphis, TN 38103

This festive standby bookends Beale Street on the opposite end of B. B. King's. Larger, less polished, and with a slightly cheaper cover charge than its counterpart, Rum Boogie is

In addition to the main stage, Rum Boogie Café connects to Mr. Handy's Blues Hall, a more intimate venue open seasonally on weekends.

dominated by a large horseshoe bar and, of course, the stage. Nearly two hundred auto-graphed guitars hang from the ceiling throughout, and the exposed brick walls are covered in concert posters, vintage ads, and memorabilia ranging from Isaac Hayes's cape to the original Stax Records sign. Most nights, house band James Govan and the Boogie Blues Band puts on a fun, crowd-pleasing show, with other acts generally filling the early-week slots. In addition to live music nightly, Rum Boogie offers a full menu of Cajun specialties like gator gumbo, red beans and rice, and down-home combos that let you sample a little bit of everything.

Silky O'Sullivan's
901-522-9596
www.silkyosullivans.com
183 Beale St., Memphis, TN 38103

Since 1992, Silky O'Sullivan's (Silky's to the locals) has been a beloved Beale Street standby for good times, cold beer, and, of course, their world-famous Divers (a full gallon of booze served in a bucket with a handful of straws for sharing—seriously). Inside, you'll find a jovial crowd living it up at the long bar or seated at the tables surrounding a pair of dueling pianos. If that scene gets too loud or wild for your mood, head out back and take refuge in the New Orleans–style courtyard. In addition to Silky's resident goats, the courtyard bar area regularly features live music and dancing. If you work up an appetite, Silky's serves up barbecue ribs, burgers, and pub grub.

More Nightlife on Beale

There truly is a little something for everyone on Beale Street, from theme bars to cozy dives. For cowboys and country girls, there's **Double Deuce** (340 Beale St.; 901-527-9002) with its spring break party vibe, country music, and a mechanical bull. If that's the kind of party you're looking for, you may also want to check out **Coyote Ugly** (326 Beale St.; 901-888-8459), which is pretty much like the movie, with girls dancing on bars and plenty of shots. The biggest bar on Beale Street is the three-level **Club 152** (152 Beale St.; 901-544-7011). On the first floor, live music runs the gamut from R&B to techno; the second level (dubbed Mustang Sally's) is open on weekends for hip-hop DJs and dancing, while the third floor is dedicated to the late-night party scene. Wanna beat the heat with a frozen daiquiri? Head to **Wet Willie's** (209 Beale St.; 901-578-5650), where the superpotent treats come in more than 10 flavors. If you're looking to escape the flashier blues clubs and catch some live blues at a small, unassuming joint where the locals go, try **Black Diamond** (153 Beale St.; 901-521-0800). **People's Billiard Club** (323 Beale St.; 901-523-7627) is the place to go if you want to shoot some pool or catch a game.

Downtown: Off Beale

Ernestine & Hazel's

901-523-9754
531 S. Main St., Memphis, TN 38103

Take one step inside this weathered old joint, and the mouthwatering scent of a Soul Burger sizzling behind the bar is guaranteed to draw you in. The one-time brothel features dark, cavernous "working-girl" rooms up a well-worn staircase, where a second small bar and pianist draw boozed-up young crowds on weekends. With her retro R&B- and soul-anchored jukebox, exposed brick walls, and photos of legendary musicians that once frequented the place, Ernestine & Hazel's may be the closest thing to a time machine east of the Mississippi. Plant yourself on a bar stool, sip an ice-cold beer (they don't serve liquor), sink your teeth into a juicy burger, and listen to the owner recount this old haunt's colorful history. Stop by on Sunday for live jazz music.

The Flying Saucer Draught Emporium

901-523-8676
www.beerknurd.com/stores/memphis
130 Peabody Pl., Memphis, TN 38103

Sure, the Memphis outpost may be one in a chain of 13, but don't think for a second that this is a generic restaurant and bar. Like beer? If so, come thirsty, as it's the only booze the Saucer serves, and they offer a *lot* of it. By a lot, we mean more than two hundred beers from around the world, all served by resident "beer goddesses." Those with an appetite for something other than beer will delight in the Saucer's upscale pub fare, and cigar enthusiasts will feel at home perusing the house humidor for the perfect smoke to complement their draught. A comfortable, laid-back spot, the bar's windows remain open in nice weather for prime downtown people-watching. Decked out in couches, tables, and—you guessed it—saucers covering every inch of wall space, the Saucer also has a pool table and regular live music.

Ground Zero Memphis

901-522-0130
www.groundzerobluesclub.com
58 Lt. George W. Lee St., Memphis, TN 38103

Co-owned by Mississippi native and acclaimed actor Morgan Freeman, Ground Zero Memphis opened its doors in the spring of 2008. Located next to the Westin, just a hop, skip, and a jump away from the touristy hoopla of Beale Street, Ground Zero aims to be the downtown destination for authentic, down-home blues music. A close approximation of the popular Ground Zero club in Clarksdale that it's modeled after, the club's interior takes its style cues from old-school Delta juke joints: Think walls scribbled with random graffiti, mismatched yard-sale chairs, weathered beer signs, and a jar of pickled eggs propped on the bar. Better yet, it's all served up with a heaping side of soul food. With a full bar and authentic regional menu, the club, like its flagship location, caters to those looking to relax, listen to some live music, and walk away with a genuine Delta experience.

Marmalade Restaurant & Lounge

901-522-8800
153 G. E. Patterson Ave., Memphis, TN, 38103

Located adjacent to the recently gentrified South Main Arts District, Marmalade is a long-time neighborhood staple specializing in Southern soul food and live music. Open for dinner, the restaurant dishes up fried chicken, catfish, barbecue, spaghetti, steaks, and chops served alongside gumbo, turnip greens, black-eyed peas, and all other manner of Southern goodness. A full bar is available, and the staff couldn't be more pleasant and accommodating. Call ahead to find out about upcoming entertainment.

Molly Fontaine Lounge

901-524-1886
679 Adams Ave., Memphis, TN 38105

Located in Victorian Village across from the Woodruff-Fontaine House, this trendy lounge is housed in an elegant Victorian mansion that dates back to 1886. The brainchild of Karen Carrier, who's behind some of the city's most stylish eateries (Beauty Shop, Automatic Slim's, Do), Molly Fontaine's offers cocktails and tapas in an atmosphere that's at once historic, eclectic, and plenty hip. Originally a wedding present for Molly Woodruff Fontaine—whose ghost is said to haunt her parents' house across the street—the gorgeous home offers Victorian architecture combined with cozy nooks and crannies done up with plenty of contemporary style. Thursday through Saturday you'll find local jazz and blues chanteuse DiAnn Price at the baby grand in the main lounge area. Be aware that the neighborhood surrounding quaint Victorian Village is a little rough around the edges, so use common sense and don't leave valuables in your car.

Raiford's Hollywood Disco

901-528-9313
www.hollywooddisco.com
115 Vance Ave., Memphis, TN 38103-4217

If you're looking for a dance club with an overzealous smoke machine, hazy red party lights, pole-dancing patrons, an illuminated dance floor, and mirrored walls, then

Raiford's is your dream destination. Decor at this tiny spot on the outskirts of downtown consists of handprints-in-paint covering the walls, a disco ball, and a drum set next to the dance floor that anyone can take a whack at. The bar only serves 40-ounce beers, there's a $10 cover charge (ladies get in free on Thursday), and it's cash only. In 2007, after 32 years keeping Memphis dancing, the club closed when Robert Raiford retired, only to be reopened shortly thereafter under new management that vowed to preserve the funky vibe. Some locals will tell you that the club lost something in translation since it reopened, but newbies will probably be too overwhelmed by the smoke machine and drunken sorority girls grinding on the dance floor to care. You can still catch the legendary Raiford at the DJ station spinning funk, soul, and R&B on some weekends.

Sauces

901-473-9573
www.saucesmemphis.com
95 S. Main St., Memphis, TN 38103

Downtown's only mojito bar is located on the Main Street trolley line. Contemporary and artsy, the space's exposed-brick walls are covered with vibrant local artwork. The narrow front room, dominated by a large bar that glows red thanks to a funky backlight, opens up into a slightly larger dining area down a few stairs at the back. There's also a small, festive patio out front on the trolley line. Sauces doubles as a restaurant, with a menu that features she-crab soup, a selection of fish dishes, crabcakes, and mojito mango chicken. But the main star here is clearly the mojitos, made with fresh mint leaves and just-squeezed lime juice. There are around 10 varieties to choose from, including pomegranate, spiced peach, and vanilla. Mojito Mondays feature $6 mojitos all day.

Midtown

Alex's Tavern

901-278-9086
1445 Jackson Ave., Memphis, TN 38107

Open since 1953, Midtown's favorite dive is known for serving some of the coldest beer in town. Alex's is a neighborhood joint in every sense of the word. Famous for their ridiculously delicious Rocky Burgers, this cozy, dimly lit, beer only bar has a kitchen that stays open until 5 AM, drawing everyone from Rhodes College students to neighborhood barflies. The TVs are usually tuned in to sports or whatever movies happen to be on cable, and the shuffleboard table against the back wall always has a crowd around it. Unconsciously retro, the room rocks a soul-heavy jukebox and wood-paneled walls lined with black-and-white photos of Babe Ruth and other past pop-culture icons.

The Blue Monkey

901-272-2583
2012 Madison Ave., Memphis, TN 38104

Located in Midtown's Overton Square area, the Blue Monkey is a quintessential neighborhood joint for the twentysomething set. With its casual, laid-back atmosphere, a wide variety of beer and wine, pool tables, and frequent live music, the bar is a favorite place to start—or end—a night out. Expect a packed, heavy-drinking house on weekends. Those looking to nosh will find the Monkey's pizza-heavy menu appealing. There's a second Blue

Monkey outpost downtown in the warehouse district at 513 South Front Street; it draws a young professional crowd and has a slightly mellower atmosphere.

Buccaneer Lounge
901-278-0909
1368 Monroe Ave., Memphis, TN 38104

Walking up to the Buccaneer, you'll probably think that it looks like a house, and you would be correct. The retro abode is now the site of one of the city's best underground and indie music rooms, with all the requirements for a good night out. Solid jukebox? Check. Full bar? Check. Intimate room with solid bookings? Check. Expect a laid-back, hipster, rock 'n' roll vibe and plenty of atmosphere to boot (the bar, in keeping with the pirate theme, is naturally called "the poop deck"). Its funky decor, wood-paneled walls, and old brick fireplace make a night out at the Buccaneer feel more akin to a good house party than a club night. Those who need a bit of fresh air or a more laid-back experience can escape the club's close quarters and relax outside on the front patio.

Celtic Crossing
901-274-5151
www.celticcrossingmemphis.com
903 S. Cooper St., Memphis, TN 38104

Here we have a little taste of Ireland smack in the middle of Memphis's Cooper-Young district. With its roomy shaded patio out front, and cozy bar and dining areas inside, the pub provides a surprisingly genuine Irish atmosphere in which to relax whilst enjoying some fine Irish fare with a side of whiskey or stout. Depending upon the night (and season), you're as likely to catch a session of Celtic musicians as you are to see a soccer match on the TV.

The Hi-Tone Café
901-278-8663
www.hitonememphis.com
1913 Poplar Ave., Memphis, TN 38104

Driving around Memphis, you'll no doubt see hordes of bumper stickers touting MEMPHIS IS MIDTOWN, and the Hi-Tone very much plays into the hype. Located off funky Poplar Avenue across from Overton Park, the Hi-Tone is one of the city's premiere live music rooms, drawing both local talent and national touring acts. A rock club in every sense, the four-hundred-person-capacity room is dark, often sweaty, and an almost guaranteed good time—all of which surely played into Elvis Costello's decision to use the venue as the backdrop for his 2005 *Club Date—Live In Memphis* DVD. Beyond the main room and bar area, patrons can relax in the adjacent lounge or play Ping-Pong in the side room. Don't be surprised if you find yourself challenging the guitarist of a band waiting to go onstage.

Lamplighter Lounge
901-726-1101
1702 Madison Ave., Memphis, TN 38104

This tiny old bar is just too cool—in a retro, time-warpy sort of way. Dive-bar connoisseurs will swear they're in Bukowski heaven, or quite possibly a David Lynch film. With an eclectic, neighborhood vibe, the Lamplighter Lounge is big on character and even bigger on atmosphere. Bric-a-brac and cloth place mats are reminiscent of Grandma's, but the vibe is more house party than weekend at Mamaw's. Grab a seat at the bar, order up a cheap, ice-cold PBR (Pabst Blue Ribbon) (there's no liquor), or pile in a cozy booth and treat yourself to a world-famous Shirley Burger. (Hint: That would be Shirley behind the bar.) Need to stretch your legs? Shoot some pool with the locals at the old-school table next to a jukebox that still plays vinyl 45s. Naturally, the jukebox is as eclectic as its surroundings, with everything from Otis Redding to Lou Reed. Fans of Cat Power may recognize the place from her 2007 "Lived in Bars" video.

Newby's
www.newbysmemphis.com
901-452-8408
539 S. Highland St., Memphis, TN 38111

A far cry from the lights of Beale Street, Newby's has been dealing in good times for University of Memphis students since 1975. Located on the Highland strip, the music venue/bar/restaurant draws all types. A young crowd packs the bar side of the space to shoot pool, fill up on bar bites, and sip Long Island Teas on Speed (so named for the energy drink mixed in). The venue side books a wide variety of music from roots rock to country, including national touring acts that draw the college crowd. The patio out back sometimes features live music of the acoustic variety.

P&H Café
901-726-0906
1532 Madison Ave., Memphis, TN 38104

Come for a beer and stay for a burger—or, you know, vice versa. Hailing itself as "the beer joint of your dreams!" the P&H (that would be Poor and Hungry) has been in existence, in some form or another, since JFK was in office. A Midtown staple, the P&H draws its poor and hungry patrons from the immediate neighborhood and beyond, with billiards, darts, a jukebox, free wireless Internet, live music, and a generally laid-back vibe. And that's not even mentioning the suds and grub. The regulars swear by the stuffed burgers—for example, El Espanol (cheddar and jalapeños) or Greek (feta cheese and capers)—washed down with an ice-cold pitcher of domestic draft served in ice-covered beer mugs. Feeling brave? Top it off with a Bunny Cream, a deep-fried honey bun smothered in vanilla ice cream and super-rich chocolate syrup. The beer joint took on added notoriety in 2000 when local filmmaker Craig Brewer (*Hustle & Flow, Black Snake Moan*) named his first film after the P&H.

Wild Bill's
901-726-5473
1580 Vollintine Ave., Memphis, TN 38107

Looking for a throwback, real-deal juke joint in Memphis proper? If so, you'll undoubtedly be directed, time and again, to Wild Bill's. A classic juke that seems to defy both time and popular trends, Wild Bill's delivers live blues, 40-ounce beers, dancing, all manner of local characters, and a healthy sense of living life for the moment. While Bill's is open during the workweek, things really get cranking on the weekends, when folks flock here for two things: good times and great blues. Thankfully, the joint delivers plenty of both. This establishment is a must.

Young Avenue Deli

901-278-0034
www.youngavenuedeli.com
2119 Young Ave., Memphis, TN 38104

Arguably Memphis's best live-music hall, the Deli has been packing 'em in since the late '90s, with an ear for both local talent and national touring artists. While the space may resemble a large warehouse, the atmosphere remains relatively cozy and intimate, with a spacious bar on the side, pool tables and a jukebox in the rear, booths flanking the opposite wall, and tables scattered across the cement floor. There's also a nice sidewalk patio that's perfect for soaking up the Cooper-Young scene. When a big show comes to town, expect the tables in front of the stage to be jettisoned in order to make room for those looking to shake a leg. In search of late-night eats? If so, the Deli is a godsend, with a kitchen that stays open well past midnight. Beer snob? You, my friend, are also in the right place, as here you'll find just about every brew imaginable.

More Midtown Favorites

Midtown is home to a high concentration of neighborhood bars. If you want to rub shoulders with the locals, there's no better place than one of these popular spots. If you're driving through Midtown, you can't miss **Neil's** (1835 Madison Ave.; 901-278-6345) where patio signs promise FREE BEER TOMORROW and WHERE THE FAT MAN ROCKS. In addition to the expansive deck, Neil's offers pool tables, karaoke, and down-home American eats that include a cheeseburger served in a bowl. Down the street, **Zinnie's** (1688 Madison Ave.; 901-726-5004) is popular with the Rhodes College set and twenty- and thirtysomethings from the neighborhood. Drop a quarter in the jukebox, order a beer, grab a free basket of the saltiest popcorn this side of the Mississippi, and settle into a booth. A few doors down, **Zinnie's East** (1718 Madison Ave.; 901-274-7101) offers a nice front deck and a full menu. A neighborhood staple since 1977, **Murphy's** (1589 Madison Ave.; 901-726-4193) is a cozy Irish pub with live music, a patio, and a great happy hour. Newer on the scene, **Yosemite Sam's** (2126 Madison Ave.; 901-726-6138) is best known—and loved—for karaoke, but the neighborhood dive also offers darts, air hockey, and pub grub.

Gay Nightlife

Backstreet Memphis

901-276-5522
2018 Court Ave., Memphis, TN 38104

This popular gay club features a huge dance floor and cabaret entertainment.

Lorenz's

901-274-8272
1528 Madison Ave., Memphis TN 38104

Expect country music on the stereo in this gay-friendly dive.

Metro Memphis

901-274-8010
1349 Autumn Ave., Memphis, TN 38104

This gay bar and dance club in Midtown offers happy hour, karaoke, and amateur drag shows.

Pumping Station

901-272-7600
1382 Poplar Ave., Memphis, TN 38104

A leather and beer scene where televisions are tuned to gay porn, plus darts, pool tables, and a patio.

RESTAURANTS

A city with truly diverse culinary offerings, Memphis is both the pork barbecue capital of the world and home to some of the mid-South's finest white-tablecloth restaurants. Foodies will feel right at home with fantastic steakhouses, New American menus spiked with Southern flavor, and award-winning fine-dining establishments. Just don't skip the 'cue. It truly is some of the country's best, from dry ribs to tangy pulled-pork sandwiches served up at a slew of legendary joints throughout the city. You'll also find down-home soul food, meat 'n threes, country breakfasts, and several unbeatable burgers.

Dining Price Codes

Inexpensive	Up to $15
Moderate	$15–30
Expensive	$30–65
Very Expensive	More than $65

The following abbreviations are used to identify what meals are served:

B—Breakfast
L—Lunch
D—Dinner
SB—Sunday brunch

Downtown

Alcenia's

901-523-0200
317 N. Main St., Memphis, TN 38103
Open: Tues.–Sat.
Price: Inexpensive
Credit Cards: Yes
Cuisine: Southern, soul food
Serving: B (Sat.), L
Handicap Access: Yes

Alcenia's serves up authentic soul food with a heaping side of Southern hospitality. Located on the Main Street trolley line practically in the shadow of the Pyramid, it is a friendly, festive spot where owner BJ Chester-Tamayo greets everyone with a hug. The decor is Mardi Gras meets the jungle, with black-and-white checkered floors, orange walls, beads, the occasional animal-print chair, and plastic tablecloths in yellow, green, and purple. The down-home delicacies are made to order (locals who don't want to wait call in orders ahead) and generally include fried, baked, and barbecue chicken; pork chops; fried catfish; and the like. The sides rival the main entrée, with flavor-packed veggies like cabbage, green beans, slaw, lima beans, and mac 'n cheese—all served in large portions on colorful plastic plates and bowls, along with discs of hot water corn bread. For Alcenia's Saturday breakfast, you can get salmon croquettes, fried chicken and waffles, and Southern standards like eggs, grits, biscuits, and fried green tomatoes. Wash it all down with sweet tea or "ghetto-aid," which is rightfully billed as "super sweet Kool-Aid." Alcenia's, officially named Alcenia's Desserts & Preserves, is also touted for the sweet stuff. In addition to all sorts of fruit preserves and BJ's famous apple butter, Alcenia's offers tempting desserts like pecan, sweet potato, and custard pie; pound cake; cobblers; and the celebrated pecan-crusted bread pudding.

Arcade Restaurant

901-526-5757
www.arcaderestaurant.com

The Arcade Restaurant has been featured in numerous movies, including The Firm, Elizabethtown, *and* Walk the Line.

540 S. Main St., Memphis, TN 38103
Open: Daily
Price: Inexpensive
Credit Cards: Yes
Cuisine: Southern, American
Serving: B, L
Handicap Access: Yes

You can't miss the neon glow of the classic sign at this prominent corner café, which anchors the South Main Arts District at the end of the trolley line. Established in 1919, the retro landmark has been owned by the same family for three generations and was once a favorite of none other than Elvis Presley. Regulars on their lunch breaks and occasional tourists fill vintage tan and turquoise booths in the diner-style main room or settle in a narrow back room with checkered floors and walls covered in historic photos and local artwork. Something look familiar? The Arcade is a popular film location and has appeared in numerous movies over the years. The simple but varied menu features popular thin-crust pizzas; sandwiches like Elvis's favorite, fried peanut butter and bananas; and a few Greek dishes. Southern-style plate lunches served on weekdays are filling and fantastic, with selections like creamy chicken and dumplings, crispy fried catfish, country fried steak with gravy, fresh veggies, corn bread, and gooey cobbler for dessert. Homestyle breakfasts are just as popular, with everything from sweet potato pancakes to Eggs Redneck, with biscuits and sausage smothered in country gravy, eggs, and hash browns.

Automatic Slim's Tonga Club

901-525-7948
83 S. Second St., Memphis, TN 38103
Open: Daily
Price: Expensive
Credit Cards: Yes
Cuisine: Caribbean, Southwestern, New American
Serving: L (Mon.–Sat.), D
Handicap Access: Yes
Special Features: Live music some nights

A Memphis mainstay for more than 15 years, this funky spot still stands out for its creative cuisine and hip, artsy atmosphere. The prime downtown location is just across from the Peabody on a street that has seen a proliferation of restaurants in the past few years. The interior is dominated by a long bar where locals belly up for fun tropical cocktails and fruit-infused vodkas. Eclectic decor includes copper-leaf tables, zebra-print bar stools, and retro, mismatched chairs. An assortment of glowing lanterns hangs from the mile-high ceiling over the main room, while a second dining area is just up the stairs in a small, loftlike space. Heavy on Caribbean flavors, the creative menu also features a splash of Southwest spice and Southern soul. Starters are all over the map—literally—with everything from pulled chicken rolled in corn tortillas to Thai-style pork dumplings. Entrées may include seafood-infused Caribbean Voodoo Stew, coconut mango shrimp, and generally at least one Jamaican jerk selection, be it fish, duck, or chicken. Sides are equally creative, with tobacco onion rings, grits, and plantains.

Kooky Canuck

901-578-9800
www.kookycanuck.com
97 S. Second St., Memphis, TN 38103
Open: Daily
Price: Moderate
Credit Cards: Yes
Cuisine: American
Serving: L, D
Handicap Access: Yes

Come for the burgers and stay for the bargain steins of beer. Centrally located downtown, this relatively new local favorite gets packed for lunch and dinner. Notorious for their Kookamonga Challenge (finish a 4-pound burger in under an hour, and it's free!), The menu also offers creative comfort food like a deep-fried Cornish hen, a BLT spiced up with fried green tomatoes, and meat loaf served cold. Made-at-your-table s'mores are a fun way to finish any meal. The funky, lodgelike space features log cabin walls, stone pillars, a fireplace, and plenty of taxidermy staring down from the walls. The bustling bar area features TVs tuned into sports and, yes, beer. And lots of it. Giant glass beer mugs cover 75 percent of the room's tables, which begs the question, who's *really* the Kooky Canuck's mascot—that life-size Bigfoot in the corner, or the ubiquitous 1-liter mug full of brew? Jury's still out . . .

Bluefin Edge Cuisine and Sushi Bar

901-528-1010
www.bluefinmemphis.com
135 S. Main St., Memphis, TN 38103
Open: Daily
Price: Moderate–Expensive
Credit Cards: Yes
Cuisine: Sushi, Asian fusion
Serving: L (Tues.–Fri.), D
Handicap Access: Yes

Located on the Main Street trolley line amid the Peabody Place offerings, this trendy spot offers sushi and creative fusion cuisine in a hip, loungy setting. The multitiered space includes a bar area, separate sushi bar, private dining room with cushioned floor seating, and a main dining area with low-slung couches and a few plain old tables and booths. Decor is contemporary and bold, with purple and orange hues, and pockets of cushy lounge areas tossed with plenty of pillows. There's also prime outdoor patio seating where you can watch the trolley go by. The extensive sushi menu includes all the standards, plus creative rolls like the Louisiana roll with soft-shell crab and crawfish, and the Tasmanian Devil with Tasmanian sweet crab, salmon, cucumber, and avocado. Beyond sushi, entrées include beef and fish dishes, shabu shabu pots, and a few grill-at-your-table options. For those in the mood for something slightly more familiar, there are also pizzas topped with mushrooms, Tandoori chicken, and seared tuna. Desserts stay true to the fusion focus, with sweet concoctions like a toasted walnut and chocolate eggroll, and chocolate ganache cheesecake served with tempura bananas.

The Butcher Shop

901-521-0856
www.thebutchershop.com
101 S. Front St., Memphis, TN 38103
Open: Daily
Price: Expensive
Credit Cards: Yes
Cuisine: Steak, American
Serving: D
Handicap Access: Yes
Special Features: Cook-your-own steaks

Perched on a prime Front Street location since 1981, this rustic, casual steakhouse specializes in hickory-charcoaled steaks, aged four weeks and cut on-site. Inside, the atmosphere
is masculine and lodgelike, with hardwood floors, exposed brick walls, red-checked tablecloths, and plenty of taxidermy and antlers on the walls. Choose your steak from the display case, and decide if you'd like to cook it yourself on the large brick grill at the front of
the house. The extensive steak selection ranges from a 2-inch-thick, 14-ounce filet
mignon to a 30-ounce porterhouse. Favorites include the 9-ounce filet mignon stuffed
with portobello mushrooms, Gorgonzola, and rosemary. Entrées are served with a baked
potato, Texas toast, and the salad bar. Not in the mood for beef? Alternatives include
salmon, char-grilled chicken breast, pork chops, and Cajun shrimp.

Café 61

901-523-9351
www.cafe61memphis.com
85 S. Second St., Memphis, TN 38103
Open: Daily
Price: Moderate–Expensive
Credit Cards: Yes
Cuisine: Regional, Creole fusion
Serving: L, D, SB
Handicap Access: Yes
Special Features: Happy hour

Located in the heart of downtown Memphis across the street from the famed Peabody
Hotel, Café 61 offers a heaping helping of Louisiana bayou charm served up with a side of
down-home Delta blues. Named after the legendary Blues Highway, the funky restaurant
features a festive bar backed by an exposed brick wall opposite an orange-hued dining area
covered in vibrant folk art. Chef Derk Meitzler's self-described "Creole global fusion"
blends traditional Creole cooking with a gumbo of other techniques for highly original,
and highly delicious, meals. Warm up your palette with the Diablo: house-smoked, New
Orleans chaurice sausage topped with a dark Cajun barbecue sauce. For an entrée, try a
house specialty like the King Creole Pork Chop 61, a 12-ounce grilled chop served over
crawfish mac 'n cheese with a Creole cream sauce. For those who haven't already overex-
tended, Café 61's robust dessert menu tempts with rich treats ranging from a warm pecan
caramel brownie to rum cake.

Circa

901-522-1488
www.circamemphis.com
119 S. Main St., Memphis, TN 38103
Open: Daily
Price: Moderate–Expensive
Credit Cards: Yes
Cuisine: Regional, New American
Serving: L (Mon.–Fri.), D
Handicap Access: Yes
Special Features: Happy hour; valet Tues.–Sat. ($8)

Opened in 2007, this modern Main Street hot spot offers fine dining in a stylish, intimate setting. The slender, shotgun space is fronted by a cozy bar area that gives way to narrow rows of tables lined by wood partitions with cutouts that serve as wine racks. Billed as "regional Tennessee/contemporary American," chef-owner John Bragg's upscale cuisine is spiked with Southern flavor. For lunch, there are crawfish beignets, cornmeal fried oysters, a crabcake sandwich, and a half-pound Angus burger. At dinner, seasonal seafood starters include oysters on the half shell and panko-crusted soft-shell crab. As for entrées, selections may include duck prepared three ways, pan-roasted grouper with gulf shrimp and crabmeat, sorghum-cured rack of lamb, or a rib eye. Wine pairings from Circa's extensive offerings are suggested on the menu, and the knowledgeable staff is more than happy to lend their expertise. Circa also offers a bar menu of small plates that includes many appetizers found on the main menu. In addition to the extensive wine list, a creative cocktail menu features tempting martinis and fruit-infused concoctions.

Dyer's Burgers

901-527-3937
www.dyersonbeale.com
205 Beale St., Memphis, TN 38103
Open: Daily
Price: Inexpensive
Credit Cards: Yes
Cuisine: Burgers
Serving: L, D
Handicap Access: Yes
Special Features: Open until 5 AM on weekends

A Memphis original since 1912, Dyer's is famous for deep-fried hamburgers that are said to be cooked in the same grease since the restaurant's inception—a claim taken so seriously that the establishment hires an armed escort to transfer the grease to its various locations. The joint is styled like an old-fashioned diner—think booths, bar stools, a chrome soda fountain counter, and colorful neon signs. The menu features no-frills burgers, hand-cut french fries, onion rings, floats, milk shakes, homemade chili, and specialties like the Split Dog (Dyer's deep-fried hot dog) and the Big Rag Baloney (yep, that would be a deep-fried bologna sandwich). No matter your burger order, one thing is certain: The tender juiciness of the thin, fried patties will literally melt in your mouth. Burgers, dogs, bologna, and pretty much everything else is served with mustard, pickles, and onions.

Encore

901-528-1415
www.encore-memphis.com
150 Peabody Pl., Ste. 111, Memphis, TN 38103
Open: Daily
Price: Expensive
Credit Cards: Yes
Cuisine: Bistro
Serving: D
Handicap Access: Yes

After 20-plus years at the Peabody's Chez Philippe, Chef José Gutierrez branched out to open this sleek, French-style bistro in late 2005. Part of the Peabody Place entertainment complex, this contemporary dining gem is accessible from Second Street or from inside Peabody Place—where a few "patio" tables facing the movie theater don't exactly live up to the ambience inside. The main dining area is anchored by a backlit marble-topped bar that curves around the length of the room. Decor is minimalist chic, yet warm, with a curtained wall, modern lighting, and candlelit tables. On the menu, French-style bistro fare gets a shot of Southern flavor here and there but mostly stays true its Provençal roots. Whet your appetite with Camembert cheese beignets, crab flan, or classic steamed mussels. For the main course, seafood entrées may include lobster-stuffed sea scallops, caramelized salmon, or pan-roasted grouper. Meat dishes may feature braised short ribs, a New York strip served with *pommes frites,* or a double pork chop. There's also the Encore burger, with ground-to-order sirloin and bacon bits on a homemade roll. Encore also offers several specialty cocktails, including a mango martini, pineapple mojito, and a raspberry caipirinha—perfect for sipping at that handsome bar.

Felicia Suzanne's

901-523-0877
www.feliciasuzanne.com
80 Monroe Ave., Memphis, TN 38103
Open: Tues.–Sat.
Price: Expensive–Very Expensive
Credit Cards: Yes
Cuisine: Upscale Southern, American
Serving: L (Fri.), D
Handicap Access: Yes
Special Features: Reservations recommended

Upscale American cuisine with a heavy dose of Southern flavor is served with style at this historic space on the Main Street trolley loop. Located in a prime corner of the Brinkley Plaza building, built in 1869 as the original site for the Peabody Hotel, the space now occupied by Felicia Suzanne's combines historic ambience with contemporary style. Massive white columns prop up the lofty ceilings, while pale lavender walls and red velvet chairs add some modern pop. A gorgeous courtyard adjacent to the restaurant is one of the city's best spots to sip a cocktail, or enjoy seasonal hors d'oeuvres during warm-weather events. Sandwiched between two brick buildings, the outdoor space is adorned with hanging ferns, dripping ivy, potted flowers, wrought-iron tables, a fountain, and festive bulbs hanging overhead.

Aside from the striking ambience—both inside and out—the menu is reason enough for a visit. Chef-owner Felicia Willett launched her culinary career working with celeb chef Emeril Lagasse, and it shows. The creative seasonal menu is spiked with Southern flavor, including plenty of New Orleans influences. You may find fried Gulf oysters tossed in New Orleans–style barbecue sauce to start; a BLFGT salad, with bacon, lettuce, fried green tomatoes, and rémoulade sauce; and flavor-rich seafood entrées like pecan-encrusted redfish or shrimp and grits with andouille sausage. There's also generally a dressed-up, Southern-style steak; double-cut pork chop; and a duck option. Dessert is well worth saving room for, with indulgent sweets like Praline Pain Perdu layered with brown sugar ice cream and praline sauce.

Flying Fish

901-522-8228
www.flyingfishinthe.net
105 S. Second St., Memphis, TN 38103
Open: Daily
Price: Inexpensive–Moderate
Credit Cards: Yes
Cuisine: Seafood
Serving: L, D
Handicap Access: Yes
Special Features: Daily specials; all-you-can-eat catfish on Wed.

This casual mid-South chain serves up seafood favorites in a fun, festive atmosphere in the heart of downtown Memphis. After ordering at the counter, settle into a table or cushy retro booth with checkered tablecloths in the main dining room, or out front on the covered, open-air patio for downtown people-watching. Walls are plastered with cheeky decor like mounted fish with faux wings, oversize fishing lures, and an entire wall dubbed the "Billy Bass Adoption Center" covered in the cast-off pop-culture novelties (donate your own Billy Bass for a free basket of catfish). The extensive menu features fried seafood baskets with catfish, oysters, or shrimp, plus grilled fish plates, steamed crab legs, broiled shrimp, and crawfish (in season). You'll also find fish tacos, po' boys, and salads topped with grilled or fried seafood. Wash it all down with a bucket of beer or an oyster shooter.

Grill 83

901-333-1224
www.grill83.com
83 Madison Ave., Memphis, TN 38103
Open: Daily
Price: Expensive–Very Expensive
Credit Cards: Yes
Cuisine: Steak, New American
Serving: B, L, D, SB
Handicap Access: Limited
Special Features: Reservations recommended; valet parking

Located within the trendy Madison Hotel, this sleek, sophisticated restaurant serves celebrated steaks to well-heeled diners who don't mind dropping 30 bones on a prime cut of beef. The narrow dining room is anchored by a sizeable bar where patrons nibble on small plates and sip signature martinis served in chilled shakers. The minimalist urban vibe is more New York than Memphis, but the historic downtown photos remind you exactly where you are. Subtle lighting and limited tables create an intimate atmosphere, although the adjacent bar often fills up with locals on the weekends. While the menu changes seasonally, dinner standbys include a signature 16-ounce, bone-in Kansas City Filet and the popular seafood gumbo, which also shows up for lunch and Sunday brunch. Beyond steaks, offerings generally include creatively prepared seafood selections, and a lamb or duck entrée. Starchy sides that complement the steaks usually include potato gratin and garlic whipped potatoes. Lighter bites on the small-plates menu include Kobe beef sliders, raw oysters (in season), and beef satay. A dressed-down lunch menu features salads, pasta, burgers, and sandwiches.

Gus's Fried Chicken

901-527-4877
310 S. Front St., Memphis, TN 38103
Open: Daily
Price: Inexpensive
Credit Cards: Yes
Cuisine: Southern
Serving: L, D
Handicap Access: Yes

Located a block west of the South Main Arts District, this modest redbrick chicken shack is celebrated for its spicy fried chicken. Inside, the style is cheery juke joint, with cement floors, white brick walls covered in beer ads, checkered tablecloths, and mismatched chairs. Come lunch- and dinnertime, expect a packed house overflowing with patrons plugging money into the soul-heavy jukebox while waiting for tables to open up. Gus's "world-famous" golden brown, spicy-battered fried chicken is made to order (expect it to take 20 minutes or so) and served on a Styrofoam plate. There's not much else on the menu here, other than starters that include fried pickles and fried green tomatoes, and sides like beans, slaw, and potato salad. The best way to wash down Gus's spicy delicacy is with an ice-cold beer, served in 12-, 24-, 32-, or 40-ounce increments. The original Gus's is located a little under an hour away in a shotgun shack in Mason, Tennessee.

Inn at Hunt Phelan Restaurant & Veranda Grill

901-525-8225
www.huntphelan.com
533 Beale St., Memphis, TN 38103
Open: Tues.–Sun.
Price: Expensive–Very Expensive
Credit Cards: Yes
Cuisine: Creole, American, Southern
Serving: L (Fri.–Sat.) D, SB
Handicap Access: Yes
Special Features: Reservations recommended; valet parking

Housed in a gracious antebellum mansion, the Inn at Hunt Phelan offers four-star dining in an intimate Old South atmosphere. Dinner at the mansion is served in four elegantly appointed rooms that once served as the home's parlor, dining room, music room, and the library where Ulysses S. Grant set up his headquarters during the Civil War. Fortunately, white tablecloths and candlelit tables don't come with stuffy service here. The seasonal menu features Creole-style cuisine with a Southern twist, along with an impressive wine list. Down the hall, the less-formal Veranda Grill and bar serves the full dinner menu, plus more casual fare like burgers. With exposed-brick walls, hardwood floors, and spinning fans overhead, the grill's vibe is upscale but warm, as is the service throughout. Beyond the veranda for which the grill is named, a fountain courtyard is a pleasant place to eat or sip cocktails. Sunday brunch features Southern specialties (shrimp and grits), highbrow options (an omelet with lump crabmeat), and a New Orleans–style Pimm's Cup to wash it all down.

Itta Bena

901-578-3031
www.bbkingclubs.com
145 Beale St., Memphis, TN 38103
Open: Daily
Price: Expensive
Credit Cards: Yes
Cuisine: Southern, American
Serving: D
Handicap Access: No

On a strip chock-full of eateries that park "hype reps" on Beale to wave menus at tourists, Itta Bena is a refreshing change of pace. Located above B. B. King's, this discreet restaurant is accessible from two stairways that you'll probably only find by asking. New in 2008, this is Beale's only truly upscale eatery, and the vibe is like nothing you'll find on the well-traveled tourist stretch. Sure, you're just above B. B. King's, and while you can still hear the muffled beats below, the ruckus feels worlds away from this lofty oasis. Blue-tinted windows turn the Beale Street bustle into a cool distant sea while dim amber lighting creates a warm, intimate vibe inside. Named for B. B. King's hometown, Itta Bena is strategically designed to look stylishly rough around the edges—rustic chic, if you will, with well-worn hardwood floors, lofty ceilings with exposed beams, distressed windowsills, and well-dressed tables tucked away in cozy nooks and crannies. A large square bar is a fine spot for cocktails, and there's a private loungey nook with leather couches and a TV tucked away in the corner. The upscale menu stays true to its regional roots, with she-crab soup, shrimp served barbecue or scampi style, and shrimp and scallops served with white cheddar grits. You can also get a juicy pork chop, 14-ounce rib eye, or a fish dish. Sides include seasonal veggies and cheese grits served with sour cream and bacon.

The Little Tea Shop

901-525-6000
69 Monroe Ave., Memphis, TN 38103
Open: Mon.–Fri.
Price: Inexpensive
Credit Cards: Yes
Cuisine: Luncheon, Southern, regional
Serving: L

Handicap Access: Yes
Special Features: Catering

This landmark lunch spot has the honor of being Memphis's oldest restaurant, in business since 1918 and in the same location since 1935. Inside, the spacious dining room bustles with a lunch crowd of regulars, including many a lawyer and local businessman. Simple, cheery decor consists of pink walls covered in old photos, dark green wainscoting, and oilcloth-topped tables adorned with yellow silk flowers. To order, simply check the box next to your choice on the ballot-style menu that changes daily. Favorite entrées include fried catfish, chicken pan pie, corned beef and cabbage, and fried chicken. Main dishes are served with two vegetables, or you can opt for three or four on a vegetable plate. Fantastic veggies—shockingly cooked without pork fat—include the Little Tea Shop's famous turnip greens, fried okra, creamy mac 'n cheese, and cinnamon-and-nutmeg-spiked sweet potatoes. Crispy-edged corn sticks, another Little Tea Shop specialty, are served piping hot. The Lacy Special takes the sticks to the next level by sandwiching a chicken breast between them, then topping the whole thing with gravy. You can also get a simple chicken or tuna salad sandwich, or homemade soup. For dessert, there's cobbler and the Little Tea Shop's famous Frozen Pecan Ball, with ice cream, pecans, and plenty of hot fudge.

The Majestic Grille

901-522-8555
www.majesticgrille.com
145 S. Main St., Memphis, TN 38103
Open: Daily
Price: Moderate–Expensive
Credit Cards: Yes
Cuisine: American
Serving: L, D, SB
Handicap Access: Yes

This grand old building on the Main Street trolley line dates back to 1913, when silent films and live performances were shown at the Majestic No. 1 Theatre. Today, the lofty theater-turned-restaurant pays homage to its past with 1940s-style and silent films projected on a screen above the dining room, plus occasional live performances and art shows. There's room for more than two hundred diners on two levels of seating beneath sky-high ceilings that boast ornate crown moldings. Main-floor decor is done in sleek old Hollywood style, with an endless backlit bar, intimate booths, and rows of tables that split the room. Diners can also settle into tables overlooking the main floor on the theater's balcony level, or outside on a patio that edges up to the trolley line. The menu ranges from hand-made flatbread pizzas and pasta to seafood entrées. For lunch, there are a variety of salads, sandwiches, and burgers, while dinner consists of steaks and specialties like fall-off-the-bone barbecue ribs. The Majestic is also open for Sunday brunch, with mimosas, Bloody Marys, and indulgent Southern-style dishes like shrimp and grits, biscuits and sausage gravy, and chicken hash.

McEwen's on Monroe

901-527-7085
www.mcewensonmonroe.com
120 Monroe Ave., Memphis, TN 38103
Open: Mon.–Sat.
Price: Moderate–Expensive
Credit Cards: Yes
Cuisine: Southern, New American
Serving: L (Mon.–Fri.), D
Handicap Access: Yes

This beloved Southern-style bistro has been a go-to for locals for more than a decade.
Located in the heart of downtown Memphis, the cozy spot consists of two separate rooms.
To the left, there's a warm bar area with exposed brick walls, hardwood floors, and plenty
of bar seating. On the right, the stylish dining room features mustard walls adorned with
fine contemporary artwork. For lunch, McEwen's sandwich offerings include grilled tuna
on a Kaiser roll, roasted chicken salad, Cajun turkey, and a Cuban. You can also opt for a
salad or an entrée like grilled trout or chicken potpie. The dinner menu features upscale
Southern cuisine with an international spin. Starters may include buttermilk fried oysters
with a spicy mustard plum sauce or Southern-style spring rolls. Seafood selections may
include seared sea scallops served with stone ground cheddar grits, sweet-potato-crusted
catfish served with mac 'n cheese, or a grilled fish selection. There's also a rack of lamb,
dressed-up barbecue pork ribs, and an oven-roasted rib eye. McEwen's wine menu features a fine selection of vintages.

Mesquite Chophouse

901-527-5337
www.mesquitechophouse.com
88 Union Ave., Memphis, TN 38103
Open: Daily
Price: Expensive–Very Expensive
Credit Cards: Yes
Cuisine: Steak, American
Serving: L, D, SB
Handicap Access: Yes
Special Features: Valet parking on weekend; monthly wine tastings

Housed in a historic downtown brick storefront, this upscale steakhouse serves prime
steaks in a sleek, stylish setting. A handsome marble bar dominates the lofty main room,
which features dark hardwoods, a whitewashed brick wall, modern art, and a prominent
stone fireplace adorned with a buffalo head. In addition to white-tableclothed four-tops,
there are also large, cushy booths below crystal chandeliers. Down a few stairs, a second
dining area is topped with an atrium-style glass ceiling. Off to the side, a private dining
nook boasts deep red walls, a showpiece wine cellar, fireplace, and more modern artwork.
On the menu, tempting starters include Cajun prime rib pizza, bacon-wrapped shrimp,
and mesquite-grilled quail. Hand-cut steaks and chops include a 22-ounce bone-in rib
eye, New Zealand rack of lamb, and double bone-in pork chop. You can also opt for the
Chop House's signature hickory-smoked prime rib or filet mignon stuffed with blue crab

or blue cheese. Not in the mood for beef? Tasty salads, plus poultry, seafood, and pasta selections, round out the menu. Sunday brunch features prime rib, smoked salmon, shrimp 'n grits, omelets, and waffles.

Pearl's Oyster House

901-522-9070
www.pearlsoysterhouse.com
299 S. Main St., Memphis, TN 38103
Open: Daily
Price: Moderate
Credit Cards: Yes
Cuisine: Seafood, Cajun
Serving: L, D
Handicap Access: Yes

Housed in an atmospheric old building that used to be a tattoo parlor, this casual South Main newcomer (opened in 2007) draws crowds for seafood platters and fresh oysters. Inside, the spacious dining area features exposed-brick walls, hardwood floors, lofty ceilings with fans spinning overhead, and a slew of tables topped with butcher paper. There are also two bars, and a small patio out back. On the menu, you'll find fried seafood platters, seafood pasta, stuffed shrimp, crab legs, blackened catfish, and crabcakes. The star here, of course, is the oysters, served raw, char grilled, flash fried, or topped with jalapeños and pepper jack cheese. You can also get oysters Rockefeller or oysters Bienville with shrimp and mushroom Parmesan sauce. There's plenty of New Orleans flavor on the menu as well, including gumbo, shrimp and crawfish étouffée, po' boys, and red beans and rice. Other popular dishes include shrimp and grits, boiled shrimp, pan-roasted mussels, and crawfish (in season). Reservations are not accepted, so arrive early on busy weekend nights or expect a wait.

The Rendezvous

901-523-2746
www.hogsfly.com
52 S. Second St., Memphis, TN 38103
Open: Tues.–Sat.
Price: Moderate
Credit Cards: Yes
Cuisine: Barbecue
Serving: L (Fri.–Sat.), D
Handicap Access: No
Special Features: Bring your own wine (corkage fee applies); mail-order ribs

A local institution since Charlie Vergos set up shop in 1948, this family-run barbecue mecca draws constant crowds of tourists and locals alike. The mouthwatering smell of smoking pork lures hungry diners down the alley entrance next to the Holiday Inn Select. The wait can stretch well beyond an hour on weekends (reservations aren't accepted), but barbecue enthusiasts don't mind waiting with a pitcher of Michelob and the city's best sausage and cheese plate in the second-level parlor. Eventually, you'll be lead to the cavernous subterranean dining area that buzzes with old-school waiters toting endless racks of ribs. Dining areas feature red-checkered tablecloths and walls covered in a delightful hodgepodge of funky flea market finds, Southern relics, and photos of local legends. On the menu, dry-rubbed pork ribs are the specialty, but there's also charcoal-broiled chicken, pork shoulder, and a skillet of shrimp that must be ordered ahead. Simple sides consist of sweet baked beans, mustard-based slaw, and supersoft white bread to sop up the sauce. Whatever you order, be sure to cover it with the fantastically tangy sauce. If your tongue's not tingling after your first bite, add another squeeze. Can't get enough of the 'Vous? Mail-order ribs are available on the Web site.

Spindini
901-578-2767
www.spindinimemphis.com
383 S. Main St., Memphis, TN 38103
Open: Daily
Price: Moderate–Expensive
Credit Cards: Yes
Cuisine: Italian
Serving: D
Handicap Access: Yes

In Memphis, the name Grisanti is synonymous with fantastic Italian fare, which holds true for Chef Judd Grisanti's newest venture in the heart of trendy South Main. The narrow space is contemporary and urban, with a striking bar dominating one side of the room.

The Skinny on Memphis Barbecue

As a rule of thumb, there are some things you just don't discuss with strangers: politics, religion, and regional barbecue. No region is the same. Hell, no state, for that matter. The differences are primarily based on the choice of meat, the use of smoke and heat, the length of time cooked, and the sauce. Oh yes, the sauce, the differences in which are of utmost importance. In the Midwest—Kansas City, for example—the barbecue leans towards a thicker, sweeter, tomato-based sauce, whereas, in say, South Carolina, the barbecue masters employ vinegar and mustard as the base.

But we're here in Memphis, Tennessee, so let's talk Memphis barbecue, as it's some of the very best in the world. Home to more than one hundred barbecue restaurants and the Memphis In May World Championship Barbecue Cooking Contest, this town means business when it comes to slow-smoked pork. In Memphis (unlike Texas, where beef is the focus), pork is king, and it's served up in a variety of ways. The pulled-pork sandwiches (topped with tangy, mustard-based coleslaw) are considered by many barbecue connoisseurs to be the best out there.

But the real star here is the ribs. The pork ribs in Memphis are a mouthwatering affair, sacred to many. Many restaurants prepare their ribs with a dry rub, while some spots offer the option of having them "wet" (glazed in sauce). Memphis-style barbecue sauce is generally tomato based with plenty of vinegar. It's not too thick, not too sweet, and varies in level of heat. In addition to pulled pork and ribs, Memphis also perfects the barbecue bologna sandwich, barbecue spaghetti, barbecue nachos (excellent), and the perfect local starter: the sausage and cheese plate, served with barbecue sauce, saltines, and pickles.

Tables line the opposite wall and join a larger dining area in a back room that's anchored by Spindini's centerpiece: a glowing wood-fire oven that fits right into its sleek surroundings with copper casing and an impressive black tile facade. Striking modern art punctuates the space, and there's a cushy lounge nook with leather chairs and a flat-screen TV just off the bar. There's also a sharp covered patio area off the side of the restaurant. The menu includes a few traditional Grisanti family favorites (spaghetti, manicotti, lasagna) alongside selections that take a more modern twist on Italian cuisine. Of course, plenty of dishes are prepared in the showpiece oven, from bacon-stuffed trout cooked on a cedar plank to Spindini's signature wood-fired pizzas that come topped with everything from chicken and pesto to lobster. Pasta selections range from creamy seafood lasagna with lobster, shrimp, and crabmeat to a seared tuna steak over linguine. There's also brick chicken stuffed with prosciutto, spinach, and mozzarella; seared scallops over Parmesan risotto; and a Gorgonzola-stuffed filet mignon wrapped in bacon.

Stella

901-526-4950
www.stellamemphis.com
39 S. Main St., Memphis, TN 38103
Open: Mon.–Sat.
Price: Moderate–Very Expensive
Credit Cards: Yes
Cuisine: New American, upscale Southern
Serving: L (Mon.–Fri.), D
Handicap Access: Yes
Special Features: Catering services; private dining areas

This downtown dining gem housed in the historic Brodnax Building (former home of Brodnax Jewelers) splashed onto the scene in 2004 and has been going strong ever since. Inside the spacious building, the atmosphere is stylish and refined, with sky-high ceilings and a mezzanine level overlooking a main dining area that's crowned by a striking wrought iron chandelier. Original details like mosaic tile floors circa 1910, egg-and-dart molding, and marble columns blend seamlessly with mahogany accents, contemporary art, and a sleek crescent-shaped bar. A small patio outside on the trolley line is a favorite place for power lunchers. Chef John Kirk's upscale menu pays homage to his Delta roots with dressed-up Southern flavors, plus eclectic influences from Asia and beyond. Lunch selections include creative salads, a 10-ounce Kobe burger, and a small selection of entrées like seafood étouffée and Thai noodles. The diverse dinner menu is a global affair, with starters that range from buttermilk fried oysters and crawfish cheesecake to tuna tartare and a pâté of the day. For the main course, you'll find several dressed-up seafood dishes with influences from Asia to the American South, plus one or two pork, beef, or lamb dishes. Stella's impressive wine list includes a varied, well-rounded selection.

Texas de Brazil

901-526-7600
www.texasdebrazil.com
150 Peabody Pl. #103, Memphis, TN 38103
Open: Daily

Price: Expensive
Credit Cards: Yes
Cuisine: Brazilian steakhouse
Serving: L (Wed.–Fri.), D, SB
Handicap Access: Limited
Special Features: Reservations recommended on weekends

This upscale Brazilian steakhouse chain in the heart of downtown draws crowds for all-you-can-eat meat served up at a fixed price ($43, plus tax and tip). Endless servers outfitted in gaucho attire roam the room with swordlike skewers of meats, ready to carve as much of the fire-roasted delicacies as you'd like. Among the selections, you'll find various cuts of beef, pork, lamb, chicken, and sausages. An extensive 40-item salad bar includes everything from imported cheeses and Italian meats to ceviche and sushi. You'll also find side items like garlic mashed potatoes, fried bananas, and cheese bread. Not in the mood for meat? You can easily fill up on the salad bar alone or opt for a lobster or shrimp dinner. Desserts and drinks are not included in the fixed price.

Midtown

The Bar-B-Q Shop

901-272-1277
1782 Madison Ave., Memphis, TN 38104
Open: Mon.–Sat.
Price: Inexpensive–Moderate
Credit Cards: Yes
Cuisine: Barbecue

Spotlight on Special-Occasion Restaurants

Whether you're in town to celebrate an anniversary or simply want to splurge on a little something special, these Memphis favorites deliver a memorable dining experience.

Café Society (901-722-2177; 212 N. Evergreen St.) A longtime Midtown standby, this elegant, French-style bistro offers an upscale menu in a warm atmosphere that includes a handsome separate bar area and alfresco dining when it's nice out.

Chez Philippe (901-529-4188; 149 Union Ave.) The Peabody's opulent fine-dining restaurant offers French cuisine with Asian accents in a lavish dining room accented by marble columns and crystal chandeliers.

Erling Jensen, The Restaurant (901-763-3700; 1044 S. Yates Rd.) The menu may be one of the priciest in town, but Erling Jensen's culinary works of art are well worth the splurge at this celebrated East Memphis institution.

Paulette's (901-726-5128; 2110 Madison Ave.) A Memphis favorite for more than 30 years, this Midtown spot is popular for romantic dinners, fantastic desserts, and weekend brunch served in an atmosphere steeped in traditional European elegance.

Restaurant Iris (901-590-2828; 2146 Monroe Ave.) New in 2008, this four-star French-Creole hot spot helmed by New Orleans chef-owner Kelly English offers casual fine dining within a charming 1908 Victorian home.

Serving: L, D
Handicap Access: Yes

Like your ribs served wet? How about dry? Both? Not to worry, the folks at the Bar-B-Q Shop understand and offer up their slabs any way you like them. We recommend getting them half and half for the best of both worlds. From barbecue chicken to barbecue spaghetti, this friendly neighborhood joint packs 'em in and is especially busy during the lunchtime rush. The menu features many a Memphis favorite, including a sausage and cheese plate, barbecue nachos, and, of course, the pulled-pork sandwich. You'll also find a few unique offerings, including beef brisket and a barbecue salad. The Shop is especially proud of their sauces, which are made from family recipes more than 50 years old that are passed down from generation to generation. You can take home a bottle of hot or mild Dancing Pigs sauce or stock up on the Shop's dry rub on your way out.

Barksdale Restaurant

901-722-2193
237 S. Cooper St., Memphis, TN 38104
Open: Daily
Price: Inexpensive
Credit Cards: Yes
Cuisine: Southern
Serving: B, L
Handicap Access: Yes

This down-home diner has been serving Midtowners hearty breakfasts and meat 'n three lunches for more than 40 years. Anchoring a strip of colorful storefronts, Barksdale is a well-worn time warp, with dark carpeting, fluorescent lighting, and wood-paneled walls covered in autographed headshots, photos of local sports heroes, and a large American flag. Locals pack the place on weekend mornings for down-home country breakfasts like fluffy biscuits with sausage gravy and hotcakes with homemade maple syrup. You can get your eggs with country ham or a rib eye steak, or go exotic with a veggie, western, or Greek omelet. Daily plate lunch specials feature mains like country fried steak, meat loaf with mushroom gravy, fried chicken livers, and fried pork chops, plus three veggies that may include purple hull peas, buttered squash, turnip greens, mac 'n cheese, or baked apples, depending upon the day. All are served with homemade yeast rolls and piping-hot corn bread. Save a little room for some cobbler, rice pudding, or a slice of homemade pie of the chocolate meringue, Southern pecan, or vanilla chess variety.

Beauty Shop

901-272-7111
966 S. Cooper St., Memphis, TN 38104
Open: Daily
Price: Moderate–Expensive
Credit Cards: Yes
Cuisine: New American
Serving: L, D, SB
Handicap Access: Yes

This chic Cooper-Young favorite housed in a retro beauty shop draws a stylish crowd for upscale eats and a trendy lounge scene. Inside, a cool bar with copper-leaf accents dominates the front room opposite a wall of tables situated beneath funky, painted-glass light fixtures. Out front, a few patio tables are set up for alfresco dining. But the best tables are in the kitschy back room, where diners can cozy up in private booths surrounded by stacked glass blocks that once enclosed individual styling stations. The same glass cubes back a row of two-tops, where one lucky diner actually gets to sit in a vintage barber chair beneath a hair dryer.

The creative menu, which is updated every four or five months, takes cues from across the globe, starting with appetizers that may include anything from Spanish garlic shrimp to watermelon and wings dusted with sugar and sweet chile lime sauce. Seafood entrées with French leanings may include dishes like mussels with pork confit and lobster meunière. There's also a grilled New York strip, rack of lamb, and roasted duck with honey sherry butter. Separate sides include fries (excuse us, *frites*) prepared with your choice of cayenne sugar, or truffle oil, black pepper, and Parmesan. Simpler lunch selections include fresh salads and sandwiches like the popular bacon, lettuce, tomato, and avocado option. Dessert is hard to pass up, with Nutella and banana crêpes, root beer floats, old-fashioned cakes, and a fancy milk shake made with gelato.

Blue Fish

901-725-0230
www.thebluefishmemphis.com
2149 Young Ave., Memphis, TN 38104
Open: Mon.–Sat.
Price: Moderate–Expensive
Credit Cards: Yes
Cuisine: Seafood
Serving: D
Handicap Access: Yes
Special Features: Private dining rooms, oyster bar

Perched on prime real estate where Cooper intersects with Young, this beachy restaurant specializes in fresh fish flown in daily. Inside, the breezy decor features cool blues, Florida artwork, and tropical greenery. The main dining area is anchored by a sizeable bar, while a few choice tables are tucked away in their own cubbies behind Key West–style screened doors. Impressive fresh fish selections are the star, prepared any one of nearly 10 ways, including blackened, grilled, pecan crusted, cedar-plank roasted, and herb crusted and topped with crabmeat. The fish comes from near and far, and may include Tazmanian salmon, wild Alaskan halibut, Louisiana redfish, or Maine gray sole. In season, you'll also find soft-shell crab, Florida stone crab claws, and oysters on the menu. Desserts made in house include tempters like Key lime pie, blueberry bread pudding, and chocolate pecan pie.

Brother Junipers

901-324-0144
www.brotherjunipers.com
3519 Walker Ave., Memphis, TN 38111
Open: Tues.–Sun.

Price: Inexpensive
Credit Cards: Yes
Cuisine: Breakfast
Serving: B, L
Handicap Access: Limited
Special Features: Shop sells spreadable fruits and hot sauces

Located in a cottage-style house on the edge of Midtown near the University of Memphis, this cute spot serves up one of the city's best breakfasts. Inside, the warm, cozy dining room bustles with students and locals who fill up tables and a handful of counter stools. There's additional seating out front, nestled amid flowers and greenery within the white picket fence. You can order salads, sandwiches, or quesadillas for lunch, but the real star here is the morning meal. Patrons sip coffee out of mismatched mugs from local businesses and wait patiently for heaping plates of eggs, waffles, omelets, and more. Breakfast selections include Southern favorites like biscuits and gravy, and quite possibly the creamiest cheese grits in Memphis, but the extensive menu goes well beyond the standards. More than 15 types of omelets (not including the make-your-own option) range from the Greek-style spanakopita to an omelet with portobello mushrooms and roasted peppers. You can also get an open-faced omelet like the Desperado, with tomatoes, onions, black beans, salsa, avocado spread, mozzarella cheese, and sour cream. Potato dishes are served with everything from pesto, tomatoes, and mozzarella to chorizo sausage, onions, peppers, cheddar, and sour cream. Lighter bites include yogurt, oatmeal, and granola, and you can also get fresh-baked banana nut bread, muffins, and cinnamon rolls.

Café 1912

901-722-2700
243 S. Cooper St., Memphis, TN 38104
Open: Daily
Price: Moderate
Credit Cards: Yes
Cuisine: New American, French
Serving: D, SB
Handicap Access: Yes

Nestled amid a colorful strip of storefronts, this warm, charming bistro features a handful of cozy rooms and a small bar area. Walls painted bold reds and yellows are covered in vintage French ads. On the menu, you'll find bistro-style fare like steamed mussels, niçoise salad, goat cheese ravioli, braised short ribs, and strip steak with *pommes frites*. There are also crêpes, and tasty burgers topped with blue cheese or smoked mozzarella and bacon. Brunch is served on Sunday, and if it's nice out, there are a few sidewalk tables out front. Café 1912 also offers an accessible, moderately priced wine menu with several by-the-glass selections.

Café Ole

901-274-1504
www.cafeolememphis.com
959 S. Cooper, Memphis, TN 38104
Open: Daily

The patio at Cooper-Young's Café Ole is one of the best spots in Memphis to sip a frosty margarita or an ice-cold Mexican beer.

Price: Inexpensive–Moderate
Credit Cards: Yes
Cuisine: Mexican
Serving: L, D, SB (Sat. and Sun.)
Handicap Access: Yes
Special Features: Margarita Mondays; happy hour

This festive Cooper-Young fixture is a favorite for margaritas, Mexican food, and one of Midtown's best patios. Inside, the main room includes an exposed-brick wall lined with a row of well-worn booths, and a trellis-topped dining space dripping with the requisite chile pepper lights. A spacious bar area in the adjacent room houses a few more tables, along with a handful of TVs and a wall of tequilas. Just beyond the bar is the seating area of choice on mild Memphis days: Café Ole's patio. Tucked between two brick buildings, the narrow, tree-shaded space is stocked with a slew of tables surrounded by plants and flowers that lure chirping birds and pleasant breezes. On the menu, you'll find familiar Mexican standards like fajitas, quesadillas, burritos, and tacos. On weekends, brunch offerings include everything from huevos rancheros to shrimp omelets. Frosty margaritas, sangria, and Mexican beer are the beverages of choice.

Central BBQ

901-272-9377
www.cbqmemphis.com
2249 Central Ave., Memphis, TN 38104

Open: Daily
Price: Inexpensive–Moderate
Credit Cards: Yes
Cuisine: Barbecue
Serving: L, D
Handicap Access: Limited
Special Features: Online ordering available

Relatively new on Memphis's legendary barbecue scene (opened in 2002), this cozy Midtown spot holds its own with the city's established pork palaces. Just down the street from Central's antiques row, the casual restaurant boasts a festive front deck with picnic tables and seasonal live music. After ordering at the counter, diners retire to an adjacent narrow dining room lined with a wall of booths—a handy roll of paper towels at the ready atop each table. Starters include hot wings, a sausage and cheese plate with tangy honey mustard for dipping, barbecue nachos, and addictive, house-made barbecue potato chips. Slow-smoked barbecue sandwiches include standards like pulled pork or chicken, plus beef brisket, bologna, sausage, and smoked turkey. There's even a portobello mushroom sandwich served with smoked Gouda. Memphis-style (dry) pork ribs are a menu favorite. Tasty sides include mac 'n cheese, greens, and onion rings. If you're in the mood for something a little stronger than sweet tea, beer is served by the pitcher or the bucket. There's also dessert, including cheesecake and peanut butter pie. Central BBQ has a second location, east of this one, at 4375 Summer Avenue.

Cozy Corner

901-527-9158
www.cozycornerbbq.com
745 N. Parkway, Memphis, TN 38105
Open: Tues.–Sat
Price: Inexpensive
Credit Cards: Yes
Cuisine: Barbecue
Serving: L
Handicap Access: Yes

Located in a nondescript strip of shops in a rather rundown area of town, this beloved barbecue joint doesn't look like much from the outside. But there's a reason why locals, St. Jude workers, and tourists in search of real Memphis barbecue have been packing the place for more than 30 years. This is the real deal, from the rub-smothered barbecue to the cracked plastic booths and wood-paneled walls. Order from friendly staff at the counter, where you can watch slabs of ribs smoke oh-so-slowly over hickory in the pit oven. This is a Styrofoam-plate and cafeteria-tray kind of place, where meaty ribs require you to roll up your sleeves. Sides include tangy barbecue spaghetti, slaw, and fresh-from-the-factory Wonder Bread that's made right down the street. The celebrated Cornish hen requires hard work with plastic utensils, but it ultimately delivers tender meat smoked with potent seasoning. Order it mild for a piquant kick or hot to get the sweat glands going. Other favorites include a sliced beef sandwich topped with slaw and the somewhat intimidating barbecue bologna sandwich. Expect to leave with spice under your fingernails, sauce on your shirt, and a big fat smile on your face.

Cupboard Restaurant

901-276-8015
1400 Union Ave., Memphis, TN 38104
Open: Daily
Price: Inexpensive
Credit Cards: Yes
Cuisine: Southern
Serving: B, L, D
Handicap Access: Yes

Down-home Southern cooking at its finest. Since moving across the street into a space formerly occupied by a Shoney's, there's a lot more space (and less wait time), but the ambience remains warm and friendly. Not that atmosphere is the reason you come to the Cupboard, which has been a local favorite for fresh vegetables since 1943. Meat 'n threes are anchored by country-style specialties like fried chicken, catfish, meat loaf, and chicken and dumplings. But the true star here is the side dish. Order a vegetable plate and load up on fried green tomatoes, mac 'n cheese, candied yams, corn pudding, eggplant casserole, black-eyed peas, turnip greens, squash casserole . . . you get the picture. The menu changes daily, but there are always plenty of sides to choose from. Warm rolls and sweet mini corn muffins accompany the meal, and the only way to wash it all down is with a sweet tea. To-die-for desserts include gooey berry cobblers and mile-high lemon meringue pie.

Dish

901-276-0002
www.dishmemphis.com
948 S. Cooper St., Memphis, TN 38104
Open: Daily
Price: Moderate
Credit Cards: Yes
Cuisine: Tapas, Mediterranean
Serving: D
Handicap Access: Yes
Special Features: Late-night tapas; DJs

This sleek urban restaurant and lounge draws a hip Cooper-Young crowd in search of cocktails and tapas (served into the wee hours on weekends). The contemporary space features cement floors, Eastern-style floor cushions, and cushy "beds" to lounge on. DJs spin several nights a week after the dinner hour, when the dance floor fills up under the disco ball in the front bar. The sushi-style tapas menu (mark what you want) includes hot and cold plates featuring mainly Asian selections with a few Mediterranean influences here and there. There are also handmade flatbreads, Japanese-style skewers, and entrées that range from grilled tofu to rack of lamb. Specialty cocktails include the Italian Russian with vodka, amaretto, coconut rum, pineapple, and cranberry, and the Dishwater, the restaurant's sweet, strong version of a Long Island Iced Tea.

Do Sushi

901-272-0830
964 S. Cooper St., Memphis, TN 38104

Open: Tues.–Sat.
Price: Moderate
Credit Cards: Yes
Cuisine: Sushi
Serving: D
Handicap Access: Yes

This trendy sushi spot is hip but comfortable, with funky style that includes a copper-leaf wall you may recognize from hot spots like Beauty Bar (next door) and downtown's Automatic Slim's. All three, along with Molly Fontaine's Lounge, are brainchildren of popular restaurateur Karen Carrier. Space is somewhat limited, and seating at the sushi bar, window lounge areas, sidewalk tables, and private, curtained-off tables tend to fill up quickly as the dinner and cocktail crowd trickle in for the evening. Beyond traditional sushi selections, Do offers creative hand rolls like duck cracklin,' spicy crawfish, and a BLTA (teriyaki bacon, lettuce, tomato, and avocado). Among the maki offerings, unique rolls include the Kona Strawberry, with crab, masago, seared walu (a type of fish), strawberry, and a sweet soy reduction. Or you can try a surf-and-turf roll made with seared beef tenderloin, which is also offered as sashimi. Beyond straight sushi, Do offers salads, bento boxes, teriyaki entrées, and more.

Harry's Detour

901-276-7623
532 S. Cooper St., Memphis, TN 38104
Open: Tues.–Sat.
Price: Inexpensive–Moderate
Credit Cards: Yes
Cuisine: New American
Serving: L, D
Handicap Access: Limited

Located in a cheery red house, this small, casual restaurant offers tasty, eclectic cuisine with influences that span the globe. In addition to a handful of small tables inside, Harry's offers additional seating on a fantastic front deck. The creative menu is big on flavor, with influences from New Orleans to Thailand. For lunch, sandwiches may include anything from grilled mahi to buffalo chicken tenders or an elk burger. Dinner starts with tempting appetizers like spicy shrimp rémoulade or Pacific Rim–style wontons stuffed with fruit, smoked meats, and fish. Entrées include flavor-packed chicken dishes like the Tequila Mocking Bird, stuffed with roasted peppers, herbs, lime, and tequila. There are generally several seafood selections on the menu as well, like bacon-wrapped fish of the day, scallops in lobster cream sauce, or shrimp with Detour-style Thai curry sauce over angel hair pasta. A second location in downtown's hip South Main neighborhood is located at 106 East G. E. Patterson Avenue (901-523-9070).

Huey's

901-726-4372
www.hueyburger.com
1927 Madison Ave., Memphis, TN 38104
Open: Daily

Price: Inexpensive
Credit Cards: Yes
Cuisine: American, burgers
Serving: L, D
Handicap Access: Yes

Searching for the best burger in Memphis? Locals have bestowed that honor upon Huey's in local publications for more than 20 years. While the beloved burger joint now boasts seven locations, including one in the heart of downtown (77 Second Street), this Midtown outpost is the original, open since 1970. Decor at all Huey's locations stays true to the ultracasual style found here: red-and-white checkered tablecloths; walls covered in scribbled autographs and all manner of pennants, posters, and photos; and a ceiling stuck with countless toothpicks that determined diners spit from straws below. There's also a well-worn bar area and space for the band to set up—all Huey's have live music on Sunday nights. One third of a pound burgers are the menu's cornerstone, and you can get them six ways, including a West Coast burger topped with guacamole and Monterey jack on a wheat bun, or a burger served on Texas toast with pepper jack, grilled onion, and jalapeños. Any burger can be swapped out for a veggie or turkey patty. There are also a slew of sandwiches, from a French dip to Huey's stacked club. Burgers and sandwiches always taste best with a side of thick-cut fries or crispy onion rings. Health-conscious diners will find a few salads and lighter selections, but let's be honest, most people are here for the thick, juicy burgers.

Neely's BBQ
901-521-9798
www.neelysbbq.com
670 Jefferson Ave., Memphis, TN 38103
Open: Daily
Price: Inexpensive—Moderate
Credit Cards: Yes
Cuisine: Barbecue
Serving: L, D
Handicap Access: Yes

Upon entering Neely's, you're faced with a decision: walk to the right and order up your 'cue from the to-go counter, or make a left and wait to be seated in the homey, wood-paneled dining room. And really, you win either way; it just depends on where you want to enjoy your ribs, pork sandwich, barbecue spaghetti, barbecue nachos, or smoked sausage (oh, we could go on). Founded by the Neely brothers in 1988 near downtown Memphis, the operation quickly developed a citywide reputation for mouthwatering barbecue with equally good service, spawning additional locations (including one in Nashville and one in East Memphis at 5700 Mt. Moriah). This reputation has since landed Neely's coverage on the *Today Show*, *Good Morning America*, and the Food Network with Bobby Flay, and in the *New York Times*, *Bon Appetit*, *Southern Living*, and many other publications. Located close to both downtown and Midtown, the restaurant gets busy during the lunch and dinner rush, so plan accordingly.

Sekisui
901-725-0005
www.sekisuiusa.com

Memphis's Best Burgers

Several of the city's best burgers are served at bars, and most of them taste best when ordered up late at night with an ice-cold beer. The next time you get a craving, follow this short list to burger nirvana.

Alex's Tavern (901-278-9086; 1445 Jackson Ave.) This beloved Midtown dive serves ice-cold beer and a mean Rocky Burger (named after the owner) into the wee hours.

Belmont Grill (901-767-0305; 4970 Poplar Ave.) This tiny bar/restaurant on the east side of town may stay packed, but the popular Belmont burger is a longtime city favorite.

Kooky Canuck (901-578-9800; 97 S. Second St.) Relatively new on the Memphis burger scene, Kooky Canuck's 4-pound Kookamonga Burger demands respect, as does the regular old half-pound version.

Dyer's Burgers (901-527-3937; 205 Beale St.) There's something about that legendary ageless cooking grease that makes these thin, deep-fried burgers irresistible—especially at the tail end of a night out on Beale.

Ernestine & Hazel's (901-523-9754; 531 S. Main St.) Smell that burger sizzling behind the bar? We dare you not to order one. This brothel-turned-bar is as famous for their Soul Burgers as the joint's storied past.

Huey's (901-726-4372; 1927 Madison Ave.) Quite simply, the city's favorite burger since 1970. Huey's now has a handful of locations, making it that much easier to satisfy Huey burger cravings.

Lamplighter Lounge (901-726 9916; 1702 Madison Ave.) Midtown's ultimate dive bar serves up cheap PBR (Pabst Blue Ribbon) by the pitcher and the beloved Shirley Burger.

---

25 S. Belvedere, Memphis, TN 38104
Open: Daily
Price: Moderate
Credit Cards: Yes
Cuisine: Sushi, Japanese
Serving: L (Mon.–Fri.), D
Handicap Access: Yes
Special Features: Early-bird specials daily 5–7 PM

This longtime Midtown favorite for sushi offers everything from creative rolls and noodle bowls to tempura and teriyaki. Inside the cozy space, there's ample seating at the sushi bar, plus a few tables in an adjacent dining room. When it's nice out, the festive enclosed patio with umbrella-shaded tables is a favorite spot to enjoy some fantastic sushi. On the menu, Memphis-themed rolls include the Grizzlies (shrimp tempura, smoked salmon, and mayonnaise), the Red Birds (crunchy crab, sweet and sour sauce, and shrimp on top), and, of course, the Memphis roll, which is really just a rainbow roll with cucumber and crab topped by tuna, salmon, and whitefish. For sushi newbies, there's an extensive selection of rolls made with cooked fish and tempura. The menu also includes hot entrées and bowls, seafood and veggie tempura, and more. Sushi and sashimi dinners and combinations are an ideal way to sample a wide variety at a great value. As for beverages, there are numerous wines offered by the glass, plus sake, Japanese beer, and more than 10 specialty cocktails. Additional Sekisui locations in Memphis include Sekisui Downtown in the Holiday Inn Select at 160 Union Avenue, and the East Memphis Sekisui Pacific Rim at 4724 Poplar Avenue.

Soul Fish

901-725-0722
862 S. Cooper St., Memphis, TN 38104
Open: Daily
Price: Inexpensive–Moderate
Credit Cards: Yes
Cuisine: Southern, regional
Serving: L, D
Handicap Access: Yes

Located just a couple of blocks from the Cooper-Young intersection, this catfish joint opened up shop in 2006. While fried catfish graces just about every menu throughout the Delta, the Mississippi delicacy just isn't as ubiquitous in Memphis. Enter Soul Fish, a retro, one-room operation lined with booths, tables, and a few stools at a lunch counter embedded with fishing lures. Simple decor is spruced up with a few contemporary accents: think painted cinderblock walls, antique Coca-Cola signage, modern artwork, and a neon-lit fish sculpture by the sign out front. The menu is fairly straightforward, with cornmeal-fried catfish served on a po' boy or in a basket with fries, hush puppies, and slaw. You can also order your catfish blackened and served atop a Caesar salad. Beyond catfish, there's slow-smoked chicken, a few salads, and wings. Popular po' boys include the Memphis-style option with smoked pork tenderloin, bacon, slaw, and barbecue sauce, or the Cuban po' boy, with the same tenderloin, plus ham, pickles, and Swiss cheese. Like any Southern eatery worth its salt, there's a selection of veggies cooked fresh daily, which may include black-eyed peas, Cajun cabbage, cucumber salad, or mashed potatoes. Be sure to save room for the sweet stuff, which includes root beer floats and caramel pecan pie.

Tsunami

901-274-2556
www.tsunamimemphis.com
928 S. Cooper St., Memphis, TN 38104
Open: Mon.–Sat.
Price: Moderate–Expensive
Credit Cards: Yes
Cuisine: Pacific Rim
Serving: L (Mon.–Fri.), D
Handicap Access: Yes
Special Features: Private dining is available for groups of up to 40 people

This hip Cooper-Young dining institution has remained on the Memphis hot list for more than a decade. The space is stylishly spare, with a small bar area, an intimate dining room, and a few patio tables under the awning out front. Contemporary decor includes distressed cement floors, whitewashed brick walls, modern art, and funky light fixtures overhead. Flickering candles atop the white tablecloths keep things cozy. The celebrated Pacific Rim menu features fresh seafood and is ever changing. Casual lunch selections may feature somewhat familiar salads (grilled chicken Caesar), sandwiches (chipotle chicken salad), and a small selection of exotic entrées. While the dinner menu is frequently updated, the signature roasted sea bass with soy beurre blanc on black Thai rice is a standard—and for very good reason. If it's on the menu, be sure to start with the sake-steamed mussels in red curry sauce, or opt for the always-popular crispy calamari. In addition to seafood, there's usually at least one grilled steak and roasted duck selection. Tsunami offers several small plates with the same creative Pacific Rim sensibilities. Crème brûlée fanatics will definitely want to save room for Tsunami's most celebrated dessert. Want to attempt to match chef-owner Ben Smith's legendary kitchen skills? Pick up *The Tsunami Restaurant Cookbook* from Burke's Books down the street.

Overton Square Area

While the once-thriving Overton Square area isn't the center of dining and entertainment it once was (before the resurgence of downtown Memphis), several neighborhood favorites remain, while newer additions have popped up along Madison Avenue in recent years. Among the old guard, **Memphis Pizza Café** (2087 Madison Ave.; 901-726-5343) has been serving the city's favorite slices since 1993. Around the corner, intimate **Bari** (22 S. Cooper St.; 901-722-2244) offers a more upscale take on Italian, specifically focusing on regional cuisine from Puglia, plus extensive wine and cheese menus. Across the block, **Side Street Grill** (35 S. Florence St.; 901-274-8955) is primarily a martini and cigar bar, but they also feature a full menu that includes sandwiches, pasta, seafood, and steaks.

In 2008, two longtime Overton Square favorites moved a block over to a new location on Madison. **The Bayou Bar & Grill** (2094 Madison Ave.; 901-278-8626) is a casual, warehouse-style spot for Cajun cuisine ranging from po' boys and red beans and rice to crawfish étouffée and jambalaya. Connected to the Bayou, **Le Chardonnay** (same address; 901-725-1375) offers an extensive wine selection, plus wood-fired pizzas, baked Brie, and a full bistro menu in an intimate, dimly lit atmosphere. Both boast fantastic patios. Just behind Le Chardonnay, **Bogie's Deli** (2098 Lasalle Pl.; 901-272-0022) offers some of the city's best sandwiches, plus salads, homemade soups, and outstanding desserts. Located in a converted house with a covered patio, this is the most charming of Bogie's five locations.

Nearby on Madison, **Molly's La Casita** (2006 Madison Ave.; 901-726-1873) serves up traditional Mexican cuisine in a festive atmosphere, plus some of the city's best margaritas. A couple of doors down, **The Blue Monkey** (2012 Madison Ave.; 901-272-2583) is a popular bar for twentysomethings that also serves sandwiches, bar bites, and Sunday brunch. Dubbed "the restaurant for beer lovers," **Boscos Squared** (2120 Madison Ave.; 901-432-2222) offers wood-fired pizzas, lunch specials, and more upscale entrées like wood-plank salmon—all of which should be washed down with one of the brewpub's handcrafted beers. Boscos also has a Sunday brunch with live jazz. Aside from being a popular dive bar and karaoke spot, **Yosemite Sam's** (2126 Madison Ave.; 901-726-6138) offers pub grub and plate lunches.

South Memphis

Four Way Restaurant

901-507-1519
998 Mississippi Blvd., Memphis, TN 38126
Open: Tues.–Sun.
Price: Inexpensive
Credit Cards: Yes
Cuisine: American regional, soul food
Serving: L, D
Handicap Access: Yes
Special Features: Free birthday meals with valid ID

Located in a historic African American neighborhood just down the street from Stax Museum, this soul food joint has been a local landmark since 1946. The neighborhood has seen better days, but the down-home cooking is a Memphis must. The place was once a favorite of Martin Luther King Jr. (a fan of the fried catfish and peach cobbler), and it's said that he enjoyed his last Memphis meal here. Don't be surprised to see locals bowing their heads in blessing before a meal in the spacious, no-frills dining areas. Renovated and reopened with new owners in 2002, the Four Way's hearty Southern specialties remain tasty and authentic. Inexpensive daily specials are the way to go, with one meat and two vegetables, plus moist corn bread or rolls. Depending on the day, meat selections may include meatloaf, fried chicken, turkey neck, or chitterlings. Veggies are just as good, with pork-infused black-eyed peas, creamy mac 'n cheese, crispy fried green tomatoes, and more. Top off a meal with sweet potato pie, cobbler, or caramel cake.

Jim Neely's Interstate Bar-B-Que

901-775-2304
www.interstatebarbecue.com
2265 S. Third St., Memphis, TN 38109
Open: Daily
Price: Inexpensive
Credit Cards: Yes
Cuisine: Barbecue
Serving: L, D (Mon.–Sat.)
Handicap Access: Yes
Special Features: Mail order available

The low-slung brick building may not look like much to cars whizzing by outside, but take one step inside this barbecue institution, and the thick scent of hickory-smoked meat lets you know that you're in exactly the right place. Located on the southern edge of town on a street that becomes Blues Highway 61, Neely's may be a bit out of the way, but it's well worth a trip. The cavernous dining rooms seat nearly three hundred, with a take-out counter to boot. Photos of three generations of Neelys adorn a wood-paneled wall opposite an impressive array of autographed photos, including Carl Perkins, Rufus Thomas, Cybill Shepherd, and many more. Chopping can be heard from the kitchen as meat is prepped for supersize sandwiches and barbecue platters. Beef and pork is slow-smoked in a closed pit using indirect heat, which makes for moist, extra-tender meat. In addition to the beloved pulled-pork sandwich, the well-rounded menu includes beef and pork ribs, hot links, rib tips, and chicken. Everything is topped by a generous layer of Neely's thick, slightly sweet sauce that's blessed with a magic mix of herbs. Sides include sweet baked beans, cool potato salad, and the tangy and delicious barbecue spaghetti.

Marlowe's Ribs & Restaurant

901-332-4159
www.marlowesmemphis.com
4381 Elvis Presley Blvd., Memphis, TN 38116
Open: Daily
Price: Moderate
Credit Cards: Yes

Cuisine: Barbecue, American
Serving: L (summer months, Elvis events), D
Handicap Access: Yes

Hard-core Elvis enthusiasts flock to Marlowe's for the barbecue, associated lore (Presley memorabilia covers every inch of the sprawling restaurant and bar), and its close proximity to Elvis ground zero: Graceland. Family owned and operated since 1974, Marlowe's has etched itself into the very fabric of Presley fandom over the past three-plus decades. If you're staying in a nearby hotel on Elvis Presley Boulevard, Marlowe's will pick you up and drop you off in their pink Cadillac limousine (for free). The proprietors like to bill themselves as having the best ribs in Memphis, and while the 'cue itself is good, it's by no means the best in Memphis. However, if you do find yourself in the neighborhood and have a hankering for "Don't Be Cruel" on the jukebox, coupled with a plate of barbecue spaghetti, you could do much worse.

East Memphis
Blue Plate Café
901-761-9696
5469 Poplar Ave., Memphis, TN 38119
Open: Daily
Price: Inexpensive
Credit Cards: Yes
Cuisine: Southern
Serving: B, L, D (Sun.–Fri.)
Handicap Access: Yes

Located in a cheery yellow house built by Holiday Inn founder Kemmons Wilson in 1954, this friendly café serves country breakfasts, meat 'n threes, and more. Inside, the home's rooms have been converted into charming dining areas with hardwood floors, yellow and white walls, blue-and-white checkered tablecloths, and cute touches like color-coordinated trim and decorative plates adorning the walls. Hearty breakfasts like blueberry and chocolate chip pancakes, crispy, fruit topped waffles, salty country ham, and fluffy biscuits with sawmill gravy are served all day and draw crowds of locals on the weekends. For lunch and dinner, you can get meat 'n two or three vegetables, or opt for four of the latter for an outstanding veggie plate. Country-style vegetables include green beans, black-eyed peas, turnip greens, mac 'n cheese, creamed corn, and around 15 more selections. As for the meat, there's country-fried steak with brown gravy, fried chicken, meat loaf, and turkey and dressing, plus daily specials like chicken and dumplings and fried shrimp. Friday night features all-you-can-eat catfish. The Blue Plate now has two additional locations, including the newest downtown outpost at 113 Court Square South. It may not be in a house, but the Court Square café stays true to the original's cheery decor scheme.

Corky's
901-685-9744
www.corkysmemphis.com
5259 Poplar Ave., Memphis, TN 38119

Open: Daily
Price: Inexpensive—Moderate
Credit Cards: Yes
Cuisine: Barbecue
Serving: L, D
Handicap Access: Yes
Special Features: Drive-through; mail order

This beloved East Memphis barbecue joint specializes in pork shoulders and ribs slow-cooked over hickory and charcoal. In this case, slow means 7 hours for ribs and 22 hours for the shoulder. With that much smoking, it's no surprise that Corky's flavor-packed pork barbecue has been a city favorite for more than 20 years. Inside, the vibe is rustic and always bustling. Wood-paneled walls are plastered with framed newspaper clippings and photos of famous patrons, and oldies pour out of the jukebox. Cozy dining areas separated by redbrick partitions are stocked with cubbylike booths and tables. Beyond the menu favorites—slaw-topped pulled-pork sandwiches, and ribs served wet or dry—there are Delta-style starters like hot tamales, barbecue nachos, and a sausage and cheese plate, plus Brunswick stew (in season). Beyond pork, you can get barbecue chicken, beef brisket (a rarity in Memphis), barbecue spaghetti, Cajun barbecue shrimp, and catfish served on a sandwich or as a dinner platter. Dessert includes chocolate fudge pie, fruit cobblers, and homemade banana pudding—as if you'll have room. In addition to the East Memphis location, there are two more Corky's in the Memphis area, plus franchises throughout the South. You can also mail order the Memphis original from the Web site.

Germantown Commissary

901-754-5540
www.commissarybbq.com
2290 Germantown Rd., Germantown, TN 38138
Open: Daily
Price: Inexpensive—Moderate
Credit Cards: Yes
Cuisine: Barbecue
Serving: L, D
Handicap Access: Yes
Special Features: Catering; Mon. all-you-can-eat special

Loyal locals pack this cozy Old Germantown favorite for heaping servings of hickory-smoked barbecue. Tucked away behind the tracks, the glorified shed features wood-plank walls covered in snapshots of Tennessee's finest. The help is full of "sweethearts" but short on time, so be prepared for prompt service and little else after the food arrives. Standards that would do any Memphian proud (think pulled pork and delightfully crispy dry ribs) are smoked through the night and served with warm baked beans, crispy slaw, and a deviled egg. The expansive menu is littered with standouts, including homemade Brunswick stew, tender doughy tamales, and plump barbecue shrimp. But the real star is the sauce, served mild or hot. For dessert, banana pudding is served like Grandma used to make it—packed with banana chunks and whole Nilla Wafers.

Upscale Dining in East Memphis

While locals and business travelers tend to spend plenty of time in East Memphis, the business district and suburban surroundings are a little off the beaten path for leisure travelers. The fantastic dining scene, however, rivals downtown's finest restaurants. If you find yourself on the east side of town looking for an excellent meal, try one of these popular spots.

Elfo's Restaurant (901-753-4017; www.elfosrestaurant.com; 2285 S. Germantown Rd.) The famed Grisanti family's latest Italian offering is this sharp eatery located in East Memphis's tony Germantown neighborhood.

Erling Jensen, The Restaurant (901-763-3700; www.ejensen.com; 1044 S. Yates Rd.) Well-heeled locals flock to this sophisticated, intimate restaurant for seasonal French global cuisine by master chef Erling Jensen at one of the city's most celebrated restaurants.

Folk's Folly (901-762-8200; www.folksfolly.com; 551 S. Mendenhall Rd.) A Memphis institution since 1977, this genteel steakhouse serves up prime cuts of beef and seafood in a cozy, old-school atmosphere.

Frank Grisanti (901-761-9462; www.frankgrisanti.com; 1022 Shady Grove Rd.) A Memphis tradition in Italian dining for around a century, the Grisanti family's famous Northern Italian cuisine is served up in this handsome restaurant within the Embassy Suites Hotel.

Grove Grill (901-818-9951; www.thegrovegrill.com; 4550 Poplar Ave.) This bustling, casually upscale spot in Laurelwood Shopping Center excels at seafood dishes and American cuisine spiked with plenty of Southern flavor. Favorites include shrimp and grits, roast duck, and a wood-grilled filet mignon.

The Half Shell (901-682-3966; www.halfshell-memphis.com; 688 S. Mendenhall Rd.) This longtime seafood landmark offers everything from Louisiana Gulf oysters and po' boys to crabcakes and steaks in a casual, festive atmosphere.

Interim (901-818-0821; www.interimrestaurant.com; 5040 Sanderlin Ave.) New in 2007, this sleek eatery is a feast for the senses with its open showpiece kitchen, glass-walled wine closet, and beautifully presented seasonal cuisine.

Jarrett's (901-763-2264; www.jarretts.com; 5689 Quince Rd.) Tucked away in a nondescript strip mall, this locally loved dining gem offers upscale American regional cuisine with an emphasis on seafood in a stylish, understated environment.

Jim's Place East (901-388-7200; www.jimsplaceeast.com; 5560 Shelby Oaks Dr.) This family-owned Memphis landmark has been serving fine American cuisine with Greek accents since 1921. The location may be a little out of the way, but the distinct ambience, cozy nooks and crannies, and lush grounds make it worth seeking out.

Napa Café (901-683-0441; www.napacafe.com; 5101 Sanderlin Ave.) Located in the corner of Sanderlin Shopping Centre adjacent to the Doubletree Hotel, this American bistro features vibrant, artsy decor and an outstanding wine list with an emphasis on California vintages.

Owen Brennan's (901-761-0990; www.brennansmemphis.com; 6150 Poplar Ave.) Brennan's has been bringing Creole and Cajun flavors to Memphis direct from New Orleans since 1990. Their indulgent Sunday brunch is one of the city's best.

Pete & Sam's (901-458-0694; www.peteandsamsrestaurant.com; 3886 Park Ave.) A longtime family favorite, this old-school eatery offers authentic Italian cuisine that includes homemade ravioli, lasagna, and handmade pizzas, plus tasty steaks and seafood, all served at down-to-earth prices.

River Oaks (901-683-9305; www.riveroaksrestaurant.com; 5871 Poplar Ave.) New American cuisine with French flair is served up at this popular, stylish bistro that splashed onto the Memphis dining scene in 2006.

Ronnie Grisanti & Sons (901-323-0007; www.ronniegrisantiandsons.com; 2855 Poplar Ave.) Tuscany-style Italian cuisine from the legendary Grisanti family is served with casual, old-school ambience in the Chickasaw Crossing shopping center.

Food Purveyors

Bakeries and Sweets

Located in the Cooper-Young neighborhood, the chic **Sweet** "desserterie" (938 S. Cooper St.; 901-726-4300) serves indulgent desserts ranging from bananas Foster to a Chambord milk shake, plus sandwiches, wine, and coffee cocktails. South Main's artsy **Cheesecake Corner** (113 E. G. E. Patterson Ave.; 901-525-2253) makes more than one hundred flavors of cheesecake, from almond coffee to praline fudge, plus they have a quiche and wine bar. For those craving fresh-baked bread, **La Baguette French Bread & Pastry Shop** (3088 Poplar Ave.; 901-458-0900) in Chickasaw Oaks shopping center is the place to stock up on French bread, pastries, and croissants. You'll also find a bistro menu, plus fantastic cakes including chocolate strawberry, raspberry ganache, and hazelnut praline.

Barbecue Take-Out

If you're willing to venture off the beaten path a bit, you'll be rewarded with some of the city's most celebrated 'cue, served over the counter, for very low prices. With more than a dozen locations throughout the city, **Tops Bar-B-Q** (1286 Union Ave.; 901-725-7527) has been giving fast-food chains a good name since 1952. Do like the locals and order a jumbo barbecue sandwich with a side of slaw and beans. If you're going to Graceland, consider stopping by **A&R Bar-B-Q** (1802 Elvis Presley Blvd.; 901-774-7444), where the extensive menu includes ribs (served wet or dry), barbecue spaghetti, rib tips, beef brisket, hot links, and fantastic pork shoulder sandwiches. Speaking of pork sandwiches on Elvis Presley Boulevard, **Payne's** (1393 Elvis Presley Blvd.; 901-942-7433) serves some of the city's best. The original Payne's, housed in a converted gas station, is closer to Midtown (at 1762 Lamar Ave.; 901-272-1523). Don't leave either one without trying a fried pie. Located east of the airport in an industrial neighborhood, **Tom's Bar-B-Q** (4087 Getwell; 901-365-6690) feeds a small army every day at the lunch hour. The extensive menu includes ribs, pulled pork sandwiches, beef brisket, rib tips, and more.

Beale Street Eats

A slew of Beale Street bars serve food, including longtime favorite **Blues City Café** (see Nightlife). There's also **Dyer's** (see Restaurants) for burgers, **The Pig on Beale** (167 Beale St.; 901-529-1544) for barbecue, **Miss Polly's Soul City Café** (154 Beale St.; 901-527-9060) for fried chicken, and **Superior Bar and Restaurant** (159 Beale St.; 901-523-1940) for all sorts of Southern specialties. Of course, there's also that old tourist standby, the **Hard Rock Café** (901-529-0007; 315 Beale St.). Perched above B. B. King's, **Itta Bena** offers Beale Street's only upscale dining option (see Restaurants for more information).

Coffee

In addition to the usual suspects like Starbucks, Memphis is home to several unique coffee shops. A bevy of caffeinated beverages, plus breakfast, sandwiches, smoothies, free wireless, and patio seating make funky **Otherlands Coffee Bar & Exotic Gifts** (641 S. Cooper St.; 901-278-4994) Midtown's best coffeehouse. Located in the heart of Cooper-Young, **Java Cabana** (2170 Young Ave.; 901-272-7210) is another favorite for its hip vibe, organic fair trade coffee, good eats, and events like poetry readings and live music. Midtown is also home to **High Point Coffee** (1610 Union Ave.; 901-726-6322), a small regional chain that offers coffee, tea, pastries, and free wireless. Downtown, you can grab a cup of joe—or a smoothie and a pastry—at **Bluff City Coffee** (505 S. Main St.; 901-405-4399), a cool coffee shop housed in a historic brick building in the heart of South Main. The **Center for Southern Folklore** (119 S. Main St.; 901-525-3655) is also a great spot to sip a specialty coffee while perusing the eclectic selection of folk art or catching some live music.

Delis

Memphis offers a handful of fine sandwich shops, including city favorite **Bogie's Delicatessen**. In addition to the original Midtown location (2098 Lasalle Pl.; 901-272-0022) Bogie's has numerous outposts throughout greater Memphis, including a location downtown at 80 Monroe Avenue (901-525-6764). Besides fantastic Boar's Head sandwiches, Bogie's serves salads, homemade soup, and indulgent desserts. Another local favorite, Midtown's **Fino's Italian Grocery & Deli** (1853 Madison Ave.; 901-272-3466) offers Italian-style sandwiches, plus pizzas, pastas, and salads. Be sure to order a side of the delicious pasta salad with your sandwich. Perched on the corner of Cotton Row in a building dating back to 1853, **Front Street Deli** (77 S. Front St.; 901-522-8943) has been a downtown favorite for weekday sandwiches and plate lunches since 1976. You may recognize the tiny spot from the film *The Firm*.

RECREATION

Parks, Nature, and Wildlife

Audubon Park

4145 Southern Ave., Memphis, TN 38117

This sprawling, East Memphis oasis offers more than 370 acres of green space. Ample facilities include indoor and outdoor tennis courts, picnic areas, playgrounds, a 7-acre fishing lake, sports fields, and a mile-long fitness trail. Audubon Park is also home to the city's celebrated Botanic Garden, located at 750 Cherry Road. Golf enthusiasts will appreciate the 18-hole course and practice range.

Confederate Park

Front St., between Court St. and Jefferson St.

This small, 3-acre park located in the heart of downtown Memphis is perched on the bluff overlooking the Mississippi River. Beyond fantastic river views, the urban oasis features a statue of Jefferson Davis and a cannon from World War I. A Civil War memorial, the park offered a vantage point during the Battle of Memphis, when the Confederate army fired cannons from the bluff at Union gunboats on the Mississippi.

Lichterman Nature Center

901-767-7322
www.memphismuseums.org/lichterman-overview
5992 Quince Rd., Memphis, TN 38119
Open: Tues.–Sat.
Admission: Adults $6; seniors $5.50; children (3–12) $4.50

With 65 pristine acres of lush forest, meadow, and lake, the Lichterman Nature Center is a natural oasis in the middle of metro East Memphis, providing a genuine escape without leaving the city. Start at the Lichterman's visitors center to peruse a handful of wildlife-centric exhibits before heading out to the expansive network of paths and trails that wind throughout the property. Expect to see ample varieties of trees, plants, insects, birds, reptiles, fish, and mammals. Visitors are encouraged to take part in the center's various programs and events, ranging from night hikes and plant sales to continuing environmental education.

Martin Luther King Jr. Riverside Park

South Pkwy. W. at Riverside Blvd.

This 380-acre park is located along the edge of the river (actually a tributary of the Mississippi) around five minutes south of downtown. The park is home to a marina and boat ramp with access to McKellar Lake. Visitors can enjoy tennis courts, picnic areas, sports fields, and nature trails. A nine-hole golf course is also located within the park, and a new 7,700-square-foot clubhouse with a pro shop and grill opened in 2007.

Memphis Botanic Garden

901-546-4100
www.memphisbotanicgarden.com
750 Cherry Rd., Memphis, TN 38117
Open: Daily
Admission: Adults $5; seniors (62 and up) $4; children (3–12) $3
Special Features: Admission to the gardens is free on Tues. noon–closing

With an annual draw of more than 150,000 visitors, the Memphis Botanic Garden features 96 acres of horticultural wonder in the heart of East Memphis's Audubon Park. Comprised of rolling lawns, lakes, pathways, and immaculate gardens, the grounds serve as a welcome refuge from the hustle of mid-South city life and provide a lovely place for a picnic. Visitors can stroll through rose gardens, sculpture gardens, herb gardens, butterfly gardens, and much more. Something is usually in bloom no matter when you visit, and even in the winter months, the Japanese Tranquility Garden offers a peaceful retreat. In addition to the grounds themselves, there are a variety of ancillary events and activities to take advantage of, including art workshops, horticultural classes, and art exhibitions. Garden facilities are also available for rental, serving greater Memphis as a destination for weddings, holiday parties, and corporate meetings. From June through September, the popular Live at the Garden concert series features national acts under the stars amid the gorgeous garden surroundings. Past performers have included Lyle Lovett, the B-52s, and Crosby, Stills & Nash.

Memphis Zoo & Aquarium

901-276-9453

www.memphiszoo.org

2000 Prentiss Pl., Memphis, TN 38112

Admission: Adults $13; seniors (60 and over) $12; children (2–11) $8; Tennessee residents free on Tues. after 2 PM

Open: Daily

Located within Overton Park, the 76-acre Memphis Zoo has undergone major renovations in recent years, making it one of the city's premier outdoor attractions. Thematically riffing on the the ancient capital of lower Egypt, from which Memphis got its name, the zoo is dressed in hieroglyphics throughout. With a comprehensive array of animals, birds, reptiles, and amphibians from around the globe, the Memphis Zoo is home to more than 3,600 animals representing more than 500 species. While the panda bears from China are a big draw these days (there is a small additional viewing fee), the marine species certainly get a lot of specialized attention as the zoo is also home to the Memphis Aquarium. Popular daily events include the sea lion show, penguin feedings, and the Wildlife Wonders show held in the zoo's courtyard area. Allow at least two hours to leisurely make your way through the sprawling grounds.

Mississippi River Greenbelt

Auction Ave. and Island Dr.

Located, in part, across the street from the upscale residential area of Mud Island, this narrow park features a mile-and-a-half walkway along the river's edge. Just beyond the bustle of downtown, the riverwalk offers unbeatable river views and is popular with locals who live in nearby communities like Harbortown. On the southern end of the greenbelt,

Tennessee residents get free admission to the Memphis Zoo on Tuesday after 2 pm. Memphis Convention & Visitors Bureau

the 102-acre park runs into Mud Island River Park, where there's a boat ramp, among other amenities.

Mud Island River Park

901-576-7241, 1-800-507-6507
www.mudisland.com
125 N. Front St., Memphis, TN 38103
Open: Apr.–Oct.

In addition to the Mississippi River Museum and the Mud Island Amphitheater, this 52-acre outdoor oasis set amid the mighty Mississippi offers outdoor activities on and off the water. The park is accessible via a short scenic monorail ride (for a fee) or a longer walk along the pedestrian bridge connecting downtown to the island. Admission to the park is free, although there's a fee for the museum. Lovely landscaping includes ample flowers, trees, grassy areas, benches, and picnic areas, and the park offers fantastic views of the Mississippi River and the iconic Hernando de Soto Bridge. The centerpiece, of course, is the working scale model of the lower Mississippi, an impressive five blocks long tracing the river's path from Cairo, Illinois, to New Orleans, Louisiana. Well-maintained walkways along the little Mississippi are a popular spot for walkers, joggers, and stroller-pushing parents. The scale model opens up into a re-created Gulf of Mexico, a 1-acre enclosed body of water holding 1.3 million gallons of water. While the rough waters of the Mississippi River on the opposite side of the island are for experienced boaters only, the calm re-created Gulf is an ideal spot for kayaking, canoeing, and pedal boating—all with the dramatic backdrop of downtown Memphis on the shore. Watercraft and bike rental are available in the park for around $10 per hour for a bike, and $20 an hour for a canoe or double kayak. Camping on Mud Island is permitted on the second Friday of every month. The park's Sleep Out on the Mississippi program provides tents, dinner, live entertainment, recreational activities, a campfire with marshmallows, and breakfast. Advance registration is required, and campers provide their own sleeping bags. The cost is $40 per person with a minimum of two people, or $30 per person for groups of eight or more.

Overton Park

2080 Poplar Ave., Memphis, TN 38104

This historic public park in the heart of Midtown is home to the Brooks Museum of Art, the Memphis Zoo, and the Memphis College of Art. Established in the early 20th century, the sprawling green oasis's 300-plus acres bustle with stroller-pushing parents, joggers, cyclists, and locals enjoying a leisurely day in the park. Visitors can walk marked trails through the park's mature forests, have lunch at a picnic pavilion, monkey around on one of the park's playgrounds, or even play a round of golf on the nine-hole course. Soccer fields, a baseball diamond, and tennis courts offer even more opportunity for outdoor recreation. Overton Park is also home to the recently renovated Levitt Shell amphitheater, where legends including Elvis Presley, the Grateful Dead, and Johnny Cash have played since 1936.

Shelby Farms Park & Recreation Area

901-382-0235
www.shelbyfarmspark.org
500 Pine Lake Dr., Memphis, TN 38134

Home of the Mississippi River Museum, an open-air amphitheater, walking trails, and outdoor recreation, Mud Island River Park offers ample opportunities for riverside fun. Memphis Convention & Visitors Bureau

Boasting 4,500 acres of thick forests, green pastures, sparkling lakes, and a lazy river, this former working penal farm is now the area's most impressive urban oasis for outdoor activity. Get your bearings with maps and information at the park's visitor's center, then choose among miles of trails that circle lakes, follow the river's edge, and snake through thick forests—including single-track mountain bike trails, paved walking and inline-skating paths, and hiking trails. Shady picnic areas and a Frisbee golf course provide even more opportunities for outdoor fun. If you don't want to break a sweat, pay-by-the-hour horseback rides are an ideal way to take in the scenery. As for the water, Patriot Lake is the best option for fishing, with a boat ramp, fishing pier, and tackle rental. The lake is also popular with kayakers, as is Wolf River, which flows for 3.5 miles through the lush Lucius Burch Natural Area. Paddleboat rental is available on the lake, but no matter how hot it gets, swimming is not allowed.

T. O. Fuller State Park
901-543-7581
1500 Mitchell Rd., Memphis, TN 38109

Located within the southern city limits, this 1,138-acre park was the first state park east of the Mississippi (and second in the nation) to permit African Americans. It is named after Dr. Thomas O. Fuller, a prominent African American minister, civic leader, and author dedicated to empowering and educating African Americans. A popular spot for bird-watching, the park is home to a diverse array of flora and fauna. There are 45 campsites for both tents and RVs, as well as a golf course, sports fields, a playground, a nature center (open in the summer), picnic facilities, a swimming pool, and 6 miles of hiking trails.

The Pyramid Arena

For better or worse, Memphis often takes every available opportunity to remind itself, and the world, of the ancient Egyptian city it was named after. There is no greater example of this than the 32-story Pyramid, located downtown next to the Mississippi River at 1 Auction Avenue. Opened in 1991, the twenty-thousand-seat arena once hosted national touring concerts and musicals, and it was home to both the University of Memphis Tigers basketball team as well as the NBA's Memphis Grizzlies. Both teams moved to the newer FedEx Forum off Beale Street in 2004, leaving the Pyramid quiet and unoccupied. A variety of potential new tenants have been considered, including a shopping center, indoor amusement park, casino, and even an aquarium. Most recently, plans have been discussed to move a Bass Pro Shop into the space.

Will a Bass Pro Shop move into the Pyramid? Tentative plans have been in the works since 2006. Memphis Convention & Visitors Bureau

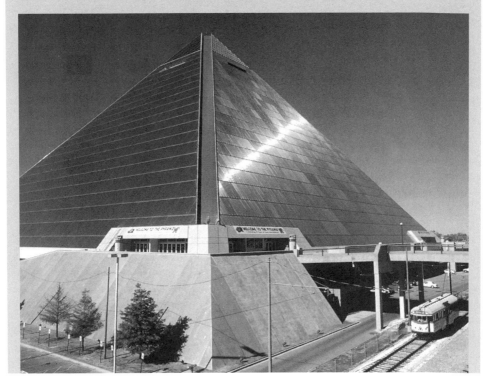

Tom Lee Park
Riverside Dr., Beale St. to G. E. Patterson Ave.

Sandwiched between Riverside Drive and the Mississippi River, this long, narrow riverfront park is the site of the outdoor concerts at Memphis in May's Beale Street Music Festival, as well as the World Championship Barbecue Cooking Contest. Running along the river for around a mile, the park encompasses nearly 30 acres. Easily accessible from downtown Memphis, this in-town escape offers pleasant walkways and seating areas with unbeatable river views. To the east, a row of homes and condos is perched on the river's bluff (don't miss the blufftop walk for more fantastic river views). The park is named for Tom Lee, an African American who rescued 32 passengers from a sinking steamboat in 1925.

W. C. Handy Park
Beale St.

Located in the heart of the Beale Street historic district, W. C. Handy Park pays tribute to the founder of the blues with a life-size bronze statue. In addition to hosting weekend concerts and an array of street vendors, the park is an ideal spot to take in some real blues from the musicians who gather here and play for tips. No bright lights here, just the music, the way it started out.

Spectator Sports

AutoZone Park
901-721-6000
www.memphisredbirds.com
200 Union Ave., Memphis, TN 38103

Home of the Memphis Redbirds, Triple A farm team for the St. Louis Cardinals, this beloved ballpark was built in 2000. Surrounded by downtown's skyscrapers, the urban stadium features picnic areas overlooking the outfield, an open concourse so fans can keep track of the action, and one of the largest video displays in minor league baseball. Seating options range from a grassy bluff out in center field ($6) to club-level suites ($20.)

In addition to Redbirds games, AutoZone Park features special events like firework nights, giveaways, and family campouts.

Remarkably, there's not a bleacher in sight; even the stadium's cheap seats are sturdy, plastic-backed numbers. The iconic rooftop sign for the Peabody Hotel makes a nice backdrop looking towards home plate from the outfield. Concessions include delicious barbecue nachos piled high with pulled pork from the legendary Rendezvous, plus fried chicken, seafood po' boys, and more. Kids love the plaza boardwalk, featuring carnival-style booth games, a batting cage, and a climbing wall.

FedEx Forum

901-205-1234
www.fedexforum.com
191 Beale St., Memphis, TN 38103

Opened in 2004, the FedEx Forum, located just off Beale Street, is home to the NBA's Memphis Grizzlies as well as the NCAA's University of Memphis Tigers. In addition to basketball, the Forum also hosts concerts, ice skating, wrestling, and musicals. With its expansive grounds covering 14 acres, the Forum anchors downtown's entertainment district and also houses the Memphis Rock 'n' Soul Museum.

Memphis Motorsports Park

Ticket Office: 1-866-40-SPEED (7-7333)
www.memphismotorsports.com
5500 Victory La., Millington, TN 38053

Vrroooom. Located across the Loosahatchie River, the Memphis Motorsports Park features a multitrack complex with a 0.75-mile NASCAR oval as well as a 0.25-mile NHRA champi-

The city's largest public building construction project, the FedEx Forum cost a whopping $250 million dollars to erect. Memphis Convention & Visitors Bureau

onship drag strip. Founded in 1986, the park seats 35,000 auto enthusiasts and boasts a track length of 0.75 mile, with a race length of 150 miles. In addition to racing, fans of Bigfoot will note that, since 2007, Memphis Motorsports Park has been the proud home of the Major League of Monster Trucks.

Mississippi River Kings
www.riverkings.com

Founded in 1992, the Mississippi River Kings are a minor league hockey team (Central Hockey League) that plays their home games just south of Memphis at the DeSoto Civic Center in Southhaven, Mississippi. Formerly known as the Memphis River Kings, the team officially became the Mississippi River Kings in 2007.

Located 20 minutes north of Memphis in Millington, Memphis Motorsports Park is one of Tennessee's top attractions. Memphis Convention & Visitors Bureau

Golf
The following courses are all open to the public.

Audubon (901-683-6941; www.thelinksataudubon.com; 4160 Park Ave.) Built in the early 1950s, this popular par 70 public course features gently rolling terrain.

Davy Crockett (901-358-3375; www.davycrockettgolf.com; 4382 Range Line Rd.) Located on the banks of the Loosahatchie River, Davy Crockett offers a scenic setting and uncrowded fairways.

Fox Meadows (901-362-0232; www.foxmeadowsgolf.com; 3064 Clarke Rd.) This par 71 course, open since 1961, features 6,545 yards of greens, a course rating of 70, and a slope rating of 115.

Galloway (901-685-7805; www.cityofmemphis.org; 3815 Walnut Grove) One of the city's most beautiful courses, Galloway is an 18-hole, par 71 course with flat, narrow fairways.

Overton Park (901-725-9905; www.cityofmemphis.org; 2080 Poplar Ave.) Tee off in Midtown's historic park; this nine-hole, par 34 course runs for 2,222 yards.

Pine Hill (901-775-9434; www.cityofmemphis.org; 1005 Alice Ave.) Open since 1932, this 18-hole, par 70 course designed by Kevin Tucker features 5,894 yards of fairways.

Riverside/Martin Luther King Park (901-576-4296; www.cityofmemphis.org; 465 S. Parkway W.) The closest course to downtown Memphis, this nine-hole, par 35 course has been around since 1913; a new, 7,700-square-foot clubhouse opened in 2007.

T. O. Fuller Park Golf Course (901-543-7581; www.state.tn.us; 1500 Mitchell Rd.) Located in the southwest corner of Memphis, this state park course features rolling hills, 5,986 yards, and a par of 72.

Whitehaven (901-396-1608; www.cityofmemphis.org; 750 E. Holmes Rd.) Formerly Whitehaven Country Club, this nine-hole, par 36 course designed by Kevin Tucker reopened in 2006 under city management.

SHOPPING

While Memphis may not be known as a shopping mecca, there are plenty of gems to be found among the city's diverse neighborhoods, which include an antiques district. Suburban East Memphis is home to most of the city's chain-store shopping and clothing boutiques, but plenty of unique finds can be found closer to downtown Memphis.

Shopping by Neighborhood

SOUTH MAIN ARTS DISTRICT (SOUTH MAIN STREET BETWEEN PATTERSON AND LINDEN AVENUES)
In the 1930s, the neighborhood surrounding Central Train Station bustled with activity. Not so long ago, however, the mostly deserted area on the southern edge of downtown was a place you'd steer clear of after dark. Today, this newly rejuvenated arts district thrives once again. Historic brick buildings now house an eclectic mix of galleries, unique boutiques, and upscale specialty stores. It's the kind of emerging neighborhood where warehouses are being converted to condos, and an American Apparel store now shares real estate with the Arcade—one of Memphis's oldest restaurants, established in 1919. The trolley line runs right in front of the quaint storefronts, making a day of shopping and gallery hopping easy on the feet.

The best way to explore the district's many galleries is on the South Main Art Trolley Tour, held the last Friday of every month from 6 to 9 PM. Gallery hoppers can pick up the free trolley downtown at the corner of South Main and Linden (south of the Orpheum Theatre) or anywhere along the way. Galleries and shops stay open late for the event and generally offer wine, snacks, and entertainment. Note that South Main is a dynamic neighborhood, and while we've made every effort to keep the listings below up-to-date, businesses and galleries often change.

American Apparel (901-528-1722; 530 S. Main St.) The first major chain to move into the neighborhood in 2006, this Los Angeles—based clothing and accessory shop specializes in hipster wear, tees, and comfy basics.

Art Village Gallery (901-521-0782; 410 S. Main St.) Showcasing the vibrant, contemporary works of Nigerian-born Ephraim Urevbu, this gallery also features works by artists from "exotic" lands, including Columbia, Zimbabwe, and Ethiopia.

D'Edge Art & Unique Treasures (901-521-0054; 550 S. Main St.) Contemporary folk art includes blues-themed paintings by famed artist George Hunt, plus works by NJ Woods, Debra Edge Taylor, and many more.

Delphinium (901-522-8600; 107 G. E. Patterson Ave.) Trendy jewelry and accessories include stylish laptop bags, scented candles, and antiqued brass necklaces, plus cosmetics, skin care, and bath and body products.

Disciple Gallery (901-386-4299; 390 S. Main St.) While this small gallery exhibits spiritually focused paintings and photography, the artwork does not generally feature blatantly religious subjects.

Divine Rags (901-572-7241; 300 S. Main St.) Located across from Pearl's Oyster House, this fashion boutique offers trendy clothes and accessories from labels including French Connection, Frankie B Denim, Jessica Simpson, William Rast, and English Rose.

Hollis Arts (901-522-8300; 408 S. Front St.) Part studio, part showcase, this Huling Row gallery features contemporary and abstract works in a variety of mediums by artist Mickey Hollis.

Jay Etkin Gallery (901-543-0035; 409 S. Main St.) Spacious, Soho-style gallery features local, regional, and national works from more than 30 artists on three floors of gallery space, plus a collection of ethnographic art.

Joysmith Gallery (901-543-0505; 46 Huling Ave.) In addition to paintings by Brenda Joysmith, this gallery showcases the works of both emerging and established African American artists, plus contemporary work from Africa, Asia, Latin America, and beyond.

Mode du Jour (901-527-7970; 506 S. Main St.) Designer jeans, trendy clothes, jewelry, purses, and shoes range in style from contemporary to conservative at this shop, run by a mother and daughter.

Muse Inspired Fashion (901-526-8737; 517 S. Main St.) One of Memphis's most distinctive clothing boutiques, this upscale shop offers unique clothing and accessories by everyone from Betsey Johnson to trendy new designers like Hale Bob. There's also a section for style-conscious men; Muse owner Lisa Doss has outfitted everyone from Joaquin Phoenix to Isaac Hayes.

Power House Memphis (901-578-5545; 45 C. E. Patterson Blvd.) The brainchild of the Delta Axis arts group, this industrial plant—turned—exhibition space houses contemporary art, installations, performances, and more in a dramatic urban setting.

Rivertown Gallery (901-527-7573; 125 S. Main St.) Beyond paintings and local artwork, this artist-run gallery offers jewelry and home decor, plus classes, workshops, and more.

The Robinson Gallery (901-619-4478; 44 Huling Ave.) Works by *Vogue* photographer Jack Robinson, plus an assortment of vintage images, are showcased at this unique gallery; '60s and '70s celeb subjects include Warren Beatty, John Lennon, Sonny and Cher, Tina Turner, and many more.

Second Floor Contemporary (901-521-1514; 431 S. Main St.) Alternative space on—you guessed it—the second floor features around five shows a year that range from installations and sculpture to abstract oils.

Sub Space South (1-800-519-5230; 502 S. Main St.) With additional locations in Houston, Washington, and Seattle, this gallery features contemporary painting, photography, and sculpture by artists from around the country.

Sue Layman Designs (901-527-2872; 125 G. E. Patterson, #103) Sue Layman's contemporary, abstract paintings feature vibrant colors and multiple layers that inspire individual interpretation.

CENTRAL AVENUE ANTIQUES DISTRICT (CENTRAL AVENUE BETWEEN EAST PARKWAY AND COOPER STREET)
Also known as the Memphis Antique and Design District, this Midtown strip is packed with unique shops offering antiques, art, vintage items, furniture, and gifts. It's easy to spend a few hours or an entire afternoon scouring the treasures within Central Avenue's shops. If you need a lunch break, Central BBQ is located amid the shops, and charming Café Palladio is nestled within the Palladio Antique Market.

Artists on Central (901-276-1251; 2256 Central Ave.) This 3,000-square-foot fine-arts gallery features paintings and three-dimensional pieces by local artists. A new show is featured each month with a reception that's open to the public.

Barbie Pepper's European Antiques (901-757-5233; 2231 Central Ave.) In addition to restorations, this antiques shop offers a gorgeous selection of furnishings from the 17th, 18th, and 19th centuries.

Consignments (901-278-5909; 2300 Central Ave.) This upscale consignment shop offers estate items and antique furnishings that include 18th- and 19th-century pieces, plus fine silver, porcelain, and cut-glass treasures.

Flashback (901-272-2304; 2304 Central Ave.) This vintage department store is stocked with retro furniture, clothing, and accessories, ranging from denim, hats, and shoes to deco vanities, funky collectibles, and '50s-era barware.

Gary's Antiques (901-276-0089; 2158 Central Ave.) There's nothing highbrow about Gary's, which offers everything from flea market treasures to antique finds in a funky, haphazard atmosphere.

Ivy's Antiques and Interiors (901-276-9912; 2266 Central Ave.) Located in a charming house, Ivy's is stocked with antique furniture and reproductions, home accessories and decor, plus designer fabrics and wallpaper.

Market Central (901-276-3809; 2215 Central Ave.) This sprawling Palladio Group merchant offers nearly one hundred stalls packed with decorative arts and antiques, plus gallery space with work by local artists.

Memphis Waterworks (901-276-3806; 741 S. Cox St.) Housed in a restored, century-old shed just south of Central, the collection here consists of antique garden accents, stone fountains, and antique hardware. Don't miss the lovely courtyard out back.

Midtown Galleries (901-725-0049; 2232 Central Ave.) Contemporary arts are the focus here, with works by local and regional artists, plus a selection of antiques and unique furnishings.

Palladio Antiques and Art (901-276-3808; 2169 Central Ave.) Endless stalls of gorgeously displayed antiques, fine arts, and decorative pieces are easy to get sucked into. Bonus: Shoppers can break for lunch at the charming Café Palladio, located amid the lovely collections.

Second Hand Rose Antiques (901-278-3500; 2288 Central Ave.) A handful of rooms are chock-full of antique leather books imported from Scandinavia and South America, stacked furniture, oil paintings, lighting fixtures, and all sorts of bric-a-brac.

Toad Hall Antiques (901-726-0755; 2129 Central Ave.) Located on the west end of Central's antiques row on the corner of Cooper, this two-story shop oozes character and charm. A diverse array of offerings include English, French, and Continental furnishings; unique home accessories; gift items; and jewelry.

Xanadu Music & Books (901-274-9885; 2200 Central Ave.) In addition to guitars, amps, and musical equipment, this Central Avenue shop offers new and used books, including hard-to-find selections.

COOPER-YOUNG DISTRICT

This hip, walkable Midtown neighborhood at the intersection of Cooper Street and Young Avenue is packed with funky shops, trendy eateries, and everything in between. The first Thursday of every month is Cooper-Young Night Out (5 9 PM), when merchants offer food and drink specials, discounts and freebies, and DJs and live music. Some shops even pick up the sales tax. For more than 20 years, the neighborhood has also hosted the Cooper-Young Festival in September, with live music, more than three hundred vendor booths, lots of food, and much more.

Amazing Lace (901-274-5223; 888 S. Cooper St.) This trendy lingerie boutique offers everything from lace to fishnets. Shop for camis, corsets, garter sets, sexy costumes, and more.

Bella Note (901-726-4131; 2172 Young Ave.) This cute, friendly gift boutique offers a fantastic selection of items packed in a hodgepodge of cozy rooms. Stock up on fancy soaps, candles, jewelry, journals, stationery, baby clothes, and all manner of unique goods that you can't live without.

Burke's Book Store (901-278-7484; 936 S. Cooper St.) An independent favorite since 1875, Burke's is a Memphis institution. See the Bookstores section for more information.

Goner Records (901-722-0095; 2152 Young Ave.) A gem of an independent music shop, this popular spot also puts on the annual Gonerfest. See the Music Stores section for more information.

Hi-Octane Vintage (901-272-0917; 2160 Young Ave.) Cool vintage clothes for men and women, plus retro furniture, rock 'n' roll memorabilia, and vintage guitars. You'll also find accessories and all sorts of kitschy collectibles.

House of Mews (901-272-3777; 933 S. Cooper St.) Cat lovers simply can't miss this non-profit feline fantasyland. In addition to oodles of cats up for adoption, the retail offerings include everything from cat treats to feline-friendly artwork.

Loudeans (901-722-9681; 2174 Young Ave.) This women's boutique offers handmade purses, hats, scarves, and accessories, plus linen clothing by Flax, vintage linens, and jewelry made by local artisans.

Lux (901-726-6600; 906 S. Cooper St.) Designer clothes and accessories for men and women from labels including Diesel, Farmer, Trade, and Andrew Christian.

Memphis Drum Shop (901-276-2328; 878 S. Cooper St.) Voted one of the five best drum shops in America, this percussion palace features six showrooms packed with everything from acoustic and electric drums to cymbals, sticks, and vintage drums. Repair services and lessons are also available.

Bookstores

Barnes & Noble (901-386-2468, 2774 N. Germantown Pkwy.; 901-794-9394, 6385 Winchester Rd.) With locations at Wolfchase Galleria and the Hickory Ridge Pavilion, plus the Bookstar affiliate, Barnes & Noble is well represented in Memphis. In addition to the fantastic selection that Barnes & Noble is known for, these expansive bookstores also feature events like children's story time and occasional book signings and readings. There's also a café where you can linger with your new selections over a snack and a cup of coffee.

Bookstar (901-323-9332; 3402 Poplar Ave.) Housed in a converted theater on the edge of Midtown, this bookstore features all of the selection and amenities of a large chain (it's actually a Barnes & Noble affiliate), but it has the character of an independently owned shop. The marquee and retro box office of the Plaza Theatre are still intact, as is the black-and-white tiled entryway. Inside, deco accents and neon lights running up the side of the sky-high ceilings are reminders of the space's former life. In addition to an extensive book selection, the large main room is stocked with writing journals and gifts. A nice adjacent café area connected to the expansive children's book section offers Starbucks coffee, plus soft pretzels, sandwiches, pastries, and cookies.

Borders (901-754-0770; 6685 Poplar Ave.) Located in upscale Germantown's Carrefour Center, this expansive book and music store offers quite possibly the city's biggest selection of both books and music. In addition to titles and tunes of national interest, there are also extensive selections of books by Memphis writers and Memphis music. Bargain hunters will appreciate the store's large inventory of value-priced titles. The on-site Seattle's Best Cafe serves sandwiches, pretzels, and baked goods, and hosts occasional live music on weekend afternoons. Borders also hosts book signings, children's story time, and more.

Burke's Book Store (901-278-7484; 936 S. Cooper St.) A Memphis institution since 1875, Burke's Book Store specializes in rare and hard-to-find books, Civil War histories, first editions, and all manner of Southern literature. The store's new location on Cooper lacks any manufactured corporate pretense, instead focusing its energy on the business at hand: books. Seemingly overflowing books, journals, magazines, and more are tucked in every corner and stacked on any available surface, yet the cozy shop somehow retains order and precision. You'll find both used and new titles here, including one-dollar bargains. Need a recommendation? Ask Burke's owners, Corey and Cheryl Mesler, the husband-and-wife team who met working at the store years ago. Blues enthusiasts should be sure to ask to see the shop's signed first edition of W. C. Handy's autobiography. Burke's frequently hosts book signings, often welcoming Delta luminaries like native son John Grisham, who has been known to give his first signings here.

Davis-Kidd Booksellers (901-683-9801; 387 Perkins Ext.) While technically a chain bookstore, Davis-Kidd, located in East Memphis in the Laurelwood shopping center, skillfully retains all the charms of an independent bookshop. An expansive space, the store provides all the amenities of the big boys (say, a Barnes & Noble) with its café, CD/DVD section, and extensive assortment of periodicals. The trick is that they do all this *and* have a knowledgeable staff on hand to recommend titles, authors, and genres. The store is also known for, and plays host to, many book signings, readings, and discussion groups. Davis-Kidd is also home to Bronte, a bistro and wine bar with indoor and patio seating.

Music Stores

If you're searching for anything related to Memphis music, don't discount the museum stores. In addition to all manner of gear sporting the cool Stax logo, **Satellite Record & Gift Shop at the Stax Museum** (901-942-7685; www.staxmuseum.com; 926 E. McLemore Ave.) carries a nice selection of music, books, and DVDs. Sure, you can pick up a pair of Elvis glasses and all manner of logo gear at **Sun Studio** (901-521-0664 or 1-800-441-6249; www.sunstudio.com; 706 Union Ave.), but you'll also find Sun recordings, including several CD compilations. The **Memphis Rock 'n' Soul Museum shop** (901-205-2533; www.memphisrocnsoul.org; 191 Beale St.) is another good spot to stock up on music-related merchandise. Of course, if Elvis tunes are what you're after, **Graceland** (1-800-238-2000; 3734 Elvis Presley Blvd.) is chock-full of endless recordings, and just about any other Elvis-related souvenirs you can dream up. Beyond the gift shops, be sure and stop by the city's can't-miss independent record stores.

Goner Records (901-722-0095; 2152 Young Ave.) Home to everything relating to the Memphis underground and punk rock since 1993, Goner Records retains the independent record store atmosphere that's quickly fading in an era of corporate monoliths. Boasting a collection of punk, indie, jazz, soul, blues, country, and metal, Goner offers both used and new CDs, vinyl, seven-inches, and 78s. The outfit has since spun off Gonerfest, the fantastic annual music festival boasting such acts as the Black Lips, Jay Reatard, King Khan & BBQ Show, Impala, and Reigning Sound, among many others.

Poplar Tunes (901-525-6348; 308 Poplar Ave.) Opening its doors in 1946, Poplar Tunes (aka Pop Tunes) is still in business. In the early 1950s, a teenage Elvis Presley would haunt the record store in his free time to listen to gospel, R&B, country, and everything in between. Years later, those varied musical influences would converge to become rock 'n' roll—a new genre that Elvis would champion. Fans of the King will be interested to note that the first Elvis Presley 45 RPM record was sold right here at 308 Poplar Avenue. The address also served as a temporary home for the seminal Memphis R&B label Hi Records that released LPs by Al Green, Ann Peebles, and Willie Mitchell, among others. Poplar Tunes has a second location in Whitehaven at 4622 Faronia Drive.

Shangri-La Records (901-274-1916; 1916 Madison Ave.) A truly great independent record store (remember those?), Shangri-La is lined top to bottom with vinyl and CDs ranging from local soul to the most obscure crate-digger treats. A relatively small shop, its selections feel truly curated, with an eclectic sense of the classics mixed in with the new up-and-comers. You're as likely to hear Guided By Voices or Cat Power on the stereo as you are Bobby Rush, Jim Ford, or Charles Mingus. Located in Midtown, the store and its offshoot Shangri-La Projects (see the Culture section) have become indispensible cornerstones of the Memphis music scene. In its 20th year in 2008, the store continues to present events, shows, and countless in-store performances from the most interesting national touring acts coming though town. Simply put, this is a music geek's paradise.

Spin Street (901-327-8730; 3484 Poplar Ave.) Located at Poplar and Highland near the Bookstar, Spin Street is a large retail music store similar to a Tower Records or Virgin in that they sell CDs, DVDs, magazines, T-shirts, video games, toys, and music memorabilia. The store also has a vinyl section (nice) and hosts occasional in-store performances.

Only in Memphis

A. Schwab Dry Goods Store (901-523-9782; 163 Beale St.) One of many shops hawking souvenirs along touristy Beale, this historic spot provides entertainment value along with cheap trinkets. For starters, it's the only original business remaining on Beale Street, family owned since 1876. Step into this one-of-a-kind variety shop and you're immediately hit with sensory overload. A veritable hodgepodge of goods covers every nook and cranny of the expansive store: counters stacked with sunglasses, tables packed with boxes of underwear and socks, and display cases filled with samurai swords. Where else can you find ginormous overalls, a jug of hot sauce, voodoo potions, and a certified "Bucket of Blues" under one roof? Just don't forget your cash—A. Schwab doesn't accept credit cards. The multilevel shop also displays a small collection of Beale Street memorabilia on an upstairs landing. You can easily lose an hour sifting through all sorts of quirky treasures. The store motto is "If you can't find it at A. Schwab's, you don't need it!" Indeed.

Graceland Shops (1-800-238-2000; 3734 Elvis Presley Blvd.) If you're looking for Elvis souvenirs, there's only one place to go—where else but Graceland? An entire plaza here is dedicated to souvenir shops selling everything from Elvis ornaments to replicas of the King's stage costumes.

The Grizzlies Den at FedEx Forum (901-205-1551; 191 Beale St.) The most extensive selection of Memphis Grizzlies NBA gear can be found inside the FedEx Forum at the Grizzlies Den, where you'll find jerseys, caps, polo shirts, T-shirts, and more.

Lansky's (901-529-9070; 149 Union Ave.) Dressing Memphis men for six decades, Lansky's is most famous for outfitting a young Elvis Presley during his rise to fame in the 1950s. In addition to the King, the shop also clothed Jerry Lee Lewis, Carl Perkins, Roy Orbison, Johnny Cash, B. B. King, and a host of other rock and blues royalty. Today, the store continues to thrive in its present home in the lobby of the Peabody Hotel. Among the shop's distinct, bold styles, Lansky's Clothier to the King line features retro, Elvis-inspired styles and Memphis-themed clothing. You'll also find pants, jackets, shirts, and accessories from various brands, including Robert Talbott shirts and ties, Kangol hats, and Tommy Bahama watches. Lansky 126, a sister shop, carries more casual styles, including Johnny Cash T-shirts, jeans, and a few selections for women. Lansky operates the Lucky Duck gift shop as well, also located in the lobby of the Peabody Hotel.

Memphis Redbirds Store at AutoZone Park (901-721-6050; 175 Toyota Plaza) Stock up on Redbirds fan gear at this expansive shop inside the downtown stadium. Beyond the Redbirds, you'll find autographed major league memorabilia and collectibles.

Shopping Centers and Malls

Chickasaw Oaks (901-324-8325; 3092 Poplar Ave.) Positioned between Midtown and East Memphis, this small shopping center is home to chains like Pier 1 and Hallmark, plus a few women's clothing stores including Ella, a popular boutique. For a quick sandwich or pastry, La Baguette is a longtime favorite.

Beale Street Shops

You'll find all manner of souvenirs, trinkets, cheap T-shirts, and Elvis everything at the endless shops along Beale Street. For Memphis gifts and souvenirs, try **Strange Cargo** (901-525-1516; 172 Beale St.) or **Alley Cats Gifts** (901-528-1055; 156 Beale St.). If you're looking for a little something different, stop in **Tater Red's Lucky Mojos and Voodoo Healings** (901-578-7234; 153 Beale St.) for chicken feet, Lucky Casino oil, bobbleheads, and plenty of novelties. **Memphis Music** (901-526-5047; 149 Beale St.) carries all sorts of souvenirs, plus blues CDs and gospel, rock, and jazz selections.

Laurelwood Shopping Center (901-682-8436; Poplar Ave. between Grove Park Rd. and Perkins Ext.) Located near the Oak Court Mall, this upscale shopping center is home to James Davis (offering designer lines like Armani, Burberry, and Rock & Republic), King Furs and Fine Jewelry, Talbots, Chico's, J. Jill, and Zoe cosmetic boutique. This is also the home of the popular Grove Grill, the fantastic Davis-Kidd Booksellers, and David Lusk Gallery, one of the premier art dealers in Memphis.

Oak Court Mall (901-682-8928; 4465 Poplar Ave.) An East Memphis standby, this is the closest mall to both Midtown and downtown with a full selection of stores (the shopping options at Peabody Place are somewhat limited). Dillard's and Macy's are the anchors, with a decent selection of standard mall stores to round out the offerings.

Peabody Place (901-261-7529; 150 Peabody Pl.) Peabody Place offers mall shopping and more in the heart of downtown Memphis. In addition to a small selection of standards like

The Peabody Place Retail & Entertainment Center is part of a complex spanning eight city blocks that includes apartments, offices, and restaurants. Memphis Convention & Visitors Bureau

Gap and Victoria's Secret, the shopping center is home to a movie theater, Jillian's entertainment and dining for adults, Dan McGuinness Irish pub, and the upscale Encore restaurant.

The Shops of Saddle Creek (901-753-4264; 6410 Poplar Ave.) Tony Germantown's popular shopping center features chains like Ann Taylor, the Apple Store, Banana Republic, Chico's, J.Crew, Talbots, and Williams-Sonoma. The spread-out complex is also the site of Yia Yias Eurocafe, a popular bistro that serves Mediterranean cuisine.

Wolfchase Galleria (901-372-9409; 2760 N. Germantown Pkwy.) This suburban shopping center in Cordova is Memphis's most popular mall, anchored by Macy's, Dillard's, JCPenney, and Sears. There are also a slew of well-known shops that include Brooks Brothers, Banana Republic, Abercrombie & Fitch, Gap, and plenty more.

4

CLARKSDALE

Cradle of the Blues

Birthplace of Ike Turner and John Lee Hooker, Clarksdale, Mississippi, has been home and host to countless blues legends throughout the years—many of whom are honored on Clarksdale's Walk of Fame, new in 2008. W. C. Handy lived here for a spell around the time he discovered the blues at a nearby Tutwiler train station, and Muddy Waters's first recordings were made at his Stovall Plantation cabin just outside of town. Blues queen Bessie Smith took her final breath at Clarksdale's Riverside Hotel, now a Blues Trail landmark. There's loads of history in this small Mississippi town, and thankfully, it has been preserved and promoted better than anywhere else in the Delta.

Like all tiny Delta towns, Clarksdale has remained a quiet, sleepy place since the historic exodus following World War II through the mechanization of agriculture. As jobs dried up, working folks moved north in record numbers for alternate employment opportunities and a better quality of life. Today, the population hovers around twenty thousand. But if you're here for the blues, there's no better place to be. Leading the way for its sister Delta cities, Clarksdale has fully embraced its rich blues heritage through festivals,

Clarksdale has paved the way for other Delta towns by embracing and promoting the area's blues heritage.
Justin Gage

Built in the early 1940s, Clarksdale's original Greyhound bus station closed in 1980 and was restored in 2002.

landmark preservation, the Delta Blues Museum, and the rejuvenation of downtown. Sure, there's still plenty of work to be done—namely in the once thriving African American community known as the New World District—but in recent years, Clarksdale's preservation efforts have set a new standard.

For live music, the best time to visit is during a festival—the Juke Joint Festival in the spring, or the Sunflower River Blues & Gospel Festival in late summer. Book rooms well in advance for these popular weekends. Otherwise, be sure to visit on a weekend, as live music early in the week is virtually nonexistent. Clarksdale is also a fine jumping-off point for exploring the rest of the Delta—think of the town as your Mississippi blues headquarters. What better place for the landmark crossroads of Blues Highway 61 and US 49? While the blue guitar monument perched above Clarksdale's busy intersection may not be the true site of Robert Johnson's mythical deal with the devil, it's a favorite photo op for the increasing number of blues travelers who pass through town for an authentic Delta blues experience.

LODGING

While there are plenty of familiar motel chains located along State Street, Clarksdale also offers a handful of unique lodging options. You may not find standard features like phones, TVs, and Internet access at every property, but what you can expect is a true taste of the Delta. Rooms in Clarksdale are housed in sharecropper cabins, a cotton gin, a converted icehouse, a cotton warehouse, and even the former African American hospital where Bessie Smith took her final breath. Rooms in town are limited, so book in advance—several months in advance for blues festivals, even at the larger chain motels.

Lodging Price Codes

Inexpensive	Up to $90
Moderate	$90–130
Expensive	$130–225
Very Expensive	More than $225

Unique Accommodations

Big Pink Guesthouse
662-313-0321, 662-313-0028
www.bigpinkguesthouse.com
312 John Lee Hooker La., Clarksdale, MS 38614
Downtown Clarksdale next to the Delta Blues Museum
Price: Expensive
Credit Cards: Yes
Handicap Access: None

Located just a few steps from the Delta Blues Museum, this tiny inn oozes charm. The main building consists of a two-story pink brick rectangle that once served as an icehouse. On the lower level, guests have access to an antiques-filled Victorian parlor and dining room, a lovely New Orleans—style atrium with a trickling fountain, and a music nook with a baby grand honoring Nashville songwriter—and Big Pink owner—Tommy Polk. A large outdoor patio off the atrium is a prime spot to catch live music on the Blues Museum stage during festivals.

Upstairs, the Eudora Suite (named after Mississippi writer Eudora Welty) features lace curtains, a king-size four-poster bed, a large marble bathtub, and a private spiral staircase to the atrium. A separate room attached to this suite, the Writing Room, can be booked for additional guests; it features hardwood floors, exposed-brick walls, two twin beds, a desk, and plenty of bookshelves. The Stella Suite, named for the character in Tennessee Williams's *A Streetcar Named Desire,* has a double bed,

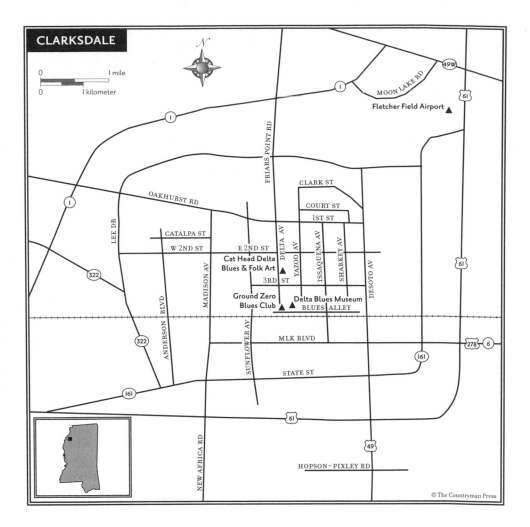

Next to the main building by the patio area, a former farm commissary (also painted pink) houses three funky rooms that are more rustic than the refined accommodations next door. Dubbed the Mississippi Music Hall, the main room is equipped with a full kitchen and retro touches like a '50s jukebox and Coca-Cola box. The tropical Isla Mujeres Suite features a tin-roofed bathroom that resembles an outhouse. Odie's Room, named for country music songwriter Odie Blackmon, is where the songwriter stays when he's in town to work on new tunes. When the Big Pink is full, the owner sometimes rents rooms in the absolutely gorgeous Honey Hill House nearby on a wooded lot off State Street.

Blues Hound Flat

901-272-0230
www.blueshoundflat.com
309 Issaquena Ave., Clarksdale, MS 38614
Downtown, two blocks from Ground Zero

Price: Moderate–Expensive
Credit Cards: Yes
Handicap Access: Limited
Special Features: Two-night minimum;
free wireless

Located in the heart of downtown
Clarksdale across from the historic
Greyhound station, this apartment-style
accommodation offers 1,500 square feet of
space. Loft-style living, dining, and
kitchen areas consist of stained concrete
floors, local artwork, and casual, laid-back
decor. The loft sleeps up to four people,
with one king bed plus a foldout couch. A
hinged screen lends privacy to the king
bed. There's one bathroom, a fully
equipped kitchen (minus a dishwasher), a
stereo with a CD player, and 52-inch TV
with a DVD player, but no cable. There's
also a washer and dryer in the utility room,
but no maid service—guests are responsible for cleaning up after themselves.
Guests also have access to a private outdoor patio out back.

Delta Cotton Company Apartments
662-645-9366
www.groundzerobluesclub.com/apartment
.php
387 Delta Ave., Clarksdale, MS 38614
Downtown, one block west of the Delta
Blues Museum
Price: Moderate–Expensive
Credit Cards: Yes
Handicap Access: None
Special Features: Discounts for more than
seven nights; laundry facilities; wireless
Internet

Located above Ground Zero Blues Club,
these seven apartment-style rooms are
housed in a converted cotton-grading warehouse built in 1903. Each spacious room is
named for a grade of cotton, from Low
Middling to Strict Good Ordinary. The popular Apartment 1, or Good Middling, is also
known as Morgan's Apartment, as in co-

*Before it was an inn, the Big Pink Guesthouse
played host to many a wild party.*

owner Morgan Freeman. The hallway connecting the rooms showcases artifacts from
the Delta Grocery & Cotton Co., including a
cotton sample table, old kitchen appliances,
and the building's original toilet.

Units boast full kitchens and baths, living areas with couches and TVs, and small
tables. The hardwood floors are glossy, the
ceilings high, and the decor retro. What you
won't find are telephones, microwaves, or
an iron. But with around 7,500 square feet
to stretch out in, guests may be tempted to
stay a while. Loft-style apartments (2 and 3)
don't have separate bedrooms, while others
(5 and 7) have multiple bedrooms that can
sleep up to four. Apartment 7 is the most
spacious, while apartment 6 is a down-
home efficiency with funky tiger lamps and
an animal-print couch. Keep in mind, a
blues club is right below your feet, and live

music is a regular occurrence Wednesday through Saturday nights. As the Web site admonishes, "You should be downstairs partying anyway . . . shame on you!" Guests bypass the club's cover charge—just be sure to get downstairs before 8 PM.

The Loft at Hopson Plantation

662-902-2378, 662-902-3866
www.hopsonplantation.com
Hopson-Pixley Rd. and Commissary Circle, Clarksdale, MS 38614
US 49 South from Clarksdale around 3 miles; turn right on Hopson-Pixley Road, cross railroad tracks, and take first right; pass Commissary on left, and the Loft will be on the right
Price: Moderate–Expensive
Credit Cards: Yes
Handicap Access: None

Part of the Shack Up and Cotton Gin Inn complex on historic Hopson Plantation, the Loft is a recent single-unit addition to Hopson's ever-expanding array of unique accommodations. Inside the converted seed house, the spacious loftlike space is equipped with a roomy king master, a separate cozy loft with a double bed, and a pull-out couch in the living area. In keeping with the funky Shack Up style, the walls are unfinished wood, and the decor consists of eclectic antique furnishings, quilts, guitars, and a piano. The full kitchen features an antique stove, and the no-frills bathroom is plenty functional. A spacious front porch with rocking chairs, hanging ferns, and spinning fans overhead is an ideal spot to take in the action across the way at the Commissary during events and blues festivals. Every October on the Sunday after the Arkansas Blues & Heritage Festival, hundreds of blues fans and musicians descend upon Hopson for the annual Pinetop Perkins Homecoming Jam.

Riverside Hotel

662-624-9163
615 Sunflower Ave., Clarksdale, MS 38614

Perched between the Hopson Commissary and the Juke Joint Chapel, the Loft is in the heart of the action when there's live music at the Commissary.

Part rooming house, part hotel, and part historical site, the Riverside Hotel is deeply rooted in Clarksdale's blues heritage.

Next to Red's Lounge, less than a mile from downtown Clarksdale
Price: Inexpensive
Credit Cards: No
Handicap Access: None

Despite its humble exterior, the Riverside Hotel played an integral role in not only the history of the blues, but the origins of rock 'n' roll itself—hence the Blues Trail marker proudly standing beside the property. Prior to its life as a hotel, the building served as the G. T. Thomas Hospital. It was here in 1937 that famed blueswoman Bessie Smith died after sustaining fatal injuries in a car accident on the Blues Highway (Highway 61). A decade and a half later, Ike Turner and his band recorded a demo for "Rocket 88" in the hotel's basement—the song that gave birth to rock 'n' roll. Turner lived in room number 7 for several years and was treated like a son by hotel proprietor Z. L. "Momma" Hill, who helped design and sew the stage outfits for Turner and the Ikettes.

Today, the Riverside is a treasure trove of history that's now run by Momma Hill's son, the friendly and knowledgeable Frank "Rat" Ratliff, who freely admits that he throws nothing away. Photographs line the walls in this living, breathing testament to the blues, and discarded bluesmen's belongings continue to find a home in the rooms' dresser drawers. The bed frames remain the same from when guests such as John Lee Hooker, Muddy Waters, Sam Cooke, and Robert Nighthawk called the Riverside home. Nighthawk even left his suitcase in his room shortly before his death, which, not surprisingly, is still here.

While the rooms (including what is now known as the Bessie Smith room) are small, modest, and no-frills, Rat takes pride in his property's cleanliness, from the accommodations to spick-and-span shared hallway bathrooms, including a ladies room, men's bathroom, and coed option. Those who prefer private bathrooms should inquire about the newly renovated side units located next door to the hotel.

The Shack Up Inn and Cotton Gin Inn

662-624-8329
www.shackupinn.com
001 Commissary Circle, Clarksdale, MS 38614
US 49 S. from Clarksdale around 3 miles, then right on Hopson-Pixley Road; cross railroad tracks and take first right, then first left past the Commissary to get to lobby on right
Price: Inexpensive
Credit Cards: Yes
Handicap Access: None
Special Features: Two-night minimum on weekends; guests must be at least 25 years old to rent a room

Located just south of town on historic Hopson Plantation, these unique accommodations consist of nine sharecropper shacks (more on the way) transplanted to the grounds where the mechanized cotton picker was first used. The rural property is dotted with classic cars, rusted out farm equipment, and bottle trees. The shacks are authentic enough to be rough around the edges but modernized with heat, air-conditioning, indoor plumbing, kitchens or kitchenettes, and even wireless Internet—although the corrugated tin roofs sometimes interfere with the connection. The walls are raw Mississippi cypress, and the decor is pure junk store chic. The commode may be cracked and the faucets squeaky, but the owners wouldn't have it any other way; keeping things funky is the point. Every surface is covered with blues memorabilia and thrift-store finds, and each shack has a TV that only picks up the blues station. Units, which sleep from two to four shackers, are stocked with everything from pianos to a copper moonshine still. Front porches with ancient couches are the perfect place to sip a cold one. There's a reason

The 300-square-foot Cadillac Shack is the Shack Up's coziest shed.

While they don't have full front porches like the shacks, the upper-level "bins" at the Cotton Gin have nice patios.

why *B&B* stands for "bed & beer" at the Shack Up.

Guests who are looking for a little less "personality" may consider staying in one of 10 rooms (dubbed "bins") across the lawn in the converted cotton gin. New, modern rooms are equipped with funky furniture, bathroom murals painted by local artists, and TVs with more than one channel. A large portion of the gin's lower level has been converted into the Juke Joint Chapel, where blues lovers fill church pews to listen to live music during festivals and other special events. A recording studio is also in the works—music to the ears of the many musicians who shack up on the premises.

Standard Accommodations

These State Street motels feature basic rooms with a minifridge, microwave, and coffeemaker; continental breakfast; and free Internet. There are also handicap-accessible rooms. The Comfort Inn has a seasonal outdoor swimming pool, and the Executive Inn has an indoor-outdoor version.

Comfort Inn
662-627-5122
www.comfortinn.com
818 S. State St., Clarksdale, MS 38614

America's Best Value Inn & Suites
662-621-1110
www.americasbestvalueinn.com
350 S. State St., Clarksdale, MS 38614

Executive Inn
662-627-9292
710 S. State St., Clarksdale, MS 38614

Budget Beds

If you're pinching pennies and don't mind some rough edges, the no-frills motels below offer very basic accommodations for around $35 to $50 a night. All have in-room minifridges and microwaves, but not much else. The Uptown Motor Inn's downtown location is a plus if you want to walk to nearby attractions.

Budget Inn
662-624-6541
420 State St., Clarksdale, MS 38614

Royal Inn
662-624-4391
1910 State St., Clarksdale, MS 38614

Southern Inn
662-624-6558
1904 State St., Clarksdale, MS 38614

Mississippi Blues Trail

When it's completed, the Mississippi Blues Trail will consist of more than 120 historical markers placed throughout the state. Headed by the Mississippi Blues Commission, the Blues Trail project pays tribute to the state's incredibly rich blues heritage and the fertile soil from which so many blues greats sprung. Beginning at the Louisiana/Mississippi border, the trail winds north throughout the state to Tennessee. The inaugural marker was placed in 2005 in Holly Springs, honoring the Father of the Mississippi Delta Blues, Charlie Patton. Since then, markers have gone up around the state paying tribute to blues luminaries and noteworthy blues locations, including Robert Johnson, Howlin' Wolf, the Riverside Motel, Dockery Plantation, Son House, Memphis Minnie, and Bo Diddley, among others. In addition to the physical markers, the Blues Commission has created an excellent Web site, www.msbluestrail.org, that has maps and directions to markers throughout the state's five regions: Delta, Hills, Pines, Coast, and Capital/River. The Web site is also a fantastic resource for current listings of blues festivals and events throughout the state.

Uptown Motor Inn
662-627-3251
305 E. Second St., Clarksdale, MS 38614

Camping
Coahoma County Expo Center
662-627-7337
1150 Wildcat Dr., Clarksdale, MS 38614

More than four hundred RV pads with water and electricity, plus some sewer hookups.

Hopson Plantation/Shack Up Inn
662-624-8329
001 Commissary Circle, Clarksdale, MS 38614

Tent and RV camping is available on the grounds of Hopson Plantation. No hookups, and guests must call in advance.

CULTURE

The majority of Clarksdale's attractions are blues related, from tiny museums that are only open during festival time to the historic sites scattered around town. The must-see attraction, of course, is the Delta Blues Museum. There are also a few interesting literary sites in Clarksdale, courtesy of Tennessee Williams, who spent many of his childhood years in the area. As with any type of business in the Delta, always call ahead; hours at many of these attractions can be sporadic.

Aaron Cotton Company Cotton Museum
662-902-9069
311 Delta Ave., Clarksdale, MS 38614
Open: Festival weekends
Admission: Donations

Part museum, part gift shop, this one-room operation offers a glimpse into the days when cotton was king. A handful of displays include a cotton rolling table, cotton classing boxes, cotton samples, and the original desk, typewriters, and office equipment from the company's heyday. Getting equal space and attention are the cotton-themed retail items like cotton bolls, seeds, T-shirts, hats, and more. The shop also has a selection of old records, magazines, and prints for sale.

Cat Head Delta Blues & Folk Art
662-624-5992
www.cathead.biz
252 Delta Ave., Clarksdale, MS 38614
Open: Mon.–Sat.; Sun. on event weekends or by appointment

This funky, must-see shop is packed with folk art, blues CDs, books, memorabilia, and much more. If you're in town for live music, Cat Head should be your first stop. Owner Roger Stolle—who also books local clubs, runs a boutique blues record label, and hosts a blues show on WROX—is the go-to source for gig info in Clarksdale and throughout the Delta. Cat Head also hosts occasional live music and mini blues fests. See the Shopping section for more information.

The Crossroads Monument

Intersection of Hwy. 61 and US 49

Here at the intersection where Blues Highway 61 meets US 49, you'll find a massive, some-what gaudy steel monument honoring "the crossroads" with replicas of the bluesman's weapon of choice: the guitar. An obvious tourism grab, Clarksdale's crossroads monument pays tribute to the legions of bluesmen who, for years, traveled these highways in search of work and pleasure. Of course, no discussion of the crossroads would be complete without a mention of Robert Johnson selling his very soul to the devil at midnight with the promise of unparalleled musical gifts. While Johnson is most often cited as the protagonist of this tale, it is in fact a composite story derived from African American folk traditions. These days, you're more likely to find tourists posing for photos than mysterious deals with the devil.

The Delta Blues Museum

662-627-6820
www.deltabluesmuseum.org
1 Blues Alley, Clarksdale, MS 38614
Open: Mon.–Sat.
Admission: Adults $7; children (6–12) $5; children under 6 free

Located in the former home of Clarksdale's historic freight depot, the Delta Blues Museum is home to both permanent and traveling collections. Built in the early 20th century, the former depot exudes an atmosphere of reverence that easily lends itself to the folk art, photography, and memorabilia preserved within its brick walls. Tracing the blues back to

Established in 1979 by the Carnegie Public Library, the Delta Blues Museum moved into the historic freight depot in 1999.

its Delta beginnings, the single expansive room houses a medley of blues artifacts, including paintings, photographs, instruments, salvaged letters, original sheet music, and, perhaps most famously, a section of Muddy Waters's cabin. A life-size re-creation of the blues legend sits inside the shack where he lived on Stovall Farms just outside of town. It was here that Alan Lomax first recorded Muddy's music for the Library of Congress in 1941. Today, the re-created cabin houses a display tracing the bluesman's career from the Delta to the Chicago spotlight. Don't miss the guitar that Billy Gibbons (of ZZ Top fame) had constructed out of discarded wood from Waters's cabin. The guitar, appropriately named *Muddywood,* now rightfully sits within the shack. Speaking of guitars, aficionados will want to pay special attention to the museum's impressive six-string collection belonging to legends like John Lee Hooker, B. B. King, Son Thomas, Big Joe Williams, and Jimmie Burns. Of course, no blues museum would be complete without a nod to the crossroads. If Robert Johnson did indeed sell his soul to the devil, the Three Forks store is where the hellhounds finally caught up to him. On display in the museum, the Three Forks sign is one of the last remnants from the juke joint where Johnson was (reportedly) poisoned the night of his final gig in 1938. In addition to its variety of exhibits, the museum also hosts a number of seasonal music events and serves as a main stage during festivals. Check the Web site for a schedule of upcoming events.

Greyhound Bus Station
210 Third St., Clarksdale, MS 38614

Time seems to have stood still at Clarksdale's downtown Greyhound bus station, an immaculately restored art deco building. When bluesmen left Clarksdale for Memphis, Chicago, and beyond, those who didn't take the nearby train often hopped on a bus instead. Needless to say, the station was a bustling place during the massive exodus that followed the mechanization of agriculture in the area. No longer a busy thoroughfare, the station now acts as a visitor's center and auxiliary space for the Delta Blues Museum's exhibitions and events. The space can also be rented out for private events.

Hambone Art Gallery
662-253-5586
www.stanstreet.com
111 E. Second St., Clarksdale, MS 38614

Artist-musician Stan Street's downtown gallery features vibrant blues- and Delta-themed folk art. In addition to art, Stan occasionally hosts live music and serves cold beers—generally during blues festival time or at his own small Hambone Music Festival held each Halloween weekend. The comfy seating area and laid-back vibe make the gallery a friendly spot to enjoy art, music, and conversation. For more information, see the Shopping section.

Hopson Plantation
www.hopsonplantation.com
US 49 and Hopson-Pixley Rd., Clarksdale, MS 38614
US 49 South from Clarksdale around 3 miles; turn right on Hopson-Pixley Road, cross railroad tracks, and plantation will be on the right

Located about five minutes south of Clarksdale, this historic plantation is where the mechanized cotton picker was first introduced in 1944, forever changing the cotton industry and the lives of its employees. It's also where legendary blues pianist Willie "Pinetop" Perkins worked as a tractor driver when he wasn't playing gigs in Clarksdale and around the Delta. When the Blues Trail marker honoring both Hopson and Perkins was erected here in 2008, the 94-year-old Pinetop attended the ceremony. Today, the picturesque grounds are home to some of the town's funkiest places to stay—the Shack Up Inn, Cotton Gin, and Hopson Loft. There are also three stages where live blues can be heard during festivals: the Juke Joint Chapel located in the Cotton Gin, and Hopson Commissary's main stage and acoustic back porch area. See individual venue listings for more information. Each October on the Sunday following the Arkansas Blues & Heritage Festival (formerly the King Biscuit Blues Festival), hundreds of blues fans descend on Hopson for the annual Pinetop Perkins Homecoming Jam.

Ike Turner's Home
304 Washington St., Clarksdale, MS 38614

Born the son of a Baptist preacher in 1931, Ike Turner spent his early life in this modest home on Washington Street. Turner, as controversial a figure as he was gifted, began his musical journey at the age of eight when a local DJ at WROX showed him how to handle records. In time, Turner would go on to DJ at the station before putting together the band that would eventually cut the track "Rocket 88" (whose demo was recorded in the basement of the Riverside Motel), which history would later hail as the first rock 'n' roll record. While you can't tour the private home, Ike fans sometimes drive by to see where the legend lived.

Muddy's Mound on Stovall Farms
From downtown, drive northwest on Oakhurst Avenue/Stovall Road; the site is around a mile north of the Farrell Rd. intersection on the left

Although Muddy Waters's rustic sharecropper cabin now resides inside the Delta Blues Museum, a Blues Trail marker honors the home's original location on Stovall Farms. Located around 6 miles northwest of downtown, the site stands on the edge of a picturesque cotton field. It was here that folklorist Alan Lomax first recorded Muddy Waters in 1941, and these cotton fields are where the legendary bluesman drove a tractor for less than 50 cents an hour. Soon after McKinley Morganfield (Waters's birth name) heard

Alan Lomax
Alan Lomax (www.lomaxarchive.com) is nothing less than a musical anthropologist and archaeologist—a true folklorist in the deepest sense of the word. As the son of noted musicologist John A. Lomax, Alan came by it naturally, scouring the earth for new sounds. Working for the Library of Congress, John and Alan Lomax were charged with collecting field recordings of various musical genres from not only the United States, but around the world. Alan Lomax, in particular, is heralded as shining a light on not only the blues of the Delta, but, through his journals and photography, the lives and plight of the people who lived there.

The Blues Trail marker at Muddy's Mound includes Eric Clapton's quote, "Muddy Waters's music changed my life, and whether you know it or not, and like it or not, it probably changed yours, too."

Lomax's recordings, he was inspired to move to Chicago to play the blues. The rest, as they say, is history.

New World District
Issaquena St. and Martin Luther King Blvd. (Fourth St.)

Located across the tracks from the Blues Museum, this historic district once hopped with African American businesses and juke joints—much like Beale Street in Memphis before it became a tourist attraction. Situated roughly between Sunflower Avenue, Issaquena Street, the old railroad underpass, and Martin Luther King Boulevard, the area—like so much of the Delta—is a shadow of its former self. Juke joints like Messengers and Club 200 occasionally liven up the scene with music at night, but by day, cracked sidewalks and empty buildings characterize much of the neighborhood. Historic sites include the New Roxy, once an African American movie theater where a young Ike Turner worked, and also a live music venue. Clarksdale's first Walk of Fame marker honoring Sam Cooke was dedicated here in 2008 outside of the New Roxy, where Cooke once performed. In late 2008, a new owner began restoration on the New Roxy as well as a property across the street; tentative plans are to convert the old theater to a multi-purpose arts venue and open a hostel in the other building.

Riverside Hotel
662-624-9163
615 Sunflower Ave., Clarksdale, MS 38614

The angel statue in Tennessee Williams Park is a nod to Summer and Smoke, a Williams play set in Clarksdale.

This is where Bessie Smith took her final breath and bluesmen like Ike Turner, Robert Nighthawk, and Muddy Waters once stayed on their way through town, or, in some cases, lived for a while. See the Lodging section for a more detailed history of this Blues Trail landmark.

Tennessee Williams District
Clark St., Court St., and Sharkey Ave. at First St.

Tennessee Williams spent part of his childhood growing up in Clarksdale, where his grandfather served as rector of St. George's Episcopal Church—still in operation at 106 Sharkey Avenue. Williams lived with his mother and grandparents in the church's parsonage. The town's colorful characters made an indelible impression on young Tom, many showing up later in plays like *A Streetcar Named Desire, The Glass Menagerie, Summer and Smoke,* and many more. Among these real-life characters was the infamous Blanche Dubois from *Streetcar,* whose father, John Clark, founded Clarksdale. Blanche's father built the antebellum Belle-Clark mansion, located at 211 Clark Street, in 1859. After Blanche married J. W. Cutrer, the couple lived down the street in the gorgeous Italian Renaissance villa at 109 Clark Street. Site of many an opulent party, the Cutrer Mansion was Williams's model for Belle Reve, the family estate that Blanche reminisces about in *Streetcar.* Take a walking tour through the lovely historic district, and be sure to stop by the tiny Tennessee Williams Park at the corner of Court Street and Polly Place, where a young Tom used to play. Literary fans should plan to visit for Clarksdale's annual Mississippi Delta Tennessee Williams Festival, held in the fall. For even more Williams history, be sure and visit Uncle Henry's Place north of town in Dundee; see the Restaurants section for details.

Theo's Rock 'n' Roll & Blues Heritage Museum

901-605-8662

www.rockmuseum.biz

113 E. Second St., Clarksdale, MS 38614

Open: Some weekends; every event weekend, Thurs. and Sun. by appointment

Admission: $5

Curated by a Dutch expat, this spacious museum (originally located in the Netherlands) documents blues, R&B, and rock 'n' roll from the 1920s through the 1970s. Six rooms deep, the museum's 3,000 square feet are filled with memorabilia, including original first pressings of blues 78s, antique gramophones, artist contracts and autographs, kitschy retro movie posters, and all other manner of music-geek curios. Patrons are encouraged to pick out and play vinyl 45s, handle ancient eight-track cassettes, and watch DVDs of living local blues legends like Super Chikan in action.

Wade Walton's Barbershop

317 Issaquena Ave., Clarksdale, MS 38614

Wade Walton may have been known as the "blues barber," but his legacy runs much deeper than cutting the hair of the likes of Sonny Boy Williamson II, Howlin' Wolf, and Ike Turner. Besides being a man of the shears, Walton also performed and recorded the blues, often keeping the beat by sharpening a razor against a leather strop. These days, the barbershop is home to Big D's Blues Club, which comes to life during local blues festivals when musicians perform out front and the barbecue smokers are fired up all day. Stop by the nearby Delta Blues Museum to see one of the well-worn barber chairs from Wade Walton's heyday.

Wade Walton's Barbershop is the site of one of the Juke Joint Festival's downtown stages.

W. C. Handy Home Site

Issaquena Ave. next to Wade Walton's Barbershop

While the Father of the Blues primarily hung his hat in Memphis, Handy lived in Clarksdale on Issaquena Avenue for a couple of years during the early 20th century. While in Clarksdale, Handy made a living leading a nonblues band, but it was around this time that he had a life-altering revelation that forever changed the course of his career. While waiting on a train in nearby Tutwiler, Handy came upon an old bluesman scraping a knife against the fret board of his guitar and singing, "goin' where the Southern crosses the Dog." The tune made a lasting impression on Handy, who went on to record his own version of the song, hence "founding" the blues. Today, the homesite is simply a marker next to an empty lot neighboring Wade Walton's Barbershop.

WROX Museum

662-645-8874
www.wroxradio.com
257 Delta Ave., Clarksdale, MS 38614
Open: Varies during festival times
Admission: $5 for adults; children 13 and under free

Hailed as the oldest radio station in northwest Mississippi, WROX first hit the airwaves on June 2, 1944. Originally located at 317 Delta Avenue, the station moved down the street to 257 Delta Avenue in the 1950s, which is now the home of the WROX Museum. Around this time, Elvis Presley had an early on-air appearance, and Ike Turner was the house janitor before becoming a regular DJ. While the station itself is now located on DeSoto Avenue, the WROX Museum pays tribute to its early role as a musical and cultural ambassador across the Delta. It's a far cry from satellite radio: Visitors can witness the early days of terrestrial radio in the museum's re-created control room from when the station ran off a 250-watt RCA transmitter. While WROX's focus is "rock and soul's greatest hits," Saturday night is dedicated to the blues. Tune in to 1450 AM to listen.

GUIDED TOURS

Birdsong Historic Tours

662-624-6051
birdsong@clarksdale.com

Fourth-generation Clarksdale resident Robert Birdsong provides custom tours based around the town's history, blues heritage, agriculture, Tennessee Williams, and more. There's not much Mr. Birdsong doesn't know—or won't share—from juicy tidbits about the colorful characters of Tennessee Williams's time to the rise and fall of Clarksdale's juke joints.

Quapaw Canoe Company

662-627-4070
www.island63.com
291 Sunflower Ave., Clarksdale, MS 38614

Canoe guide—musician—artist—boat carver John Ruskey offers canoe and kayak trips down the mighty Mississippi and its tributaries, including Clarksdale's Sunflower River. Explore wilderness areas, backwaters, bayous, and levees for a few hours, a few days, or a few weeks. For the adventurous, extended overnight trips include a two-week float from Cairo (Illinois) to Memphis and a four-week expedition from Memphis to New Orleans. Shorter day trips include full-moon floats under the night sky. No matter how long you decide to take to the water, you're guaranteed to see the Mississippi River in a whole new light.

SEASONAL EVENTS

We've said it before, and we'll say it again: Be sure to book accommodations well in advance for blues festivals. Clarksdale's limited rooms fill up quickly—and early—during these popular weekends.

April

Cat Head Mini Blues Fests
662-624-5992
www.cathead.biz
Cat Head
252 Delta Ave., Clarksdale, MS 38614

Held in conjunction with larger festivals throughout the area, these free Sunday festivals, also held in August and October, are a fine way to top off a weekend packed with live blues. A lineup of regional blues acts set up shop on the sidewalk in front of the store and generally play from around 10 AM to 5 PM. Folding chairs are set up, and tents block out the hot Mississippi sun, making this a comfortable, laid-back live music experience. Be sure to stop in Cat Head for a little between-act browsing.

Juke Joint Festival
662-624-5992
www.jukejointfestival.com

This popular annual blues festival, held at venues throughout Clarksdale, has been celebrating the local juke joint since 2004. The official festival consists of a full day packed with live blues music at downtown stages by day and local juke joints by night—including many jukes where live music has become a rarity. Local and regional acts like Big Jack Johnson, Jimbo Mathus, T-Model Ford, and Honeyboy Edwards play five outdoor stages throughout the day until night falls and the juke joints take over. In addition to live music, downtown comes to life with small-town fair-style fun, including pig races, kids' activities, crawfish boils, and plenty of food and drink. Vendor stalls are set up in the streets, and Robert Birdsong usually gives history bus tours throughout the day (free with wristband). While the all-day festivities are held on Saturday, the juke joints crank all weekend long, and many attractions that are otherwise closed remain open throughout the weekend. A $10 wristband gets you into all the clubs and allows you to hop on a bus that circles the juke joints and motels at night—no driving required.

May

Caravan Music Festival

901-605-8662

Outside the Rock 'n' Roll & Blues Heritage Museum and Cat Head, downtown Clarksdale

One of the newest music festivals to spring up in Clarksdale is the Caravan Music Festival, founded in 2007 by Theo Dasbach, who runs downtown's Rock 'n' Roll & Blues Heritage Museum. Held annually the Saturday after the Memphis Blues Music Awards, the festival features both local and national artists in a variety of genres, including blues, rock, pop, and country. Daytime concerts outside the Rock 'n' Roll Museum and Cat Head are free, and Second Street is blocked off from Yazoo to Delta avenues for spectators. During the night, there's additional live music at venues like Ground Zero, Red's, and Super Chikan's Place at the Bluesberry Café. Previous performers include T-Model Ford, Robert Belfour, Terry "Harmonica" Bean, Memphis Snake Doctors, Mississippi Rose Lee, and Thompson Ward "Light."

June

Delta Jubilee

662-627-7337

Coahoma County Expo Center at the fairgrounds

1150 Wildcat Dr., Clarksdale, MS 38614

This family-oriented community event is designed for locals, but visitors are welcome. The Jubilee offers a true taste of small-town Americana with family activities that range from cook-offs to a frog-jumping competition. There are also carnival rides and fireworks along with arts and crafts booths, live music, and even a pet show. The annual event is a fund-raiser for the Rotary Club. Coolers are not allowed.

August

Sunflower River Blues and Gospel Festival

www.sunflowerfest.org

Sunflower River Blues Association

Box 1562, Clarksdale, MS 38614

This free, nonprofit, weekend-long festival held in downtown Clarksdale has been going strong for more than 20 years. Regional artists and big-name national headliners grace the main stage in Blues Alley (by the Delta Blues Museum) and an acoustic stage by the Sunflower River. Sunday is reserved for gospel acts. It's no secret that the Mississippi Delta can be sweltering in August, but that doesn't stop more than 25,000 fans from 17 countries and 37 states from showing up for the festivities—making this one of Mississippi's biggest blues festivals. It's also a prime time to visit local juke joints, which come to life during festivals.

October

Hambone Festival

662-253-5586

www.hambonefestival.com

Hambone Art Gallery
111 E. Second St., Clarksdale, MS 38614

This recent addition to Clarksdale's blues festival lineup is hosted by artist-musician Stan Street every year on Halloween weekend—which also happens to be Street's birthday weekend. The festivities include a Saturday street party with soul food and live blues from local favorites like Big T and Terry Harmonica Bean, plus Street's blues artist friends from beyond the Delta—and, of course, Stan Street himself. In addition to the gallery, there are shows at venues like Ground Zero, the Depot, and Red's throughout the weekend. The fun culminates in a "Bloody Mary chill-out" on Sunday morning.

Mississippi Delta Tennessee Williams Festival
662-621-4157
www.coahomacc.edu/twilliams

This annual festival honors renowned playwright Tennessee Williams, who spent many of his childhood years in Clarksdale—during which time he drew a great deal of inspiration from the town's colorful characters. Fifteen-minute front-porch plays are held at gracious homes in the historic Tennessee Williams District, including the home of Tom's childhood best friend, Walter Clark; the mansion built by Mississippi governor Earl Brewer; and the double-galleried porch where the Tennessee Williams postage stamp was unveiled in 1995. There are also lectures, plays featuring Broadway stars, a competitive acting contest for high school students, dinners, and receptions. At least one event is usually held at the gorgeous Cutrer Mansion, home of the real-life Blanche and model for Belle Reve. The celebration, sponsored by the Coahoma Community College, has been drawing literary buffs since 1992.

Pinetop Perkins Annual Homecoming
www.hopsonplantation.com
Hopson Plantation/Hopson Commissary
001 Commissary Rd., Clarksdale, MS 38614

Held every year on the Sunday after the Arkansas Blues & Heritage Festival (formerly known as the King Biscuit Blues Festival), this one-day event honoring Pinetop Perkins's birthday is a full afternoon of live blues on Hopson Plantation, where the legendary bluesman was once employed. Hundreds of blues fans and musicians fill up the grounds for the festivities. Music gets going around 2 PM or so and continues into the early evening.

NIGHTLIFE

There are a couple of things every blues fan needs to know about juke joints and blues clubs: First and foremost, be sure to visit on a weekend if you're looking for live music. Second, always call ahead, as hours and bookings can be sporadic. Fortunately, Clarksdale is the most reliable Delta town for live blues. To get up-to-the-minute information about who's playing, stop by Cat Head downtown or check the store's Web site. Juke joints are no-frills, makeshift affairs, and many come and go at a rapid clip. We've done our best to cover current spots where you're likely to hear live music, but always ask around. The best time for live blues anywhere in the Delta is during a festival. When there's not live music, the tunes are generally provided by a jukebox or DJ.

Always have cash on hand, as juke joints don't typically accept plastic, and expect to pay a cover between $5 and $10, depending upon the band. Some jukes serve basic food like burgers and fried catfish, but the beverage options are limited. You won't find hard liquor anywhere other than Ground Zero. Instead, expect to drink ice-cold beer out of giant 32-ounce bottles or cans, which are served with a pair of plastic cups for you and a buddy. If you must have the hard stuff, most jukes allow you to bring your own bottle and will provide a bowl of ice and the mixer of your choice (aka, a "setup"). Be aware that smoking is pretty much always permitted. Finally, exercise common sense and courtesy. Ask before you start snapping photos, and don't get in the way of that local who's spending his hard-earned dollars for a little Saturday-night entertainment. And whatever you do, don't forget to tip the band.

Anniebell's Lounge

662-624-2320
1406 N. State St., Clarksdale, MS 38614

If you're looking for a real-deal roadside juke, look no further than Anniebell's Lounge. Located next to an abandoned gas station not far from the infamous crossroads, this joint is most definitely—as the sign next to the front door proclaims—A PARTY FOR GROWNUPS. Step inside, buy a great big bottle of ice-cold beer, sit back, and enjoy the music. The spacious, dimly lit club provides plenty of room for socializing, shooting stick, and dancing beneath the disco ball. Unlike most jukes, Anniebell's features a spacious bar as well as a stage area that's separated from the dance floor. Tunes are provided by the house DJ, or more rarely, a down-home electric blues band. If you work up an appetite, the attached burger joint is usually open late.

Located beyond downtown's limits, Anniebell's Lounge offers an authentic juke-joint experience down the street from the Crossroads.

Most Sundays, Mr. Tater the Music Maker plays at tiny Club 2000 in the New World District.

Club 2000
No phone
Issaquena Ave., Clarksdale, MS 38614

Pool table? Check. Warped, water-stained ceiling panels? Check. Video poker? Check. Fading posters advertising beer and liquor? Check. An authentic, old-school, juke-joint experience? Absolutely. Located in Clarksdale's New World District, next door to the New Roxy Theatre, this tiny juke looks like it's seen better days, and it very well may have, but make no mistake—the blues are alive and well within its four walls. A small room with low ceilings and no more than 10 to 12 tables, Club 2000 is a funky throwback that specializes in a good time. When the club has live music, the band sets up right in front, sandwiched between the video poker machines and the door. When crowded, it's hard to tell where the band ends and the dancing patrons begin. Besides cold beer, the club serves up typical juke-joint fare (burgers and so on), which you can order up at the window/bar in the back of the room.

Delta Blues Room
662-624-9200
220 Sunflower Ave., Clarksdale, MS 38614

Located on the Sunflower Avenue strip, this handsome spot is about as classy as a juke joint gets. Exposed brick walls lined with a neat row of holiday lights are covered in black-and-white portraits of blues legends. Spinning fans overhead surround the obligatory disco ball.

When there's live music, the band plays in the middle of the room. Surrounding tables boast matching chairs, tablecloths, and even candle jars. A small bar is located in the back, and if you're lucky, the kitchen may be serving up its famous hot wings or burgers.

The Depot Blues Club

662-624-8132
200 Blues Alley, Clarksdale, MS 38614

Housed in historic Clarksdale Station, this restaurant, bar, and live-music hall is located downtown next to the Blues Museum. Named after the passenger train depot in which it sits, the establishment is halved down the middle, with generous space given to both the music hall and the dining area. Additional patio seating is out back. The restaurant's menu originally focused on traditional Southern cooking (plate lunches, meat 'n threes) and steaks but has since added pizza to its offerings. Predominantly a blues club, the Depot offers live music most weekends and occasional karaoke nights. Credit cards are accepted.

Ground Zero Blues Club

662-621-9009
www.groundzerobluesclub.com
0 Blues Alley, Clarksdale, MS 38614

Cofounded by acclaimed actor and Mississippi Delta native Morgan Freeman, the Ground Zero Blues Club brings the soul of the rural Mississippi juke joint to the heart of historic downtown Clarksdale. Housed in a converted cotton warehouse, the club's front porch is littered with seasoned couches and lawn furniture that beg patrons to take a load off. Inside, the warehouse-style space is packed with prototypical juke joint graffiti, mismatched yard sale chairs, holiday lights, and all manner of carefully curated Southern decor in a state of stylish disrepair.

Renowned for giving local blues musicians a steady place to gig, Ground Zero also occasionally books national touring acts (including the North Mississippi All-Stars and others) and is one of the very few places to hear live blues on weeknights—or at least from Wednesday on. It's not uncommon to share a beer and a game of pool with a patron one night only to see him take the stage the following evening. Ground Zero boasts a full bar (a luxury in Clarksdale), accepts credit cards, and serves up delicious regional fare like barbecue, soul food, and plate lunches on weekdays. Enjoy a hearty meal before taking in a night of live music in the town that purists consider the ultimate ground zero for the blues.

Hopson Commissary

662-624-5756
www.hopsonplantation.com
001 Commissary Rd., Clarksdale, MS 38614

Anchoring the funky-cool Shack Up Inn complex on Hopson Plantation, the Commissary is one of Clarksdale's most interesting venues. The cavernous historic building features a large stage area and bar in the front room, and a smaller bar and acoustic stage on a screened back porch. Tables are scattered throughout the main room, on a second-level loft area overlooking the main stage, and in nooks and crannies throughout the mazelike building. Every surface is covered with antiques and artifacts from the deep South, from

The original Ground Zero Blues Club is the most reliable spot in Clarksdale to catch live blues.

The Hopson Commissary turns into a huge party during the Juke Joint, Sunflower, and Pinetop Perkins Homecoming festivals.

Ole Miss flags and blues memorabilia to mannequins, barber chairs, and retro road signs. It all makes for a festive, fun vibe that seems to be especially popular with college-aged partiers. While live music and barbecue are generally reserved for group events, the Commissary is usually open for Shack Up and Loft guests around 5 PM for happy hour. Everyone can get in on the action on blues festival weekends, when the Commissary is often an official venue. One of the biggest annual bashes takes place the Sunday after Helena's Blues & Heritage Festival (formerly known as King Biscuit), when hundreds of visitors and a slew of musicians descend upon Hopson for a day of live music, barbecue, and plenty of beer.

Juke Joint Chapel in the Cotton Gin Inn
662-624-8329
001 Commissary Circle, Clarksdale, MS 38614

New in 2007, this one-of-a-kind venue is housed in half of the huge tin cotton gin on the Shack Up grounds. The other half of the building is dedicated to 10 rooms, or "bins," for overnight guests. A row of church pews make up the seating, and yes, a disco ball hangs from the sky-high ceiling. The sizeable stage platform is up a handful of stairs in front of a backdrop of old signs, including the Red Top Lounge sign from the old favorite (but now closed) Clarksdale juke. There's plenty of room to dance between the stage and the pews, and cold drinks are usually sold at the back of the venue.

Messenger's
No phone
133 MLK Dr., Clarksdale, MS 38614

Family owned since the 1930s, and quite possibly the oldest known juke joint on record (county files date the establishment to 1907), Messenger's is an all-in-one good-time operation featuring a pool hall, domino den, café, and juke joint under one roof. The expansive structure takes up two large rooms split down the middle—billiards on one side, and the café/juke joint on the other. Old soul, blues, R&B, and hip-hop rule the jukebox in the smoky pool hall. Next door, notable blues artists like Jimbo Mathus get the crowd going during blues festivals and other rare live-music weekends. If you work up an appetite, a basic menu of burgers and sandwiches is available, all ready to wash down with an ice-cold beer . . . or two.

Red's Lounge
No phone
395 Sunflower Ave., Clarksdale, MS 38614

Red's Lounge is *the* local juke joint in Clarksdale. Expect fatback beats, tall cans of Budweiser, impromptu booty-shakin',' and, most importantly, real-deal authentic blues. While it doesn't look like much from the street, Red's boasts regular players such as T-Model Ford, Big T, Big Jack Johnson, and Wesley Jefferson, all of whom call the juke a second home. Adding to Red's lore is the building's former life as Levine's Music Center, where Ike Turner and his Kings of Rhythm purchased the instruments used to cut "Rocket 88"—the song widely regarded as the birth of rock 'n' roll. Be sure to drop some bucks into

One of Clarksdale's roomiest jukes, Messenger's features pool tables, live music, and good eats.

Big Jack Johnson, T-Model Ford, Lightnin' Malcolm, Wesley Jefferson, and Robert Belfour regularly play at Red's Lounge.

the metal bucket center "stage" because, as the band will surely remind you, "if you don't tip, the band don't get a sip." Crowds pour out onto the sidewalk during festivals, when Red grills up his famous sausages on the smoker out front.

Sarah's Kitchen
662-627-3239
278 Sunflower Ave., Clarksdale, MS 38614

This cozy juke joint tucked in the strip across from the Sunflower River is a fine place for live blues with a side of soul food. A narrow main room features simple juke-joint style—wood-paneled walls covered in concert and festival posters, water-stained ceiling panels, and a small stage in front. A handful of booths and tables fills the small space, while the kitchen and order counter are located in an adjoining room. The handwritten menu features down-home favorites like fried chicken, catfish, and pepper steak served with soul-pleasing sides like fried green tomatoes, lima beans, rice and gravy, and corn bread. Lunch is generally offered Thursday through Saturday, with occasional live blues on Thursday and during festivals. If you're lucky, you may even catch an all-you-can-eat biscuits and gravy breakfast with live blues during a festival weekend.

Super Chikan's Place at the Bluesberry Café
662-627-7008
235 Yazoo Ave., Clarksdale, MS 38614

The display windows lining the entrance of this downtown café/music venue let you know that you're entering SUPER CHIKAN'S HOWSE. Several of the local bluesman's folk art guitars, aka "chik-can-tars," are on display, along with concert posters and blues memorabilia. Inside, the carpet is green, the walls are purple, and the chairs are metal, but the main focal point is a spacious raised stage that dominates the room. In addition to hosting live blues acts some weekends and during festivals, Bluesberry is also a café. Wings, burgers, and fried green tomatoes share menu space with a muffuletta, stromboli, and tempting desserts like éclairs and red velvet cake. And, of course, there's plenty of cold beer in the cooler.

RESTAURANTS

Don't plan on dieting when you're in the Delta. Regional specialties like fried catfish and tamales are anything but light, and lunch is more about barbecue and meat 'n threes—that's one meat, three vegetables for the uninitiated—than a dainty deli sandwich. Embrace the rib-sticking menus, and you'll be rewarded with the deep-fried goodness of Delta-style cooking. Whatever you do, don't leave town without trying a tamale. Slightly smaller than the Mexican version, this Mississippi Delta specialty is made with spicy beef wrapped in cornmeal and is generally served with a side of chili and crackers. Of course, there are a few grease-free exceptions below, but even the town's fine-dining establishments (Madidi and Rust) and sandwich shop (Dutch Oven) retain some Delta flavor. While many restaurants serve beer, hard liquor is a rarity, although some spots do allow you to bring your own wine. As always in the Delta, opening hours can be sporadic, so always call ahead, and keep in mind that most of these eateries allow smoking.

The Delta Blues Scene

While the Delta blues may not be as prevalent as it once was, there are still many great bluesmen out there traveling Highways 61 and 49 practicing their trade. Favorite local bluesmen who still gig fairly consistently include T-Model Ford, Super Chikan, Big Jack Johnson, Bill "Howlin' Mad" Perry, Big T, Terry "Harmonica" Bean, and Jimmy "Duck" Holmes. These gentlemen represent a small pool of musicians who are keeping the traditional blues alive throughout the Delta.

Blues travelers should note that since the 1990s, with the legalization of gambling, many of the blues players have taken to gigging at casinos in lieu of juke joints and blues halls. While understandable (better payday, reliability), it has diminished the opportunity for catching the music in its natural setting. Most jukes and clubs that do offer live blues are only open on weekend nights (and sporadic at that), so be sure to plan ahead and call before you haul. A great way to catch a whole lotta blues in a small time frame is to hit up one (or more) of the Delta's growing number of blues festivals. Often beginning on Thursday night, these festivals present the opportunity to catch blues artists in clubs with set dates and times (although no one's really watching the clock too hard). Blues travelers come from every walk of life and from practically every state and country. You're as likely to be standing at the bar next to a 22-year-old Sigma Chi from Ole Miss at Red's in Clarksdale during the Juke Joint Festival as you are a 52-year-old gentleman on holiday from Stockholm, Sweden. It truly takes all kinds.

Dining Price Codes

Inexpensive   Up to $15
Moderate $15–30
Expensive $30–65
Very Expensive   More than $65

The following abbreviations are used to identify what meals are served:

B—Breakfast
L—Lunch
D—Dinner
SB—Sunday brunch

Abe's Bar-B-Q

662-624-9947
www.abesbbq.com
616 N. State St., Clarksdale, MS 38614
Open: Daily
Price: Inexpensive
Credit Cards: Yes
Cuisine: Barbecue
Serving: L, D (Mon.–Sat.)
Handicap Access: Limited
Special Features: Barbecue sauce available for sale

Famous performers who have stopped by for a bite at Abe's include Paul Simon, ZZ Top, and Conway Twitty.

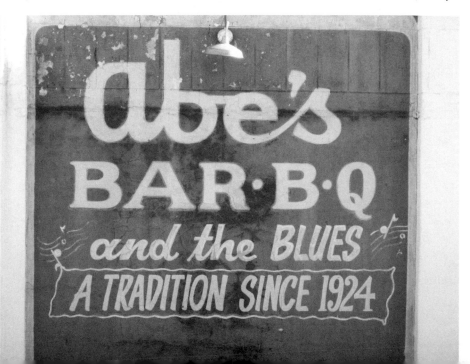

Locals and tourists alike have been flocking to this unassuming spot since 1924 for slow-roasted Boston butt barbecue cooked over hickory. The low-slung brick building is located just steps away from the famous crossroads monument. Inside, diners can grab a stool at the small counter or opt for a table in a cozy dining room that's plastered with blues paraphernalia and pig art. Skip the burgers and dogs for anything barbecue: pork, beef, or ribs. The real standout is the thin-sliced, crispy-edged pork, offered as a plate meal or pressed between a white sandwich bun after it's topped with crisp slaw and tangy barbecue sauce. The oversize Big Abe is more of the same: a double-decker sandwich chock-full of pork, slaw, and an extra slice of bread. Cigar-size hot tamales, made of corn husks stuffed with a slightly spicy mix of pork and beef, are another one of Abe's delights. Like everything else on the menu, tamales are served on paper plates with plastic-wrapped utensils.

Rest Haven
662-624-8601
419 State St., Clarksdale, MS 38614
Open: Mon.–Sat.
Price: Inexpensive–Moderate
Credit Cards: Yes
Cuisine: American, Lebanese, Italian
Serving: B, L Mon.–Sat., D Wed.–Sat.
Handicap Access: Limited

A unique eatery in a town that favors barbecue and fried catfish, Rest Haven goes beyond the basics with an extensive Lebanese and Italian menu. In the mornings, locals whom servers know by name fill up a diner-style room with counter stools, leatherette booths, Formica tabletops—and a wall dedicated to maps and photos of Lebanon. Hearty Southern breakfasts feature standards like creamy, butter-drenched grits, fluffy biscuits, and salty country ham. Lunch is also familiar, with hearty meat 'n three plate lunches that change daily. Orders get more adventurous at dinner, when diners spill over to a second, larger dining room for traditional Italian entrées ranging from lasagna to veal Parmesan. An entire page of the menu is dedicated to Middle Eastern specialties centered around Kibbie, a traditional Lebanese dish made with ground-round beef, cracked wheat, onions, and "special seasoning." The tasty Kibbie is prepared every which way: fried, baked, or raw, and served on sandwiches or as patties. Stuffed grape leaves, cabbage rolls, and hummus round out the eclectic menu. For dessert, there's really only one way to go: the pie. Rest Haven coconut, meringue, and chocolate cream pies have been a favorite since this friendly spot opened in 1947.

Delta Amusement Café
662-627-1467
318 Delta Ave., Clarksdale, MS 38614
Open: Mon.–Sat.
Price: Inexpensive
Credit Cards: Yes
Cuisine: American, regional
Serving: B, L
Handicap Access: Limited
Special Features: Crawfish boils in season

Located down the street from Ground Zero, Delta Amusement has been a local favorite since 1969. Back in the early days, it was primarily a gambling joint for dominoes and poker, which is where the *Amusement* comes in. Today, gambling is confined to a handful of video poker games and the occasional Monday-night poker. While the café does a steady take-out business with locals, visitors can settle in for breakfast and hearty plate lunches in one of two small dining areas with wood-paneled walls covered in photos of locals and college pennants. Served on paper plates, daily lunch specials range from beef tips on rice to fried catfish, plus sides like creamy mac 'n cheese, turnip greens, lima beans, or corn bread. Chili cheeseburgers have been a menu favorite for years, and popular Friday-night crawfish boils draw crowds in season. During festivals, the café features live music on a lively back patio stocked with picnic tables and a bar.

Dutch Oven
662-621-9766
100 Blues Alley, Clarksdale, MS 38614
Open: Mon.–Fri.
Price: Inexpensive
Credit Cards: Yes
Cuisine: American, regional, bakery
Serving: L
Handicap Access: Limited

Located in downtown's old train depot building, this popular lunch spot offers a refreshing alternative to heavy plate lunches and ubiquitous fried Delta dishes. Owned and operated by local Mennonites, the friendly one-room café serves outstanding sandwiches, salads, and quite possibly Clarksdale's best baked goods. Sandwiches made with fresh-baked, melt-in-your-mouth butterhorn bread include the popular chicken salad, and creamy pimento cheese with a bit of a kick. There are also grilled panini sandwiches, salad combos, and fresh side orders like fruit or zesty pasta salad. Soups and casseroles are also popular. The real star, however, is the sweets. Almost everyone tops off a meal with a slice of made-from-scratch pie or cake. The outstanding selection of sweets usually includes fresh fruit, chocolate chess, and cream pies, plus everything from red velvet cake to German chocolate. The Dutch Oven has plans to expand when it moves into the lower level of downtown's Lofts Above The Five & Dime, which is currently under construction.

Delta Tamale Trail
Tamales? In Mississippi? Yes, it's true, and while not quite as famous as the Blues Trail, the Delta's tamale trail (www.tamaletrail.com) runs a close second in the eyes (and stomachs) of foodies. While no one seems to know exactly how this south-of-the-border staple became a mainstay in the Delta, everyone agrees that tamales have been a part of the regional cuisine for the better part of one hundred years. Blues fans know this—just listen to Robert Johnson's "They're Red Hot." It makes you wonder what was hotter—the tamales, or the hellhound on Johnson's trail. Plan your tamale pilgrimage through the Delta with the help of the Web site's interactive map.

Tamales in the Mississippi Delta, like these from Hick's, are traditionally served with saltines and chili.

Hick's World Famous Hot Tamales & More

662-624-9887
www.hickstamales.com
305 S. State St., Clarksdale, MS 38614
Open: Mon.–Sat.
Price: Inexpensive
Credit Cards: Yes
Cuisine: Barbecue, regional
Serving: L, D
Handicap Access: Limited

Corn-shucked hot tamales are served via drive-through, take-out, or dine-in at this humble local institution. Inside, diners can order at the counter and settle in to one of the few plastic booths that line the one-room operation. Fading newspaper clippings cover the walls; one section features President Clinton's visit, while another is dedicated to the late Dale Earnhardt Sr. The world-famous menu item is served by the dozen, half dozen, or quarter dozen and presented in paper boats—all the better to catch the inevitable pool of grease. Made of gritty cornmeal stuffed with flavor-spiked ground beef, the famous Delta concoctions are best enjoyed with a dollop of spicy beef chili on top and a pack of crackers on standby. Chopped barbecue pork sandwiches are served in foil and piled with juicy pork, slaw, and enough sweet barbecue sauce to soak through the bun and create a delicious mess. Burgers, Italian sausage, catfish plates, and ribs are also available, along with an intimidating 14-inch Big Daddy sandwich that's topped with pork, turkey, ham, sautéed onions, barbecue sauce, steak sauce, and more. No matter what you order, expect to leave with sticky fingers and a satisfied stomach.

Madidi

662-627-7770
www.madidires.com
164 Delta Ave., Clarksdale, MS 38614
Open: Tues.–Sat.
Price: Expensive–Very Expensive
Credit Cards: Yes
Cuisine: Fine dining
Serving: D
Handicap Access: Yes
Special Features: Reservations recommended; full bar

Flickering gas lamps outside a redbrick building that dates back to the turn of the 20th century signify your arrival at Clarksdale's original fine-dining establishment. Co-owned by actor Morgan Freeman, the upscale eatery swept into town in 2000 with much fanfare and hasn't slowed down since. With white tablecloths, subtle lighting, and lofty ceilings, this dining destination has managed to breathe new life into downtown Clarksdale. Sleek but warm, the space features hardwood floors and exposed brick walls covered in contemporary local artwork. A separate bar area is off the main dining room, and several private dining rooms make up the second floor.

The seasonal menu ranges from dressed-up local favorites to entrées with global flair. For starters, you may find anything from cornmeal fried oysters to rare ahi. Main entrées generally include well-prepared fish, lamb, and steak dishes, with a quail or duck selection often thrown into the mix. Rich desserts, a nice wine list, and a full bar complete this superb dining experience.

Ramon's

662-624-9230
535 Oakhurst St., Clarksdale, MS 38614
Open: Tues.–Sat.
Price: Moderate
Credit Cards: No
Cuisine: Italian, regional, seafood
Serving: D
Handicap Access: Limited
Special Features: Bring your own wine

Tucked away in a residential neighborhood just off the beaten tourist path, this hidden gem is a local favorite. Admittedly not much to look at, the low-slung brown restaurant has been family run since 1945. Inside, the modest dining room is a throwback to the '70s, with wood-paneled walls, mismatched chairs, an ancient jukebox, and a low ceiling that has seen better days. Candles flicker on the tabletops, and although the atmosphere is free of frills, the neighborhood vibe is cozy and friendly. Besides, you're here for the food, right? While Ramon's menu features Italian dishes like spaghetti and meatballs and ravioli, the real favorite is the fried seafood. Enormous jumbo fried shrimp can be ordered on a platter (with 6, 8, or 12 shrimp), or on a Rich Boy sandwich dressed with creamy tartar sauce and served with a surprisingly tasty side of buttered noodles. Fried chicken livers are another specialty, served on their own or with a side of spaghetti. Expect the food to be heavy and delicious, so arrive with an appetite.

The Ranchero

662-624-9768
www.theranchero.com
1907 State St., Clarksdale, MS 38614
Open: Mon.–Sat.
Price: Moderate
Credit Cards: Yes
Cuisine: American, regional
Serving: L, D
Handicap Access: Limited
Special Features: All-you-can eat catfish Fri.; barbecue sauce available for sale

This cozy, family-run establishment has been a go-to for locals since 1959. The homey dining areas feature wood-paneled walls covered with black-and-white photos of local sports heroes, news clippings, and memorabilia. Most everyone knows each other, and regulars greet waiters by name. The hearty menu features a little bit of everything—aged steaks, pasta, seafood, and hickory-smoked pit barbecue made with the Ranchero's in-house sauce. Daily plate lunch specials include a meat selection like crispy country fried steak covered in brown gravy, catfish, or London broil, plus three Southern-style "vegetables," which may include rice and gravy, black eyed peas, and green beans. There's also a salad bar, which is a rarity in these parts. Other notable menu items include a varied selection of starters, including fried dill pickles, seafood gumbo, oysters on the half shell, and hot tamales.

Rust Restaurant

662-624-4784
218 Delta Ave., Clarksdale, MS 38614
Open: Wed.–Sat.
Price: Expensive
Credit Cards: Yes
Cuisine: New American, upscale regional
Serving: D
Handicap Access: Limited
Special Features: Full bar; reservations recommended

New in 2008, this downtown hot spot features rustic-chic style and an upscale menu infused with regional flavor. Funky, abstract art ranging from the top of a water fountain to a deer head painted silver adorn the walls, creating an atmosphere that would easily impress diners well beyond the Delta. Other decor elements include fine-art photography, sections of corrugated tin, and a bar made from splinters salvaged from the historic Haney House. The seasonal menu is progressive Southern with a heavy New Orleans influence. Dishes with regional flavors may include crawfish beignets with rémoulade sauce, cornmeal-crusted Gulf oysters, gumbo, and grilled pimento cheese points. Favorite entrées range from filet mignon served with mashed potatoes and wok-fried green beans to seared tuna with wasabi mashed potatoes. For something a little more simple, there's the classic Rust burger. Top off your meal with a slice of the fluffy It Ain't Your Birthday Birthday Cake, topped with a buttercream frosting and presented with an unlit candle.

SHOPPING

While Clarksdale isn't exactly a hotbed for shopping, a few gems can be found downtown. Among them are fine- and folk-art galleries, cute boutiques, and everything blues related.

Can't-Miss Spots

Brick Gallery

662-627-3939
www.thebrickgallery.com
226 Delta Ave., Clarksdale, MS 38614

Located in the heart of downtown Clarksdale, this chic, warehouse-style gallery showcases artists from across the Southeast and beyond. The exposed-brick wall, lofted ceilings, and cushy leather seating area create a vibe that's at once warm, sleek, and sophisticated. Paintings and fine-art photographs range from classic Delta landscapes to vivid contemporary works. In addition to art, the gallery also carries a small selection of well-selected antique furniture and accessories. Artist receptions are held fairly frequently, and the gallery usually has a little something planned during festival time. Open Thursday through Saturday, or by appointment.

Cat Head Delta Blues & Folk Art

662-624-5992
www.cathead.biz
252 Delta Ave., Clarksdale, MS 38614

Upon your arrival in Clarksdale, a trip to this beloved blues and folk-art odditorium is an absolute must. Want to see live music while you're in town? This is the place to find up-to-the-minute information about who's playing, when, and where—in Clarksdale and throughout the Delta. Run by blues enthusiasts Roger Stolle, the downtown store carefully caters to both the seasoned blues traveler and novice alike. Imagine a cross between your grandparents's attic (if they were, say, hip to the blues and outsider art) and that of a timeless Mississippi Delta juke joint, and you're on the right track. Effortlessly cool, the store is packed with Southern gothic paintings, figurines, sculptures, and vibrant folk art from in and around the Delta. A large section of the store is devoted to music, and the carefully chosen selection of literature, magazines, and CDs emanate a blues authority. While you're browsing, be sure to investigate Cat Head's own eponymous, boutique blues label. The shop also features occasional live music, book signings, and mini blues fests held in conjunction with area festivals.

Hambone Art Gallery

662-253-5586
www.stanstreet.com
111 E. Second St., Clarksdale, MS 38614

If ever there were a visual counterpart to the blues, it would be the South's varied and disparate folk art. Artist, musician, and gallery curator Stan Street knows this all too well and fills his gallery with local and regional paintings, sculptures, woodworks, and all other manner of inspired creative eccentricities. Located in the center of downtown Clarksdale,

In addition to selling folk art, music, and everything blues related, Cat Head produces records and hosts mini blues festivals throughout the year.

On display in his Hambone Art Gallery, Stan Street's artwork features vibrant scenes from Delta kitchens to Florida's cypress swamps.

Hambone, along with Cat Head, serves as the de facto folk art epicenter for those looking to get a general feel for the region's eclectic arts. While most of Street's paintings depict life in the South and on the Delta, expect a heavy emphasis on jazz and blues—their muses applied to canvas, tree bark, metal, and just about any found object Street deems worthy of application. In conjunction with the gallery, Street puts on the annual Hambone Music Festival each fall, drawing on local blues talent, including his own music. The gallery also hosts festivities during events throughout the year.

Miss Del's General Store
662-624-2381
www.missdels.com
145 Delta Ave., Clarksdale, MS 38614

Housed in a historic brick building that's been standing at the northern end of downtown for more than a century, Miss Del's offers a delightful hodgepodge of goods, with every-thing from antique chairs to turnip seeds sold in bulk. A general store with a modern twist, this unique shop offers "feed, seed, and stuff you need." World-traveling owner Shonda Warner, who splits her time between Clarksdale and London, brings her eclectic tastes to the shelves of her charming store. It's easy to lose an hour or so soaking up the sensory experience inside. In the front room, shoppers can stock up on gourmet goodies like pick-led okra and peach preserves, browse for stationery and bath products, or try on an impressive selection of jewelry from across the globe. In the back, a spacious room filled with antique furniture neighbors a room with fertilizers and all manner of yard and farm supplies. After shopping to your heart's content, pick up an espresso, fresh-baked sweets, or specialty treats like Rococo Chocolates from the UK to enjoy on a rocking chair out front. A splendid loftlike space on the second floor is sometimes available for lodging, events, and cocktail parties.

More Music, Art, and Boutiques

BluesSource.com
662-313-0061
www.bluessource.com
115 Third St., Clarksdale, MS 38614

Owner Gary Miller opened this tiny shop in 2007 to complement his Web site and sell off his impressive personal record collection. A man with good taste in music, his vinyl includes loads of blues, R&B, '70s rock, '80s pop, and more, plus concert posters, vintage magazines, and artist photos.

Bluestown Music
662-645-1816
317 Delta Ave., Clarksdale, MS 38614

Owned by local musician Ronnie Drew, this small shop is jam-packed with vintage guitars, amps, bass, and all other manner of musical instruments. The gear is stacked, strewn

During festivals, Miss Del's General Store often hosts events like live blues and storytelling.

across the room, and hanging off the walls. Adding to the kitchen-sink vibe, aged photographs of blues and rock 'n' roll luminaries are tacked to the walls in any available space.

Delta Blues Museum
662-627-6820
1 Blues Alley, Clarksdale, MS 38614

Stock up on blues-related books, CDs, posters, prints, and souvenirs like shirts, hats, and guitar picks.

Delta Creations
662-621-1414
243 Delta Ave., Clarksdale, MS 38614

Various vendor stalls in this spacious showroom feature a wide selection of goodies, ranging from embroidered baby clothes to antique furniture.

Gimme Gumbo Gallery
662-302-3803
Third St. and Delta Ave., Clarksdale, MS 38614

Open during festival weekends and by appointment, this small corner gallery downtown shows art featuring blues musicians and regional scenes.

Mag-Pie Gift & Art Shop
662-624-8385
253 Delta Ave., Clarksdale, MS 38614

In business for nearly a century, this local favorite offers gifts, stationery, and home accessories, plus china, crystal, and flatware. The shop is also a popular spot for bridal and baby registries, too.

Two.Two.Five Delta
662-627-1154
225 Delta Ave., Clarksdale, MS 38614

This precious shop offers a cute selection of gifts and accessories that any Southern belle would cherish, from sunglasses and jewelry to candles, art, handbags, and more.

5

Northern Delta

Between Memphis and Clarksdale

The northern Delta gets some heavy tourist traffic, but it's mainly for the casinos in and around Tunica. While it can easily be argued that casinos here and on the Mississippi Gulf Coast have led to the decline of local juke joints that can't compete, it's undeniable that gaming has brought a significant influx of revenue that's aided in the preservation and growth of towns like Tunica. Beyond the casinos, there are plenty of blues-related sites in the northern Delta. Heading south from the Tennessee state line, most of the spots listed below are on or just off the Blues Highway, Highway 61, with the exception of Helena, Arkansas, which is across the Mississippi River on US 49, and tiny Friars Point on the Mississippi side of the river. Although it's outside Mississippi, Helena boasts a rich blues history and puts on one of the country's biggest blues festivals.

The price codes used in this chapter are as follows:

	Lodging	*Dining*
Inexpensive	Up to $90	Up to $15
Moderate	$90–130	$15–30
Expensive	$130–225	$30–65
Very Expensive	More than $225	More than $65

The following abbreviations are used for restaurants to identify what meals are served:

B—Breakfast
L—Lunch
D—Dinner
SB—Sunday brunch

WALLS

Culture

Memphis Minnie's Grave
Norfolk Rd., Walls, MS 38686
Directions: From Hwy. 61, go west on Goodman Road, then left on MS 161; take a right on

First Street and continue across the railroad tracks onto Old Highway 61. After around 2 miles, turn right onto Norfolk Road. The church and graveyard will be on the right.

Commissioned by the Mount Zion Foundation, the grave of Memphis Minnie (aka Lizzie Douglas) lies in the New Hope M.B. Church Cemetery on a country road just outside the tiny town of Walls, Mississippi. Easily the tallest headstone in the small cemetery, the marker reads LIZZIE 'KID' DOUGLAS LAWLERS, AKA MEMPHIS MINNIE. JUNE 3, 1897–AUGUST 6, 1973. A Blues Trail marker stands nearby next to the road. Small in stature, and about as feisty as a man twice her size, Minnie arguably revolutionized the blues with her distinctive singing and evocative guitar playing. After a lifetime of both critical and commercial recognition, Minnie passed away at the age of 76 in the city she took her name from, Memphis, Tennessee.

ROBINSONVILLE (TUNICA RESORTS) AND TUNICA

While the Tunica area may be best known for its endless casinos, time was, it was a small town with a hoppin' blues scene. Today, you'll find a few Blues Trail markers in and around town, and possibly a blues show, although it'll most likely be on a big casino stage. Away from the casino bustle, Tunica offers a few gems worth seeking out, plus a charming downtown Main Street. Unlike many Delta towns, downtown Tunica is well preserved and thriving—thanks, in large part, to the casinos. Once the poorest county in the country, Tunica is now one of the most prosperous towns in the Delta. While Robinsonville's name was officially changed to Tunica Resorts several years ago, locals still refer to their town as Robinsonville, while casinos use the Tunica Resorts address. Keep in mind that Robinsonville and Tunica Resorts are one and the same.

Culture

Bluesville at Horseshoe Casino
1-800-303-7463
1021 Casino Center Dr., Tunica Resorts, MS 38664

Located within Harrah's Horsehoe Hotel and Casino, just outside of Tunica, you'll find Bluesville—a three-hundred-capacity club that features live blues, rock, country, and pop. Host to both local and national touring acts, the club has featured big acts like B. B. King, the Allman Brothers Band, and Merle Haggard. Due to its size and sight lines, Bluesville often offers audiences an opportunity to catch big-name artists in a much more intimate setting than larger venues afford.

Harold "Hardface" Clanton Blues Trail Marker
www.msbluestrail.org
Tunica Resorts, MS
Directions: From Hwy. 61, turn west on Magnolia Street. The marker is at Main and Magnolia Sts.

Locally known as Tunica's first black millionaire, Harold Clanton is honored here in his hometown with a Blues Trail marker commemorating his long involvement with the blues. Nicknamed "Hardface," Clanton owned a productive and profitable farm in Tunica, but it was his ties to the town's nightlife, and specifically his nightclubs, that got him close to the

Essential Listening: Top 10 CDs for the Trip
Looking for some tunes for the road? These 10 blues essentials offer a fantastic primer on the Delta blues. The artists below all began their musical life in the Delta, and while some went on to perfect their craft elsewhere, others never set foot over the state line. One thing is certain: The deep roots of the Delta blues made a permanent mark on the music of the legends listed here.

The Complete Recordings, Robert Johnson (Sony)
The Definitive Collection, Muddy Waters (Geffen Records)
Dust My Broom, The Essential Recordings of Mississippi Delta Blues (Indigo UK)
His Best, Sonny Boy Williamson (Chess)
The Land Where the Blues Began, various artists (Rounder Select)
Not the Same Old Blues Crap, Vol. 1 & 2, various artists (Fat Possum Records)
The Original Delta Blues, Son House (Sbme Special Mkts.)
The Rough Guide to Delta Blues, various artists (World Music Network)
The Sky Is Crying: The History of Elmore James (Rhino Records)
The Ultimate Collection, B. B. King (Geffen Records)

blues and the many players who performed in his clubs.

Highway 61 Blues Trail Marker
www.msbluestrail.org
Tunica Resorts, MS
Directions: East of Grand Casino Parkway on Highway 61; marker is near the intersection of Dunn/Kirby Road and Highway 61 on the north side of the highway

From Roosevelt Sykes's "Highway 61 Blues," cut in 1932, to Bob Dylan's watershed Americana LP "Highway 61 Revisited," the famed Blues Highway has long been both a physical and metaphorical symbol of escape, freedom, and new beginnings. Originally stretching north from New Orleans to the Canadian border, it was 61 that carried many a Mississippi bluesman to Chicago, where the electric blues took root and ultimately transformed the genre.

James Cotton Blues Trail Marker
www.msbluestrail.org
Tunica area
Directions: Just south of Tunica around Clayton; east side of Highway 61 at the intersection with Bonnie Blue Road

The James Cotton Blues Trail marker, which stands on the edge of Highway 61 next to a group of large metal silos, pays tribute to the man who, by the age of six, was imitating the sounds of passing trains on the harmonica. Cotton's first introduction to the blues was through the music of Sonny Boy Williamson, whose influential performances on the King Biscuit radio program out of Helena, Arkansas, were broadcast throughout the Delta. Duly inspired, Cotton eventually landed in West Memphis and began cutting sides with a pre-

The 30th marker on the Mississippi Blues Trail was erected on February 13, 2008. Honoree James Cotton was in attendance and played his harmonica for the crowd.

Elvis Sam Philips at his Memphis Recording Service studio. James Cotton soon moved on to Chicago to play with Howlin' Wolf and later played with Paul Butterfield, helping to usher in the 1960s blues revival. With a name that's practically synonymous with the harmonica in blues circles, "Mr. Superharp's" storied career was honored when he was inducted into the Blues Hall of Fame in 2006.

Son House Blues Trail Marker
www.msbluestrail.org
Tunica Resorts, MS
Directions: Old Highway 61, southwest of Grand Casino Parkway

Erected in June 2007 at the former site of the Clack Store in Tunica Resorts stands the Blues Trail marker for Son House, who is widely considered to be the father of folk blues. Known for his aggressive guitar style and prominent use of slide, House was a major influence on both Robert Johnson and Muddy Waters. During his juke-joint days in the 1940s, House was recorded by Alan Lomax for the Library of Congress. Shortly after, the bluesman disappeared from the world of music for decades until being rediscovered in the mid-1960s.

Tunica Museum
662-363-6631

www.tunicamuseum.com
4063 Hwy. 61 N., Tunica, MS 38676
Open: Mon.–Sat.
Admission: Free

The Tunica Museum boasts an impressive in-house collection and also plays host to national touring exhibits. The permanent collection focuses on the county's regional time-line over the past two centuries, covering the Delta's natural history, indigenous Native Americans, European settlement, and various facets of American life, including the sociopolitical landscape, agricultural and industrial advances, race relations, and military history. On the tour, you'll meet "Sally" (the first taxidermied mule east of the Rockies), listen to blues music rooted in the area's cotton fields, and examine the impressive details of a re-created early-20th-century farm commissary. Allow yourself approximately 45 minutes to cover the entire museum.

Tunica River Park

1-866-517-4837
www.tunicariverpark.com
1 Riverpark Dr., Tunica Resorts, MS 38664
Open: Daily
Museum admission: Adults $5; seniors and children $4

These days, the name "Tunica" is mostly associated with the gaming industry. Fair enough, but the Tunica River Park aims to showcase Tunica's historic relationship with the mighty Mississippi River. The park overlooks the river with a large (48-foot) observation deck and features an interactive museum with four separate aquariums, and 130 acres of hiking trails and natural forest. Those looking to explore the river the old-fashioned way can board the *Tunica Queen* riverboat, which offers hourlong sightseeing excursions and two-hour dinner cruises departing from River Park.

Seasonal Events

SEPTEMBER

Mid-South Fair

Tunica Resorts, Hwy. 61 across from the Tunica Visitors Center

Sportsman's Paradise

Hunting and fishing in the greater Delta is an extremely popular recreation activity for many who live in the region, as well as visitors. Sure, Louisiana's license plates may read SPORTSMAN'S PARADISE, but those in the know are well aware that Mississippi, Tennessee, and Arkansas can easily boast the same. Depending upon which season you visit, you'll likely run into groups of duck, deer, quail, and turkey hunters. Whether you choose to cast a line in a multitude of rivers and lakes, draw a bow, or squeeze a trigger, the Delta is truly a sportsman's playground. Those looking to take part in seasonal hunting and fishing will want to obtain appropriate licenses from the various states' wildlife and fisheries departments. Guided hunting tours are available throughout the Delta.

www.midsouthfair.com
This family-friendly event featuring carnival rides, games, exhibits, and live entertainment has been held annually since 1856. It moved from Memphis to Tunica County in 2009.

OCTOBER

Delta Day
Downtown Tunica
www.tunicamainstreet.com/DeltaDay.html

This daylong festival on Main Street features food, arts and crafts, various events, entertainment for kids, and live music at Rivergate Park.

Restaurants

Blue and White
662-363-1371
1355 Hwy. 61 N., Tunica, MS 38676
Open: Daily
Price: Inexpensive
Credit Cards: Yes
Cuisine: Southern
Serving: B, L, D
Handicap Access: Yes

You can't miss this landmark roadside diner with its retro sign, vibrant blue roof, and sparkling white walls. Inside, it's more of the same—blue and white checkered floors, blue booths, blue counter stools, blue and white chairs . . . you get the picture. In business since 1937, this old-timey diner used to be the only restaurant on this undeveloped, pre-casino stretch—back when Elvis was a patron and there were still gas pumps out front. Today, the atmosphere remains much the same as it always has, with locals and old-timers lingering over coffee and chatting up waitresses at the counter. Down-home country breakfasts like ham, grits, biscuits, and redeye gravy are served all day. The popular lunch buffet is a feast of Southern specialties like chicken and dumplings, fried chicken, meat loaf, turnip greens, creamed corn, field peas, green beans, yeast rolls, and corn bread. For dinner, hearty fried favorites include dill pickles, catfish, and a seafood platter. Of course, the only suitable way to wash down a fine Southern meal at the Blue and White is with a tall glass of ice-cold sweet tea.

The Hollywood Café
662-363-1225
www.thehollywoodcafe.com
1585 Old Commerce Rd., Tunica Resorts, MS 38664
Open: Mon.–Sat.
Price: Inexpensive–Moderate
Credit Cards: Yes
Cuisine: American, regional
Serving: L, D (Tues.–Sat.)

Made famous in Marc Cohn's hit song "Walking in Memphis," the Hollywood Café is also known as "Home of the Fried Dill Pickle since 1969."

Handicap Access: Yes
Special Features: Full bar; live music on weekends

Located just north of Tunica, this atmospheric local landmark was here long before the casinos ever rolled into town. Thankfully away from the casino hubbub, the brick commissary turned restaurant dates back to 1926. John Grisham wrote about this popular spot in *A Time to Kill,* and singer Marc Cohn name-drops the café in his hit tune "Walking in Memphis," in which he also mentions Muriel, who played the piano at the Hollywood for years. Inside the whitewashed brick building, photos of Marc Cohn adorn the antiqued plaster-and-brick walls, and Muriel's piano still proudly sits on the well-worn hardwood floor. A bar area anchors the back of the room, and a small stage at the opposite end regularly features live music on weekends. As for eats, the simple lunch menu features burgers, local pond-raised catfish, fried frog's legs, and the like. The dinner menu expands slightly to include fried seafood platters and steaks. The Hollywood's famous fried dill pickles are served all day, along with fried green tomatoes and onion rings.

Lula

Culture

Livin' at Lula Blues Trail Marker
www.msbluestrail.org
Lula, MS
Directions: From Highway 61, take US 49 W. Turn right on Moon Lake Road, then left on Front Street Marker is at S. Front Street and Second Street.

Beyond the Delta: Mississippi Side Trips

HOLLY SPRINGS

Located east of the Delta, just south of the Tennessee border, Holly Springs (www.hollyspringsms.us) is home to the Hill Country blues, a style characterized by a steady, driving rhythm. Local musicians R. L. Burnside and David "Junior" Kimbrough popularized this style of blues in the 1990s. For live blues music, try the Marshall Disco (on the north side of MS 4 around 2 miles west of MS 7). Elvis fans won't want to miss quirky Graceland Too, a pink house chock-full of Elvis memorabilia at 200 East Gholson Avenue.

OXFORD

South of Holly Springs, Oxford (www.oxfordcvb.com) is home to Ole Miss (aka the University of Mississippi), where the Blues Archive holds the world's most extensive collection of blues recordings. Also on campus, the Center for the Study of Southern Culture publishes *Living Blues* magazine, which sponsors an annual blues symposium. Literary buffs flock to Oxford to tour William Faulkner's home (Rowan Oak), browse the celebrated Square Books store, and explore the town where best-selling author John Grisham sometimes resides.

TUPELO

For Elvis enthusiasts, Tupelo (www.tupelo.net) ranks right up there with Memphis as a must-see site. Fans of the King can visit the Elvis Presley Birthplace (a modest two-room home), then tour the nearby Elvis Presley Memorial Museum. A self-guided driving tour takes fans by Elvis's old haunts, including sites where he went to school, ate cheeseburgers, bought his first guitar, and performed live. In June, the annual Elvis Presley Festival features music, food, and more in downtown Tupelo.

One of the cornerstones of early Delta blues activity, it was Lula, Mississippi, that facilitated the meeting of blues legends Son House and Charley Patton prior to their recording sessions together for the Paramount label in 1930. Fast forward 30 or so years, and Lula once again served as a hotbed of blues activity when two of the principals of the Delta's most beloved blues band, the Jelly Roll Kings (Frank Frost and Sam Carr), laid down roots in Lula. Erected in 2008, the Livin' at Lula Blues Trail marker can be found in a grassy area by the railroad tracks across from the small, sleepy downtown strip.

HELENA

Located just across the Mississippi River in Arkansas, Helena has a different feel than the cities on the other side of the bridge. Perched on a ridge overlooking the river, this quiet town features more hills and greenery than most of its Mississippi sisters. Once a wild and thriving port town with plenty of booze, gambling, prostitution, and music, downtown Helena is now a sleepy place, although the picturesque strip along Cherry Street is showing slow signs of restoration. The best time to visit is undoubtedly during the Arkansas Blues & Heritage Festival (formerly King Biscuit), when the town positively comes to life. It's also the only time when you're likely to hear live blues in Helena these days. Otherwise, there are a handful of attractions worth seeing, and a few lovely bed & breakfast inns.

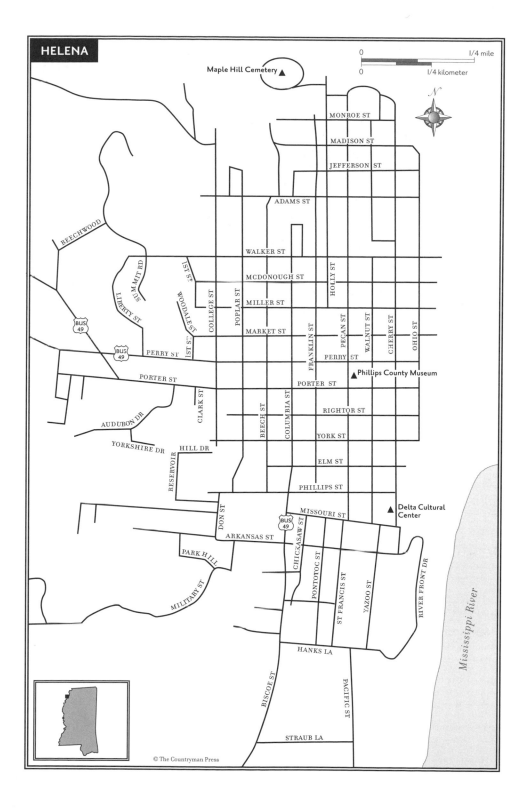

HELENA

Maple Hill Cemetery ▲

0 ————————— 1/4 mile
0 ————————— 1/4 kilometer

N

MONROE ST
MADISON ST
JEFFERSON ST
ADAMS ST

BEECHWOOD

WALKER ST
MCDONOUGH ST
MILLER ST
MARKET ST

SUMMIT RD
LIBERTY ST
1ST ST
WOODALE ST
1ST ST
COLLEGE ST
POPLAR ST

BUS 49
BUS 49

PERRY ST
PORTER ST

HOLLY ST

FRANKLIN ST
PECAN ST
WALNUT ST
CHERRY ST
OHIO ST

PERRY ST

▲ Phillips County Museum

PORTER ST

CLARK ST
BEECH ST
COLUMBIA ST

RIGHTOR ST

AUDUBON DR
YORKSHIRE DR
HILL DR
RESERVOIR

YORK ST

ELM ST

PHILLIPS ST

DON ST
MISSOURI ST

▲ Delta Cultural Center

BUS 49

ARKANSAS ST

CHICKASAW ST
PONTOTOC ST
ST FRANCIS ST
YAZOO ST

PARK HILL

MILITARY ST

RIVER FRONT DR

HANKS LA

Mississippi River

BISCOE ST

PACIFIC ST

STRAUB LA

© The Countryman Press

In 2006, the town of Helena joined with West Helena to officially become Helena–West Helena.

Plenty of bluesmen called Helena home at some point in their lives, including Robert Johnson, who taught his girlfriend's son, Robert Lockwood Jr. (just a few years his junior), a few things on the guitar. Robert Nighthawk and pianist Roosevelt Sykes were from Helena, and Howlin' Wolf lived here for a while. Perhaps most famously, Helena was home to Sonny Boy Williamson II, who hosted the tremendously popular *King Biscuit Time* blues radio program broadcast throughout the Delta on KFFA. The first blues program on the radio, *King Biscuit Time* is still broadcast from downtown's Cultural Center, making it the longest-running radio show currently on the air.

Lodging

In addition to a handful of motels on the outskirts of town, Helena's limited accommodations include three gorgeous, centrally located bed & breakfast inns, and a nearby casino. Book early for the Arkansas Blues & Heritage Festival, as there aren't nearly enough local rooms to accommodate the influx of festivalgoers.

BED & BREAKFASTS

Edwardian Inn
870-338-9155
www.edwardianinn.com
317 Biscoe, Helena–West Helena, AR 72342

Less than a mile southwest of downtown
Price: Inexpensive–Moderate
Credit Cards: Yes
Handicap Access: Limited
Special Features: Free wireless; no children under 12

This stunning 1904 Colonial Revival mansion sits atop a hill just south of downtown. Two sets of stairs lead to the grand entryway, where a columned wraparound porch is stocked with swings, rocking chairs, and spinning fans overhead. Inside the grand foyer, striking quarter-sawn oak woodwork adorns the ceiling, arched entryway, staircase, and columns. Down the hallway, just

The grand Edwardian Inn was originally built by a cotton mogul in 1904.

past the check-in area, a sunny garden room is where a full, cooked-to-order breakfast is served in the mornings. Twelve elegant, well-appointed rooms named for local history makers (including seven Confederate generals) feature rich woods, floral wall coverings, antiques, and period furnishings. All rooms have private baths, and some accommodations feature separate seating areas, decorative fireplaces, hardwood floors, and high ceilings.

Foxglove Bed and Breakfast

870-338-9391
www.bbonline.com/ar/foxglove
229 Beech St., Helena–West Helena, AR 72342
Just west of downtown
Price: Inexpensive–Moderate
Credit Cards: Yes
Handicap Access: No
Special Features: No children under 12

Perched atop Crowley's Ridge in front of a Civil War battlefield, this 1900 Georgian Revival mansion is located close to down-

town on a quiet residential street. Once-grand estates neighboring the property are sadly falling into disrepair, but Foxglove is an exception—despite some peeling paint on the exterior. Inside, well-preserved period details include quarter-sawn oak woodwork, parquet floors, and carved mantelpieces. Eight rooms with private baths feature high-end antique furnishings like four-poster beds, and half of the rooms are equipped with Jacuzzi tubs. The front porch, complete with a circular veranda area, affords lovely views of the leafy street. A full breakfast (omelets, bacon, and the like) is served every morning, and in the evenings, guests are treated to snacks and beverages that usually include beer, wine, cheese, and crackers.

Magnolia Hill Bed and Breakfast

870-338-6874
www.magnoliahillbnb.com
608 Perry St., Helena–West Helena, AR 72342
Less than a mile northwest of downtown

Magnolia Hill Bed and Breakfast is part of Helena's historic Carriage Square, which also includes Victorian Gardens and the Solomon House.

Price: Inexpensive–Moderate
Credit Cards: Yes
Handicap Access: No
Special Features: Free wireless; no children under 12

This gorgeous Queen Anne Victorian built in 1895 is situated on the former site of Helena's first courthouse. Located in the town's quaint historic district, the property once served as a Presbyterian church as well as a cadet club for World War II soldiers. Today, eight charming rooms are spread throughout the mansion's three floors. An expansive front porch offers nice views from the property's hilltop perch, while a screened-in porch on the side of the house edges up to the Victorian gardens of adjacent Carriage Square. In addition to antiques and period decor throughout, the property boasts original details like fireplaces, light fixtures, hand-carved mantels, and a fully restored bathroom with a claw-foot tub and pull-chain commode (not for guest use). Rooms with private baths include the Dogwood Room, featuring oak furniture and a private second-floor patio, and the Magnolia Room (aka the Honeymoon Suite), located within the property's octagon-shaped turret with a circular king-size bed and ceiling mural adorned with cherubs. The full breakfast is an elegant affair with service on china and crystal.

MOTELS

Best Western Inn
870-572-2592
www.bestwesternarkansas.com/hotels/best -western-inn-west-helena
1053 W. US 49, Helena–West Helena, AR 72390

Crown Inn Motel
870-572-2597
412 N. Sebastian Rd., Helena–West Helena, AR 72390

Holiday Star Motel
870-572-3717
302 N. Sebastian Rd., Helena–West Helena,
AR 72390

Isle of Capri Casino
1-800-THE-ISLE
www.isleofcapricasino.com/lula
777 Isle of Capri Pkwy., Lula, MS 38644

Motel 6
870-572-7915
www.motel6.com
1207 W. US 49, Helena–West Helena, AR
72390

Sands Motel
870-572-6774
1086 W. US 49, Helena–West Helena, AR
72390

Super 7
870-753-9701
1007 MLK Dr. and US 49, Helena–West
Helena, AR 72390

CAMPING
Pat Kelley RV Park
870-572-4036
1243 US 49, Helena–West Helena, AR
72390

Spaces with full hookups are available for
daily, weekly, and monthly rental.

River Park Campgrounds
870-338-9047
River Park adjacent to Cherry St. levee,
Helena–West Helena, AR

Camping here is only permitted during the
Arkansas Blues & Heritage Festival and the
Wild Hog Festival, organized by the
Helena–West Helena Fire Department.

Culture

Bubba's Blues Corner
870-338-3501
105 Cherry St., Helena–West Helena, AR 72342

At Bubba's Blues Corner, the blues are number one. In a way, Bubba Sullivan's little corner
of the world feels more akin to a private collector's showroom than a typical record store,
which actually makes sense, as that's how it began. An Arkansas native, Bubba is as affable
and knowledgeable a store owner as they come. His personal collection has grown into a
Delta music mecca covering all manner of blues and culture. Located on historic Cherry
Street, Bubba's shop is attached to what was once his wife's antiques store, which has since
moved shop to Virginia. In addition to Bubba's extensive collection of CDs, DVDs, and rare
vinyl, you'll find blues memorabilia, T-shirts, and other Delta curios. A few display cases
on one side of the store contain everything from vintage guitars to Frank Frost's Jelly Roll
Kings harmonica holster and stage getup. Have a question about Helena blues and culture?
If so, Bubba is your man; he is the unofficial, yet de facto, local music historian. Side note:
Fans of the Band will most definitely want to pay a visit, as Bubba has an extensive selection of local boy Levon Helm's releases.

Carriage Square
870-338-8099
www.carriagesquare.net
726 Columbia St., Helena–West Helena, AR 72342

Comprised of Magnolia Hill Bed and Breakfast, the adjacent Victorian Gardens, and the historic Solomon House, the historic block known as Carriage Square harkens back to a genteel era. The lovely Victorian Gardens feature a flower-lined pathway circling a grassy lawn that's rimmed with park benches, a covered gazebo, antique-style street lamps, a fountain, and a stage area where weddings and events often take place. Next door, the plantation-style Solomon House, built in 1926, features a parlor with a piano, crystal chandelier, and period details. Behind the French doors across the hallway is a dining area where private events are held. The second floor is home to a handful of shops where merchants offer a variety of vintage items and antiques, including dolls, toys, estate jewelry, silver, glassware, and linens—including vintage linens from the estate of silent film star Marion Davies.

Confederate Cemetery (Maple Hill Cemetery)

1801 Holly St., Helena–West Helena, AR 72342

Established in 1869, this historic cemetery contains the graves of around a hundred soldiers killed in the Civil War Battle of Helena and other engagements, including Confederate general Patrick R. Cleburne, a Helena native.

Delta Cultural Center

870-338-4350
www.deltaculturalcenter.com
141 Cherry St., Helena–West Helena, AR 72342
Open: Tues.–Sat.
Admission: Free

The Delta Cultural Center is housed within two separate buildings just around the corner from one another in the heart of downtown Helena. The first, located within a pair of restored storefronts on Cherry Street (you can't miss the Red Ball Store sign), acts as Helena's visitor's center. The focus within the space's three galleries (and gift shop) is on the Arkansas Delta's rich musical heritage, including blues, gospel, and rockabilly. In addition to ever-changing temporary exhibits, the permanent Delta Sounds display is a multimedia experience where visitors can view, listen to, and read up on Arkansas's finest musical players, from Sonny Boy Williamson to the Band's Levon Helm. Other displays include video highlights from the annual Blues & Heritage Festival and an interactive display detailing the "8 Keys to the Blues." The Cherry Street cultural center is also home of the *King Biscuit Time* radio program, where "Sunshine" Sonny Payne broadcasts weekdays at 12:15 PM from a specially built studio where visitors can watch—and even take part in—the legendary radio show.

Additional museum displays detailing the area's history are housed around the corner in the handsomely restored redbrick train depot at 95 Missouri Street. Dating back to 1912, the Missouri Pacific Depot is located next to the levee by the train tracks. Beyond the lovingly restored lobby area, the Heritage of Determination exhibit details the land of the Arkansas Delta and the men and women who called the area home, from Native Americans and slaves to planters and steamboat pilots. Upstairs, a Civil War exhibit features artifacts and photos detailing the Arkansas Confederates and Helena's role in the war.

The Cherry Street outpost of the Delta Cultural Center is where the King Biscuit Time *radio show is broadcast.*

Gist Music Company

870-338-8441
307 Cherry St., Helena–West Helena, AR 72342

Morse Gist first opened the doors of his music store on downtown Helena's Cherry Street in 1953. Over the years, the shop has been an Arkansas Delta cornerstone for musicians and fans alike, with the Gists often bolstering local artists with equal measures of enthusiasm and resources. The knowledgeable Gist waxes on guitar tune-ups and custom inlays as easily as he does on the nuances of local Delta flavor. When you're there, be sure to ask him about the time Elvis Presley came into his store in the '50s with a pressing of his first record.

King Biscuit Time on KFFA

870-338-4350
141 Cherry St., Helena–West Helena, AR 72342

"Pass the biscuits, 'cause it's King Biscuit Time!" Started in 1941, the *King Biscuit Time* radio show is one of the longest-running daily radio programs still in existence today. Famously endorsed by King Biscuit Flour, the radio show regularly featured blues heavyweights Sonny Boy Williamson and Robert Lockwood Jr. performing live, and off the cuff, in the studio. The show's influence in and around the Delta is undeniable, reaching countless blues enthusiasts and future players alike. Since 1951 the show has been hosted by "Sunshine" Sonny Payne, who—at 12:15 PM Monday through Friday—begins each broadcast

The original King Biscuit trailer that took Sonny Boy Williamson II to play in parking lots across town now sits in a pasture next to the KFFA office.

with the phrase "Pass the biscuits . . ." Visitors to Helena are encouraged to stop by the show, broadcast live from the Delta Cultural Center on Cherry Street, but know ahead of time that you may just wind up on the air discussing what brings you to Helena. Blues travelers can still see the old King Biscuit trailer parked in a field outside of KFFA's small trailer office by the transmitter at 1360 Radio Drive (870-338-8361).

Magnolia Cemetery
Wire Rd., Helena, AR 72390
Directions: North on 1st St.; veer left onto Wine Rd.

Located off Springdale Road on the windy Wire Road is the lovely Magnolia Cemetery, whose earliest internments date to 1850. With mature trees and gently rolling hills, the sprawling cemetery is as peaceful a place as you're likely to find. The final resting place of William H. Grey, one of the first African Americans elected to the Arkansas General Assembly in 1869, the cemetery is also the home to the grave sites of local blues legends Robert Nighthawk and Frank Frost, the Delta's Harmonica King. Magnolia also has plans for future local blues musician internments.

Phillips County Museum
870-338-7790
623 Pecan St., Helena–West Helena, AR 72342

This historic 1891 building, connected to the Philips County Library, is home to a museum that features Civil War relics, Native American artifacts, and a Thomas Edison collection.

Pillow-Thompson House
870-338-8535
718 Perry St., Helena–West Helena, AR 72342

This intricate, gorgeously restored Queen Anne house built in 1896 offers tours and frequently hosts private events.

Seasonal Events
APRIL

Wild Hog Musicfest & Motorcycle Rally
www.wildhogmusic.org
Downtown Helena

This three-day music festival and motorcycle rally features bike-centric events, plus live music that usually includes classic rock tribute bands and Southern rock.

MAY

Arkansas Delta Family Gospel Festival
Presented by the Delta Cultural Center, this free, daylong festival held the Saturday of Memorial Day weekend features national, regional, and local gospel performances on downtown's Cherry Street Pavilion.

Frank Frost and Robert Nighthawk are buried in Helena's beautiful Magnolia Cemetery.

JUNE

Mother's Best Music Fest

Like the Arkansas Delta Family Gospel Festival, this free, day-long event features live music at downtown's Cherry Street Pavilion. Presented by the Delta Cultural Center, the lineup is generally heavy on blues music, along with R&B, rockabilly, jazz and more genres.

OCTOBER

Arkansas Blues & Heritage Festival

Helena–West Helena, AR

www.bluesandheritage.com

Yes, the Arkansas Blues & Heritage Festival is actually the old King Biscuit Blues Festival—same place, same organizers, same people. Unfortunately, the organizers didn't trademark the name, and someone else swept in, did so, and then barred the festival from using the brand name. Yes, it's a shame, but thankfully, the name change hasn't put a damper on the event itself. The three-day event regularly draws more than 100,000 blues enthusiasts, making this one of the country's most respected blues events since 1986. The free festival boasts four stages situated in front of, and around, the river's levee. As the festival has grown, so have the ancillary events—such as the barbecue competition—with various food and art vendors lining up along Cherry Street. Notable past performers include T-Model

Sleepy downtown Helena swells with blues fans during the city's annual Arkansas Blues & Heritage Festival.

Ford, Frank Frost, Luther Allison, Big Jack Jackson, Pinetop Perkins, and many more. If you plan on attending, you'll want to book your accommodations well in advance, as hotels tend to sell out both in Helena and the surrounding towns in Arkansas and Mississippi.

Restaurants

Granny Dee's Homestyle Cooking
870-817-0200
426 Cherry St., Helena–West Helena, AR 72342
Open: Mon.–Sat.
Price: Inexpensive
Credit Cards: Yes
Cuisine: Southern, soul food
Serving: B, L
Handicap Access: Limited

Located next to the historic Malco Theatre, this cozy soul food spot offers hearty homestyle cookin' on Helena's main drag. Pull up a sturdy, upholstered chair in the main dining room, or opt for a padded metal foldout if the good seats are taken. Hanging plants and green-and-white-striped trim create a friendly vibe in the main dining area, while additional tables and a few two-person booths make up the overflow room. Southern-style breakfasts include biscuits and gravy, fried chicken and waffles, eggs, grits, and a Saturday breakfast buffet. For lunch, the menu features everything from burgers and sandwiches to hog maws, rib plates, catfish, and smoky joes. A small lunch buffet may be stocked with anything from chicken wings, beef stir fry, and rolls to veggies like sweet potatoes, corn on the cob, and green beans. Service is warm and friendly, blues is usually on the stereo, and you probably won't need to eat again for a good several hours.

Olivers' Restaurant
870-338-7228
101 Missouri St., Helena–West Helena, AR 72342
Open: Mon.–Sat.
Price: Inexpensive–Moderate
Credit Cards: Yes
Cuisine: Regional, seafood, American
Serving: D
Handicap Access: Limited
Special Features: Full bar

Located next to the Delta Cultural Center in the heart of downtown Helena, this popular restaurant and local hangout is one of the few (nonchain) restaurants in town that's open for dinner early in the week. It's a friendly place, where regulars grab a drink after work in the cozy bar area or settle in at a table in the small dining room. Candlelit tables on black-and-white checkered floors offer simple ambience that's warm and casual. The menu is reliable, if not entirely memorable, with local standards that include heavy fried items— catfish, oysters, chicken fried steak, dill pickles—plus a few more adventurous options like barbecue shrimp and a quesadilla. If you're looking for a place to grab dinner on a Monday night, or chat up some locals at the bar, Olivers' is a fine option.

Pasquale's Tamales
1-877-572-0500
www.sucktheshuck.com
Sears Parking lot, 1005 US 49 W., Helena–West Helena, AR 72342
Open: Fri.–Sat., festivals
Price: Inexpensive
Credit Cards: No
Cuisine: Regional
Serving: L
Special Features: Internet mail order

The famous tamales served from this modest trailer have a long history. After coming over to Helena from Sicily in the late 1800s, Pasquale St. Columbia made a living as a food merchant working the cotton fields and sawmills along the levee. Many of the immigrant farm workers he befriended were Mexican, and Pasquale traded his recipe for spaghetti for a recipe for traditional Mexican hot tamales. Today, the third and fourth generations of Pasquale's family continue to sell his spicy beef tamales from a trailer in the Sears parking lot. You can order the tamales alone (with crackers) or on a plate with chili, cheese, peppers, and onions. Pasquale's also serves up bowls of chili, Frito pie, and muffuletta. While the trailer is only open for business on the weekends, it regularly rolls into town at festival time. Pasquale's also has a thriving online mail-order business, which makes it all the easier to enjoy these Delta delicacies back home.

River Road
870-338-3003
115 Cherry St., Helena–West Helena, AR 72342
Open: Tues.–Sat.

Don't miss downtown Helena's levee murals behind the restored depot, which now houses half of the Delta Cultural Center.

Price: Inexpensive–Expensive
Credit Cards: Yes
Cuisine: American, steak, seafood
Serving: L (Tues.–Fri.), D (Thurs.–Sat.)
Handicap Access: Yes
Special Features: Full bar

This classy, centrally located restaurant on downtown's Cherry Street offers one of Helena's only upscale dining options. Inside, the two spacious dining rooms feature hardwood floors, white tablecloths, and an exposed-brick wall with wood trim. Well-placed decor includes historic framed photos, a collection of King Biscuit Blues Festival posters, and antique instruments. The side dining area is also home to a handsome showpiece bar. As for the food, lunch features both the familiar—burgers, barbecue, meat 'n threes—plus a few more imaginative options like an 8-ounce lunch steak, chicken-salad-stuffed tomato, quiche, and shrimp Alfredo. Dinner is a more upscale affair, starting with hors d'oeuvres like spanakopita, oysters Bienville, and lobster thermidor. For the main entrée, steaks and seafood rule the menu. Choose from six steak selections, ranging from an 8-ounce filet mignon flavored with rosemary to a 22-ounce bone-in rib eye in a Creole butter marinade. Seafood selections include crawfish étouffée, lemon herb snapper, and blackened catfish. Several chicken dishes and a 14-ounce pork chop round out the menu.

Recreation

PARKS, NATURE, AND WILDLIFE

Levee Walk

Downtown Helena

This pleasant paved walkway along the levee in the heart of downtown Helena features views of the Mississippi River, plus blues murals by the railroad tracks next to the Delta Cultural Center.

Quapaw Canoe Company

870-228-2266
411 Ohio St., Helena–West Helena, AR 72342

Riverman John Ruskey opened the Helena outpost of his Clarksdale company in the summer of 2008. Bike, canoe, and kayak rental is available, and the river put-in is just steps away over downtown's levee.

River Reach Park

East on Perry St., Helena–West Helena, AR 72342

Want a closer look at the Mississippi River? You can picnic or fish at this park, which also features an elevated boardwalk overlooking the river.

DUNDEE

Sleepy Moon Lake Road, perched on the banks of the narrow lake, is worth visiting for a fine restaurant that doubles as an inn. There's also some fascinating Tennessee Williams history here. Visitors to both Clarksdale and Helena often make the 20-odd-minute drive for dinner. North of Clarksdale off US 49/61, Moon Lake is just across the Mississippi River from Helena, Arkansas.

Restaurants

Uncle Henry's Place Inn & Restaurant

662-337-2757
www.unclehenrysplace.com
5860 Moon Lake Rd., Dundee, MS 38626
Open: Thurs.–Sun.
Price: Expensive (dinner); inexpensive (inn)
Credit Cards: Yes
Cuisine: Cajun
Serving: D
Handicap Access: Limited
Special Features: Bring your own wine and liquor; open during the week for groups of 20 or more; reservations recommended

A popular pilgrimage for Tennessee Williams fans, Uncle Henry's was the site of the Moon Lake Casino from 1931 to 1938. Williams frequented the casino and later immortalized the storied establishment in plays like *A Streetcar Named Desire* and *The Glass Menagerie.* Reborn as Uncle Henry's in 1946, the laid-back restaurant features a homey dining room with feminine touches like floral curtains, a cabinet stocked with antique dishware, linen tablecloths, and a piano in the corner. Some regulars prefer to eat at the counter in the small adjacent entryway. The restaurant is a longtime local favorite for fresh, made-from-scratch south Louisiana seafood specialties like crawfish étouffée, broiled catfish stuffed with crabmeat, barbecue shrimp, soft-shell crab, crawfish pasta, and seafood gumbo. Char-grilled Angus steaks round out the rich menu.

Upstairs, the B&B features a handful of cozy rooms with floral bedspreads and private bathrooms. Three or four rooms (one is sometimes occupied by family) are just off a comfy wood-paneled common area with shelves of books, checkers, and plenty of family photos. Guests can stay in a room where the casino used to operate or opt for the private cottage behind the main building, which features a room with two full beds and a kitchen. In the morning, lodgers are treated to a hearty, Southern-style breakfast like eggs, biscuits, and country ham. Located just across the bridge from Helena, the accommodations fill up fast during the popular Arkansas Blues & Heritage Festival in October.

FRIARS POINT

Culture

North Delta Museum

662-383-2233 (Friars Point City Hall)
Second St., Friars Point, MS 38631
Open: Tues.–Sat.
Admission: Adults $4; children (under 7) $2

Seated on the banks of the Mississippi River in the once-bustling (but now quiet) port town of Friars Point, you'll find the quirky North Delta Museum. One part museum, one part treasure trove, and two parts eclectic, pack-rat, grandparents'-attic-style collection, the museum is a dusty tribute to northern Delta history and culture. A little bit of everything (truly), the museum's four walls house a tangible Delta timeline that includes a prehistoric collection, Native American artifacts, Civil War military regalia, steamboat history, exhibits on blues luminaries, and a re-created general store. Flo Larson, the friendly woman who operates the museum, is more than willing to spend ample time giving patrons an in-depth tour of the exhibits—and beyond—so don't be shy.

Robert Nighthawk Blues Trail Marker
www.msbluestrail.org
649 Second St., Friars Point, MS 38631

In 2007, a Blues Trail marker was erected in downtown Friars Point to honor Robert Lee McCollum, better known as Robert Nighthawk. The marker stands in front of Hirsberg's Drugstore, where Robert Johnson and other blues greats once played. Nomadic in spirit, Nighthawk traveled almost constantly, but he called Friars Point home and was married here in 1936. One of the preeminent blues guitarists throughout the 1940s, '50s, and into the early '60s, Robert Lee McCollum took on the name Nighthawk after the release of his first LP, entitled "Prowling Night-Hawk." A lasting influence on fellow blues and rock 'n' roll musicians, Nighthawk is credited with introducing many a song that have become blues staples, like "Black Angel Blues," "Annie Lee," "The Moon is Rising," and "Crying Won't Help You." Nighthawk died in 1967 in Helena, Arkansas, the town where he was born.

Historic Dockery Farms, where bluesmen like Charley Patton lived, worked, and played, is a favorite Blues Trail photo op.

6

CENTRAL DELTA

The Heart of the Mississippi Delta

Beyond Clarksdale, the central Delta is home to the highest concentration of blues sites in the region. This is where W. C. Handy had not one, but two life-changing brushes with the blues, where "Father of the Delta Blues" Charley Patton inspired a new generation of musicians on Dockery Farms, and where Robert Johnson is buried—in three places, in fact, although only one of the grave sites is the true resting place of the legendary bluesman. In Bolivar County, Merigold is home to one of the Delta's most celebrated juke joints; while live music at Po' Monkey's Lounge may be a rarity, the Thursday-night parties at this country shack are legendary.

The central Delta is a fine place to hop from town to town and explore the area's rich history, from blues heritage to unforgettable, only-in-the-Delta eateries like Lusco's, Doe's Eat Place, and the White Front Café. If you're looking for live music, it's best to plan around festivals or upcoming gigs (always call ahead), or you may find yourself spending the night in a quiet town with nonexistent nightlife. Among the area's hubs, there's Greenville on the edge of the Mississippi River, B. B. King's hometown of Indianola, and Greenwood, perhaps the prettiest town in the Delta, and home to the region's only luxury boutique hotel.

The price codes used in this chapter are as follows:

	Lodging	*Dining*
Inexpensive	Up to $90	Up to $15
Moderate	$90–130	$15–30
Expensive	$130–225	$30–65
Very Expensive	More than $225	More than $65

The following abbreviations are used for restaurants to identify what meals are served:

B—Breakfast
L—Lunch
D—Dinner
SB—Sunday brunch

Blues enthusiasts often leave tokens on the graves of famous bluesmen, like the harmonicas, coins, and trinkets found on Sonny Boy Williamson's grave.

TUTWILER

Culture

Grave of Sonny Boy Williamson II
Tutwiler, MS
Directions: 15 miles south of Clarksdale on US 49; from US 49, drive west on Hancock

Avenue into Tutwiler. When the road ends, turn left and cross the railroad tracks, then continue south on Second Street. Turn right on Bruister Road; cemetery will be on right in around a mile.

Located at the edge of a patch of woods, surrounded by weeds and underbrush, you'll find the grave site of famed blues harmonica player, singer, and songwriter Sonny Boy Williamson II. Sonny, who was born in 1908 and died in 1965, was known as the King of the Harmonica, which is immediately evident thanks to the slew of harmonicas scattered around his grave site by fellow blues travelers paying their respects. An impressive stone, the marker, which boasts a photo of Williamson playing the harp, is inscribed, INTERNATIONALLY FAMOUS HARMONICA AND VOCAL BLUES ARTIST DISCOVERED AND RECORDED BY TRUMPET RECORDS, JACKSON, MS 1950–1955.

Tutwiler Murals
Tutwiler, MS
Directions: From US 49, drive west on Hancock Avenue into Tutwiler. When the road ends, turn left and cross the railroad tracks, veer left on Second Street, and park. Murals are on the north side of the tracks.

While the train station where W. C. Handy famously received his first taste of the blues in 1903 does not still stand, you will find a sizeable mural commemorating the event. Additional murals also pay homage to Sonny Boy Williamson II and Delta agriculture. Painted on the back wall of a row of brick buildings, these five murals face Railroad Park and the train tracks that once swept Handy away with a new appreciation of what would soon be popularized as the blues. Facing the wall, from left to right, the murals depict a painting of a locomotive, representing the allure of the railroad; Handy's meeting with the unknown bluesman who was scraping the blade of his knife against the fret board of his guitar, singing, "where the Southern crosses the Yellow Dog"; a Delta crop duster; the area's catfish farms; and a depiction of the final resting place of Aleck Miller, aka Sonny Boy Williamson II, along with a map detailing directions to his grave site.

PARCHMAN

Culture

Parchman Penitentiary
Parchman, MS
Directions: South of Tutwiler on US 49 W., at the intersection with MS 32

If you know your blues music, then you're most likely familiar with Parchman Penitentiary, aka the Farm, aka Parchman Farm. The oldest prison in Mississippi, as well as the state's sole maximum-security prison, Parchman has the dubious distinction of not only having been featured in various blues numbers, but having housed some of those very bluesmen. The prison is also featured in several of Faulkner's works (*The Mansion, Old Man*) and is the setting for the earliest photo of Elvis Presley, whose father was incarcerated at Parchman for three years after being convicted of forgery. While visitors are discouraged from stopping for a photo op, avid blues fans may want to drive by for a glimpse of the sign for the legendary pen.

Shelby

Nightlife

Do Drop Inn
Second Ave. and Lake St., Shelby, MS 38774

Located around 30 miles south of Clarksdale on Highway 61, Shelby is a tiny, crumbling town that used to be home to several hopping jukes. Today, only the Do Drop Inn still occasionally hosts live music, but bookings are few and far between, so be sure to check local schedules. A clapboard building painted a funky pea green, the joint is easy to spot thanks to its distinctive color and Do Drop Inn painted right above the door. Big E's Place and Where the good times are are also stenciled on the front of this authentic, old-school juke. Inside, there's plenty of room to groove, with a dance floor and a stage. On weekends when there's not live music (which is most of the time), a DJ sometimes provides tunes.

Merigold

Nightlife

Po' Monkey's Lounge
Poor Monkey Rd., Merigold, MS 38759
Directions: From Hwy. 61, turn west on Pemble Rd./South St. around Merigold; take the first left where the road forks onto a gravel road (Poor Monkey Rd.). The club is about a mile down on the left.

If you're looking for an authentic juke house, brother, you got it. Located a mile or so down a dirt road—in the middle of a cotton field—Po' Monkey's Lounge is the physical embodiment of every deep South, rural juke joint you've ever read about and/or seen in photographs and documentaries. Housed in an early-20th-century sharecropper's shack, the structure was transformed into a makeshift lounge in the 1950s by resident owner Willie Seaberry (aka Po' Monkey) and has been an off-and-on good-timin' establishment for locals ever since. (Seaberry is known to change outfits several times throughout any given evening—each time parading around the room to make sure his patrons take a gander at his new duds.) This is the real deal, and it is one of the last remaining rural jukes akin to the ones that gave the blues a home around the time W. C. Handy got wise. This is time travel sans the machine.

Mound Bayou
Located just east of Highway 61 between Cleveland and Shelby, this historic town was founded by former slaves Isaiah T. Montgomery and Benjamin T. Green in 1887. Created as a haven for African Americans and their culture, the self-governed town grew and flourished in the early 20th century, and it was home to an oil mill and one of the first African American banks in Mississippi. Mound Bayou also boasts the first brick church built in Bolivar County. In the 1920s, like much of the Delta, the community struggled with falling crop and land values. Today, Mound Bayou remains a small, quiet place that's perhaps best known for Peter's Pottery, a locally-loved shop located at 301 Fortune Ave. (662-741-2283).

Unlike some jukes, Po' Monkey's rarely has live music (usually only during festival time or special bookings), but it hosts an amazing house jock who spins on Thursday nights under the name DJ Candy Man. As for the tunes, expect a heavy dose of regional soul and R&B—most of which with overtly sexual lyrics hard-core enough to make Clarence Carter blush. Inside the shack, typical juke house decor rules: multicolored streamers, mismatched tables and chairs, pool table, retro beer and liquor posters, and—this being Poor Monkey's—endless stuffed-animal monkeys hanging from every available rafter. Next to the '70s-styled DJ booth in the back, a TV flickers between color and black and white, but it's pretty much obscured by the dancing and carousing of the over-30 patrons shaking their stuff on the dance floor. Like at most juke joints worth their salt, beer is available (and mostly sold) via oversize bottles of Budweiser accompanied by a napkin and two Dixie cups for drinking. Po' Monkey's is only open on Thursday nights ($5 cover) and for occasional live music bookings.

Restaurants

Crawdad's
662-748-2441
www.crawdads1.com
100 S. Park St., Merigold, MS 38759
Open: Tues.–Sat.
Price: Moderate–Expensive
Credit Cards: Yes
Cuisine: Cajun, steaks, seafood
Serving: D

While live music is a rarity at Po' Monkey's Lounge, DSU's Delta Center sometimes presents blues shows at the legendary juke. Justin Gage

Handicap Access: Yes
Special Features: Full bar

What started as a tiny, modest spot serving one menu item (crawfish) in 1984 has grown and expanded over the years into the expansive log cabin–like space you'll see today. Inside, the atmosphere is rustic and warm, with cypress walls covered in taxidermy, and a deer antler chandelier overhead. It feels a little like you're dining in a hunt club, especially in the safari-themed main bar. In addition to steamed crawfish (in season), Crawdad's is well known around the Delta for char-grilled steaks that are cut on-site. The seafood-heavy menu also features ample Big Easy flavor, from gumbo and raw oysters to New Orleans–style barbecue shrimp and fish entrées. You'll also find Delta specialties on the menu, including the ubiquitous fried pickles, and catfish served fried, grilled, blackened, or baked in bread crumbs and topped with a Parmesan crawfish sauce. Thanks to a liquor license and two bars, Crawdad's is also a popular spot for cocktails.

Shopping

McCarty's Pottery
662-748-2293
www.mccartyspottery.com
101 Saint Mary St., Merigold, MS 38759

Housed in a charming old barn, this shop has been producing award-winning pottery crafted from Mississippi clay since 1954. Pieces include dishes, platters, lamps, planters, sculpture, and dinnerware glazed in McCarty's signature nutmeg brown, cobalt blue, and jade. Part of the fun of a visit to McCarty's is a stroll through the lush gardens, complete with fountains, a goldfish pond, pool, and a myriad of lush greenery. A separate café on the grounds called The Gallery is open for lunch.

CLEVELAND

The largest town near popular Bolivar County attractions like Dockery Farms and Po' Monkey's Lounge, Cleveland features shopping and dining that's a step above what's available in many Delta towns. Located in the heart of downtown's historic Crosstie District, Cotton Row is home to numerous boutiques, antiques shops, and specialty stores. Among the town's impressive array of restaurants, KC's offers one of the Delta's few fine-dining experiences. Cleveland is also the home of Delta State University, where the modest Mississippi Delta Blues Hall of Fame is located, honoring winners of the Peavine Award. When it comes to blues heritage, the town's biggest claim to fame is Bolivar County Courthouse, where W. C. Handy had an experience that forever changed the course of his career.

Lodging
Cleveland offers a standard selection of the usual chain motels along Highway 61 (known in town as Davis Avenue). If you're planning on a big night out at Po' Monkey's Lounge, located around 10 minutes down the road in Merigold, this is pretty much the closest place to crash.

Days Inn
662-846-5404
www.daysinn.com
900 S. Davis Ave. (Hwy. 61), Cleveland, MS 38732

Delta Inn
662-846-1873
1139 S. Davis Ave. (Hwy. 61), Cleveland, MS 38732

Econo Lodge
662-843-4060
www.econolodge.com
721 N. Davis Ave. (Hwy. 61), Cleveland, MS 38732

Hampton Inn
662-846-2915
www.hamptoninn.com
912 N. Davis Ave. (Hwy. 61), Cleveland, MS 38732

Holiday Inn Express
662-843-9300
www.hiexpress.com
808 Davis Ave. (Hwy. 61), Cleveland, MS 38732

Western Motel
662-843-6908
907 S. Davis Ave. (Hwy. 61), Cleveland, MS 38732

Culture

Bolivar County Courthouse
662-843-2712
200 Court St., Cleveland, MS 38732

Situated on the leafy grounds of the Bolivar County Courthouse is a plaque in honor of W. C. Handy, the Father of the Blues. It was here, in 1905, while performing with his orchestra at a dance, that Handy claims to have found his muse as a composer. Not unlike his fateful night at the Tutwiler train depot, Handy's epiphany came by watching others. When his orchestra was unable to perform requested blues numbers, a local band was brought in to take over—and reportedly stole the show. As a musician, Handy was forever a changed man.

Mississippi Delta Blues Hall of Fame
Charles W. Capps Archive & Museum, Delta State University
Fifth Ave. at Court St., Cleveland, MS 38733

Housed at Delta State University, the Mississippi Delta Blues Hall of Fame is most notably home to the Peavine Awards, which were founded at the university in 1998 to honor the region's rich blues heritage. Each year, the award is given to two or three musicians who are inducted into the Mississippi Delta Blues Hall of Fame. Recipients are honored with a plaque on the wall at the archive. Past honorees include John Lee Hooker, Tommy Johnson, Charley Patton, Howlin' Wolf, Robert Johnson, and Ike Turner. The hall of fame itself isn't as grand as the name suggests; it's a row of simple plaques, and not much else to see.

Nightlife

Your best bet for live blues is probably **Airport Grocery** (see the Restaurants section), where Willie Foster recorded a live album. Located on downtown's Cotton Row, **The Pickled Okra** (201 S. Sharpe Ave.; 662-843-8510) features live music some weekends after the dinner hour, including occasional blues. **The Senator's Place** (1028 S. Davis Ave./Hwy. 61; 662-846-7434) serves up hearty country cookin' and live blues most weekends.

Restaurants

Airport Grocery
662-843-4817
3608 Hwy. 61 N. (N. Davis Ave.), Cleveland, MS 38721
Open: Daily
Price: Inexpensive–Moderate
Credit Cards: Yes
Cuisine: American, regional
Serving: L (Mon.–Sat.), D
Handicap Access: Yes
Special Features: Full bar; pool tables; live music

Although this popular spot is no longer located near the airport on the outskirts of town, the down-home vibe at "Cleveland's Home of the Blues" remains. A hodgepodge of rustic decor consists of tin Coke signs, holiday lights, autographed blues posters, an old piano, and the occasional deer head. Blues music is generally on the stereo, and once every month or two, there tends to be live blues music. Several blues greats have played the joint over the years, including Willie Foster, who recorded "Live at Airport Grocery" at the old location. Though it started out as a modest grocery and gas stop around the Depression, Airport Grocery Eat Place evolved over the years into one of Cleveland's go-to spots for casual eats in a fun, friendly atmosphere. Hearty menu favorites include burgers, barbecue ribs, an oversize pulled-pork or beef barbecue sandwich, and hand-rolled tamales served with a side of ketchup. You can also get a steak, fried catfish, shrimp, and indulgent sides like fried pickles, gravy-smothered fries, and even fried green beans. In addition to dinner and occasional live music, this is also a popular spot to sip a cold beer and shoot a game of pool.

The Bean Counter
662-846-5282
219 S. Court St., Cleveland, MS 38732
Open: Mon.–Sat.
Price: Inexpensive
Credit Cards: Yes

Cuisine: Coffee shop, sandwiches
Serving: B, L
Handicap Access: Yes
Special Features: Free wireless

The Mississippi Delta may be one of the last places in America where you won't find a Starbucks on every other corner, which makes finding cute coffee shops like the Bean Counter that much more refreshing. Located in a converted gas station across from the pretty Bolivar County Courthouse, this comfy spot serves up espresso, cappuccino, frappuccino, specialty iced mocha drinks, and more. You can also sip on an Italian soda or choose from a selection of chai teas. Breakfast items include several types of muffins, plus scones, bagels, and cinnamon rolls. For lunch, there are sandwiches, paninis, and even a flatbread pizza. If you just want a snack, biscotti, cookies, and a selection of cakes will do the trick. There are cozy tables and comfy couches, so chances are you'll want to linger for a while over your espresso.

KC's Restaurant
662-843-5301
400 Hwy. 61 (N. Davis Ave.), Cleveland, MS 38732
Open: Mon.–Sat.
Price: Moderate–Very Expensive
Credit Cards: Yes
Cuisine: New American
Serving: L (Wed.–Fri.), D
Handicap Access: Yes
Special Features: Wine tastings; catering

Fine-dining establishments in the Delta are few and far between, and KC's Restaurant was among the first. Foodies come from well beyond Cleveland for this four-star dining experience. Inside the mission-style property, vibrantly colored walls, contemporary light fixtures, and high ceilings create a sleek, modern interior with space for nearly 150 diners in three dining rooms. A separate area houses KC's bar, which may just be the closest thing Cleveland has to a see-and-be-seen spot. Celebrated chef-owner Wally Jo offers an eclectic, upscale menu with influences from France, Asia, and right here in the Mississippi Delta. Starters may include anything from caviar to crispy Gulf oysters, or maybe even an elk quesadilla. Gorgeously presented entrées have included free-range veal rib eye, seared scallops, grilled quail with fried green tomatoes, and duck breast with foie gras confit served with pecan-whipped sweet potatoes. Dessert is equally indulgent with selections like macadamia nut tart with caramelized bananas. KC's also offers one of the Delta's best wine lists; the walk-in cellar is stocked with more than seven hundred bottles.

The Southern Grill
662-843-1317
308 E. Carpenter, Cleveland, MS 38732
Open: Daily
Price: Inexpensive
Credit Cards: Yes
Cuisine: American, regional

Serving: B, L
Handicap Access: Yes
Special Features: Breakfast and lunch buffets; free wireless

Modest looking from the outside, this no-frills local favorite is an expansive affair with a slew of tables and booths packed with regulars who are mostly there for the fantastic (and inexpensive) breakfast or lunch buffet. Rib-sticking country breakfasts include omelets, pancakes, country ham, grits, and biscuits with three types of gravy: white, sausage, or tomato. The most popular dining option, of course, is the all-you-can-eat breakfast buffet, with just about all of the above, and more. The lunch buffet is another belt-busting affair, with everything from fried catfish, chicken strips, pulled pork, and spaghetti to meat 'n three standards like collard greens, beans, corn bread, and hush puppies. There's also a salad bar and usually three types of dessert, like peach cobbler, bread pudding, and banana pudding. If you insist on ordering off the menu, you'll find juicy half-pound burgers, po' boys, salads, and sandwiches. For some serious comfort food, try the hot tamale or Frito chili pie, smothered in chili and topped with cheese.

DOCKERY

Culture

Dockery Farms
662-719-1048
www.dockeryfarms.org
229 MS 8, Cleveland, MS 38732
Special Features: Hosts a limited number of private tours, lectures, and events

Established by Will Dockery in 1895, Dockery Farms is considered one of the landmark cornerstones of the Delta blues. In addition to its role in the cultivation of cotton, Dockery Farms played an equally important role in the birth and cultivation of blues music. At one time or another, the operation employed countless blues musicians, including Charley Patton, Tommy Johnson, Henry Sloan, Willie Brown, and Roebuck "Pop" Staples. It was at Dockery that traditions were born and later passed from player to player as the men congregated in the commissary and elsewhere on the grounds in their off hours. Visiting the farm is akin to a trip back in time; five of the six original buildings that made up the heart of the plantation are intact, making this one of the Delta's most coveted photo ops. In 2006, the site was placed on the National Register of Historic Places.

BOYLE

Culture

Peavine Railroad Blues Trail Marker
www.msbluestrail.org
Boyle, MS
Directions: From Highway 61, turn west on MS 446 (TM Jones Highway); marker is near where the railroad tracks intersect with 446

The precise origins of the blues are lost to time, but one of the primal centers for the music in Mississippi was Dockery Farms. For nearly three decades the plantation was intermittently the home of Charley Patton (c. 1891-1934), the most important early Delta blues musician. Patton himself learned from fellow Dockery resident Henry Sloan and influenced many other musicians who came here, including Howlin' Wolf, Willie Brown, Tommy Johnson, and Roebuck "Pops" Staples.

The 37th marker to go up, Dockery Farms became an official stop on the Blues Trail on April 19, 2008.

Made famous by Charlie Patton in his song "Pea Vine Blues," the Peavine Railroad Blues Trail marker represents the long-running metaphorical association of escape and railroad travel in early blues music. Here, the Peavine branch (officially listed as the Kimball Lake branch) of the Yazoo and Mississippi Valley Railroad met up with the Memphis to Vicksburg mainline that carried bluesmen and their music off to find work and greater opportunity.

SHAW

Culture

David "Honeyboy" Edwards Blues Trail Marker
www.msbluestrail.org
Honeyboy Edwards Park, Shaw, MS
Directions: From Hwy. 61, turn west on MS 448 (E. Peeler Avenue); marker is south of Peeler between Elm and White Oak sts.

Erected in 2007 by the Mississippi Blues Commission, Honeyboy Edwards's Blues Trail marker is located on a narrow, grassy park named in his honor. While Shaw's downtown may be marked by boarded-up and abandoned buildings, the new park's shiny street lamps, park benches, and small covered pavilion are a bright spot in the crumbling town.

Born in Shaw in 1915, Honeyboy learned from such notable Delta blues luminaries as Tommy Johnson, Charlie Patton, and Big Joe Williams. A few years after playing alongside Robert Johnson, in what would turn out to be Johnson's final performance before his death, Honeyboy was discovered by music scholar and historian Alan Lomax, who recorded him for the Library of Congress. After recording commercially in 1951 for Arc Records, Honeyboy enjoyed a career that continues today, although he now resides in Chicago.

Rosedale

Culture

Rosedale Blues Trail Marker
www.msbluestrail.org
Rosedale, MS
Directions: From MS 1, turn east on Bruce Street; marker is near the intersection of Bruce Street and Railroad Avenue.

Like many a Delta town, Rosedale is said to have been *the* place where Robert Johnson sold his soul to the devil (at the crossroads of MS 1 and 8) in return for unparalleled musical gifts. The town's blues notoriety grew even further in the 1960s, when Eric Clapton and his band Cream took some liberties with the song, renaming it "Crossroads." Both it, and the Led Zeppelin cover of "Traveling Riverside Blues," mention Rosedale by name. The Rosedale Blues Trail marker stands on the old Yazoo and Mississippi Valley Railroad depot site.

Seasonal Events

May

Crossroads Blues Festival
www.rosedaleblues.com
Rosedale, MS

It's no surprise that Rosedale, name-dropped by none other than Robert Johnson in his seminal "Traveling Riverside Blues," now has its own blues festival. Founded by Rosedale's Blues Society in 1999, the fest returned in 2008 after a three-year hiatus and was held in a new location at the River Resort, just south of town. In addition to live blues music, festivities generally include food, craft vendors, and after-fest music at the Blue Levee. Notable past performers include T-Model Ford, Sam Carr, Bill "Howlin' Mad" Perry, and Willie Foster. The date and location of the festival are subject to change, so be sure to check the Blues Society Web site and local Rosedale event listings.

Restaurants

Blue Levee
662-759-6333
1310 S. Main St., Rosedale, MS 38769
Open: Tues.–Sat.
Price: Inexpensive–Expensive

Credit Cards: Yes
Cuisine: American, Southern, regional
Serving: L, D
Handicap Access: Limited
Special Features: Live music; bring your own wine and liquor

Open since late 2005, this modest spot has become a Delta dining destination. Located by the entrance of Great River Bend State Park (at the other famed crossroads of MS 1 and 8), the casual, laid-back eatery is just over the levee from the Mississippi River on the back side of a gas mart. Diners enter through a screen-porch door and settle into a funky dining room with down-home Delta decor that includes local artwork, mismatched chairs, and vintage light fixtures. The vibe is cozy and eclectic, and there's usually live music every other Saturday, including blues, rock, bluegrass, or country. The Blue Levee also hosts bands during Rosedale's Crossroads Blues Festival. For lunch, locals pack in for popular plate lunches, soups, sandwiches, and salads. Dinner consists of regional standards along with impressive daily specials. Starters include crabcakes, fried green tomatoes, and fresh salads. For the main entrée, there are steaks, catfish and shrimp (served blackened, grilled, or fried), and less-familiar fare like Mediterranean-style stuffed chicken. Upscale specials change frequently and may include wild game, rack of lamb, duck, or butter-poached lobster served over spicy crawfish grits. Thursday night is seafood night at the Blue Levee, with a menu that features seafood platters, surf and turf, all-you-can-eat shrimp, and soft-shell or Dungeness crab. For dessert, don't pass up the homemade sopapilla cheesecake. The Blue Levee also serves up one of the Delta's most impressive beer selections.

White Front Café

662-759-3842
902 Main St. (MS 1), Rosedale, MS 38769
Open: Tues.–Sat.
Price: Inexpensive
Credit Cards: No
Cuisine: Tamales
Serving: L, D
Handicap Access: No
Special Features: Take-out, catering

Also known as Joe Pope's White Front Hot Tamales, this one-trick pony is a landmark in these parts. Joe's younger sister, Barbara Pope, took over the operation after Joe's death in 2004, but other than that, not a whole lot has changed since Joe opened the place in the '70s. Inside the unassuming white house, there are a few spots to sit and enjoy the one and only menu item. Joe's all-beef tamales are hand rolled, corn shucked, and fairly spicy. Tourists and locals alike drive from all over for what many consider the Delta's best tamales. Tourists like to linger at one of the few seats, but regulars generally order their tamales by the dozen to carry out. In-the-know locals bring their own containers for the tamale "juice," which they use on everything from salad to French bread. While tamales are the only menu item, you will find a jar of pickles, candy, and soda. Can't get enough? Order a few dozen frozen tamales to take home.

Recreation

PARKS, NATURE, AND WILDLIFE

Great River Road State Park

662-759-6762
Rosedale, MS
Directions: MS 8 at junction of MS 1; turn west on State Park Road at highway intersection

Named for the "Great River Road" that follows the Mississippi River from its humble beginnings in Canada all the way to its conclusion in the Gulf of Mexico, the park boasts a 75-foot, four-level overlook tower with stunning panoramic views of the mighty Mississippi. Perfect for hiking, fishing, camping, and picnics, the park is located on the river's levee off MS 1, just 35 miles north of Greenville. Highlights include 61 camping sites, RV hookups, trails, recreational sports fields, and a visitor's center. Don't miss the whiskey still on display outside the visitor's center, complete with a recipe. A nod to Rosedale's storied history of levee camps and bootleggers, the still belonged to Perry Martin, an infamous bootlegger who lived on a houseboat on the park's lake, which is now named for him.

GREENVILLE

The state's largest city on the Mississippi River, Greenville hosts the region's oldest and largest blues festival. Held annually in September, the Mississippi Delta Blues & Heritage Festival is a fantastic time to catch live blues in Greenville. Historic Nelson Street used to be home to several well-known juke joints, but these days, it's rather run down and crime ridden, best visited during the day or with a knowledgeable local. In recent years, the live-music scene has moved to downtown's Walnut Street, where there's plenty of live music every weekend, including some blues. On the other side of the levee opposite Walnut Street, you'll find a few casinos.

Greenville has a rich history, from its impressive literary heritage to the devastating Great Flood of 1927, when broken levees left thousands of residents stranded. Visitors can learn more about the Great Flood at Greenville's History Museum or in the back room of McCormick Book Inn. Steak lovers are encouraged to experience a little living history at Doe's Eat Place. Trust us on this one.

Lodging

INNS AND BED & BREAKFASTS

Camelot Bed & Breakfast

662-332-9477
www.camelotbedandbreakfast.com
548 S. Washington Ave., Greenville, MS 38701
North of US 82 E.
Price: Inexpensive–Moderate
Credit Cards: No
Handicap Access: No
Special Features: Free Internet access, laundry facilities

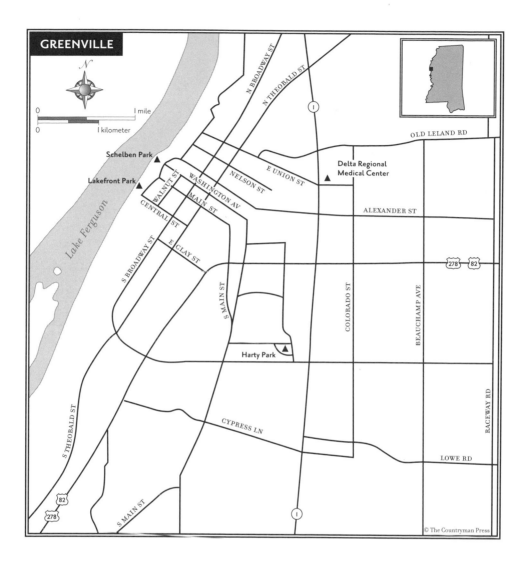

Located on a lovely tree-lined residential road just a few blocks southeast of downtown, this small bed & breakfast offers two rooms with private baths. A stay here is akin to staying in a friend's guest room, with comfortable accommodations that feature hardwood floors, floral bedspreads, and homey decor. Guests can lounge in a comfy living room where there's also a small work desk. During the week, Camelot usually hosts business travelers, while leisure travelers are common during event weekends—book well in advance for the Delta Blues Festival. Saturday and Sunday mornings, a full Southern-style breakfast with biscuits and gravy and the like is served in the dining room. During the week, continental breakfast is served and rates are lowered. Guests have access to free, on-site laundry facilities, and extended-stay rates are available.

Located in the old levee board building, the Greenville Inn & Suites is a unique place to stay in the heart of downtown Greenville.

Greenville Inn & Suites

662-332-6900
211 S. Walnut St., Greenville, MS 38701
Downtown Greenville by the levee
Price: Inexpensive
Credit Cards: Yes
Handicap Access: Yes

Built in 1883, this historic building was occupied by the levee board until 1997, making it one of Greenville's oldest commercial structures. Today, the property houses 41 rooms and suites in a prime downtown location just over the levee from Lake Ferguson (a tributary of the Mississippi River). Walnut Street's main drag is just a block away, Greenville's handful of casinos are right over the levee, and Nelson Street is a quick drive away. Thanks to its former life as the levee board building, the inn boasts plenty of character that you won't find at the local chains. Spacious accommodations feature microwaves and minifridges, while some rooms are equipped with a kitchenette and seating area with a couch. Traditional decor consists of floral bedspreads and matching trim on the wall, floral prints, dark carpeting, and dark wood furnishings. The property features free continental breakfast that you can enjoy in an outdoor courtyard complete with a trickling fountain.

MOTELS

Comfort Inn

662-332-0508
www.comfortinn.com
137 N. Walnut St., Greenville, MS 38701

Days Inn
662-334-1818
www.daysinn.com
2701 US 82, Greenville, MS 38701

Econo Lodge
662-378-4976
www.econolodge.com
3080 US 82 E., Greenville, MS 38702

Hampton Inn
662-335-7515
www.hamptoninn.com
1155 VFW Rd., Greenville, MS 38701

Holiday Inn Express
662-332-5800
www.ichotelsgroup.com
3090 US 82 E., Greenville, MS 38702

Regency Inn & Conference Center
662-334-6900
2428 US 82 E., Greenville, MS 38702

Relax Inn
662-332-1527
2630 US 82 E., Greenville, MS 38703

Culture

Greenville History Museum
Call Benjy Nelken at 662-335-5802
409 Washington Ave., Greenville, MS 38701

Inside the historic Miller Building, artifacts, photos, memorabilia, and news clippings trace Greenville's history from the late 1800s to contemporary times, including the days of the devastating 1927 flood.

Greenville Writer's Exhibit at William Alexander Percy Memorial Library
662-335-2331
341 Main St., Greenville, MS 38701

Literary buffs can see original manuscripts and more from a slew of well-known local writers, including William Alexander Percy, Shelby Foote, Ellen Douglas, Walker Percy, and many more.

Hebrew Union Temple Century of History Museum
662-332-4153
504 Main St., Greenville, MS 38701

Housed within this grand 1906 temple is a museum dedicated to the contributions and culture of the city's Jewish residents, who date back to 1867.

Old Number I Firehouse Museum
662-378-1573
230 Main St., Greenville, MS 38701

Visit this restored 1920s fire station to gawk at antique fire trucks and explore interactive exhibits. Open by appointment only.

Seasonal Events
SEPTEMBER

Mississippi Delta Blues & Heritage Festival
www.deltablues.org
MS 1 at MS 454, Greenville, MS 38701

For more than 30 years, the annual Mississippi Delta Blues & Heritage Festival has celebrated both Mississippi's blues heritage and its well of modern-day talent. The second-oldest continuously operating blues festival in the country, the Greenville fest has hosted performers including B. B. King, Sam Chatmon, Son Thomas, Willie Foster, Ruby Wilson, Robert Cray, John Lee Hooker, Muddy Waters, Stevie Ray Vaughn, Albert King, and Bobby Rush. Held at Freedom Village (site of a Blues Trail marker), south of Greenville off MS 1, the outdoor festival features three stages, including the main stage, where national acts perform; the Juke House Stage, where local musicians play; and a Gospel Stage.

Mississippi Jazz & Heritage Festival
662-247-3364
www.jazzmississippi.com
749 Main St., Greenville, MS 38701

The annual Mississippi Jazz & Heritage Festival has been celebrating Mississippi's jazz heritage for more than a decade. Dedicated to the memory of Woodville, Mississippi, native and jazzbo Lester "Prez" Young, the fest is held Labor Day weekend (call ahead to confirm). Highlights include a jazz workshop, regional cuisine, lectures, children's activities, and a concert featuring the state's homegrown jazz artists. The festival's free outdoor jazz concert takes place at the Edwards Center at 749 Main Street.

Nightlife

Nelson Street
Northeast of downtown Greenville

Once a thriving African American business and social hub—and a haven for live blues—Nelson Street is sadly now a shadow of its former self. In its heyday, bluesmen like Little Milton Campbell, Charlie Booker, Willie Love, and Sonny Boy Williamson II frequently played the strip and even immortalized the area in songs like "Nelson Street Blues" (Willie Love) and "No Ridin' Blues" (Charlie Booker). Today, you'll probably be warned to avoid Nelson Street, thanks to the presence of drugs and prostitution. Many businesses are abandoned, and popular juke joints like Perry's Flowing Fountain are sadly no longer in operation. But you will find a Blues Trail marker near the railroad tracks (best to seek out in daylight hours), and you can still hear great live blues during the Little Wynn Nelson Street Festival held the day before the Mississippi Delta Blues & Heritage Festival each year. If you're intent on visiting a Nelson Street juke on a nonfestival weekend, going with a local guide is advisable.

Walnut Street
Located in the heart of downtown Greenville by the levee

Walnut Street has become the reliable place in town to hear live music. While the strip is quiet during the day, the block comes to life at night, and on weekends, when blues, rock, and country music pour out onto the street. The best bet for live blues is the festive **Walnut Street Blues Bar** (128 Walnut St.; 662-378-2254), although rock and cover bands also frequent the stage. Down the street, **Southern Nights Bar and Grill** (138 Walnut St.; 662-334-9402) features karaoke and occasional live music. Across the street, the roomy, exposed-brick back room at **Spectator's Pub & Eatery** (139 Walnut St.; 662-335-3334) hosts weekend rock shows for a young crowd that likes to dance. In addition to live music, Walnut Street also features a few walk-of-fame-style tiles in the sidewalk honoring local blues musicians like Willie James Foster, David "Honeyboy" Edwards, and Barrington "Skeeter" Provis Jr.

Restaurants

Doe's Eat Place
662-334-3315
502 Nelson St., Greenville, MS 38701
Open: Mon.–Sat.
Price: Expensive–Very Expensive
Credit Cards: Yes
Cuisine: Steaks, seafood
Serving: D
Handicap Access: No
Special Features: Reservations recommended

The location is on the end of dodgy Nelson Street, the atmosphere is about as no-frills as it gets, and the service is a bit patchy, but this is where you come for one of the best steaks in America. Family owned since 1941, this grocery store turned restaurant resembles a small home and isn't exactly equipped as a restaurant. When you walk in, the heat from the grill and the scent of sizzling steak stop you in your tracks, and you immediately think you've accidentally walked into the kitchen. You have, but it's no accident. The famous steaks are right there in front of you, being grilled in the well-worn waiting area/kitchen next to bowls of fresh-cut fries and stacks of enormous T-bones awaiting the heat. Help yourself to a cold beer from a cooler in the corner (you're on the honor system here) and watch "Little Doe" and his crew work their magic while you decide which steak you're going to order.

In the adjacent dining area, mismatched tables and chairs are scattered around the other half of the kitchen and throughout a handful of tiny rooms with pitched floors and wood-paneled or painted-cinderblock walls covered in press clippings. Just about everyone knows each other, and there's usually not a menu in sight. Families and friends generally share gigantic 4-pound sirloins and plates of Doe's famous tamales. If you're at all put off by your haphazard surroundings (which is part of the fun), just wait for the food to start coming out, and prepare to swoon. While you could order the shrimp, do yourself a favor and go for the filet mignon. But first, there's the house salad, simple but delicious thanks to a refreshing lemony dressing. Then comes the main event. Cut on-site, the perfectly grilled steaks benefit from simple preparation. You won't find rich toppings here, and they would only hide the fantastic flavor of the tender, ultrafresh beef anyway. Use the thick, hand-cut french fries on the side to sop up the drippings. More than an amazing meal, Doe's offers an unforgettable Delta dining experience.

Jim's Café
662-332-5951
314 Washington Ave., Greenville, MS 38701
Open: Mon.–Sat.
Price: Inexpensive
Credit Cards: Yes
Cuisine: American, regional
Serving: B, L
Handicap Access: Yes

A downtown fixture owned by the same family for more than 65 years, Jim's Café has seen Main Street's glory days come and go. While run-down shops now dot the once-bustling street, the café remains a popular local meeting place for good conversation over breakfast and plate lunches. The redbrick storefront's retro neon sign and white awning certainly

Doe's Eat Place won the James Beard Foundation Award in the America's Classics category in 2007.

haven't changed much over the years. Inside, old-timers sip coffee and swap stories at a row of cozy booths lining a wood-paneled wall plastered with historic photos of Greenville during better times. In addition to plate lunches, Jim's lunch menu offers burgers and sandwiches, plus stuffed deviled crabs (in season), pork chops, veal cutlets, and even a gyro sandwich. You can also buy a bottle of the café's house-made hot sauce or salad dressing on your way out. This is down-home dining from another era and a longtime Greenville tradition.

Posecai's

662-378-3688
1443 Trailwood Dr., Greenville, MS 38701
Open: Tues.–Sat.
Price: Expensive
Credit Cards: Yes
Cuisine: Upscale regional; Creole
Serving: D
Handicap Access: Yes
Special Features: Full bar

New on Greenville's dining scene in 2007, this upscale eatery housed in a charming blue house offers a menu ranging from Delta specialties to New Orleans favorites. Located a few minutes south of downtown off US 82, Posecai's is tucked away on a quiet residential street surrounded by apartments and townhomes. Boasting one of the Delta's best dining atmospheres, the restaurant's five rooms feature hardwood floors, fireplaces, and local artwork. The vibe is sleek and elegant, but not at all stuffy, and service is professional. Owner Ted Posecai, a Louisiana native, brings Big Easy flavor to his menu, including selections like file gumbo, fresh oysters, and a barbecue shrimp and grits cake. You'll also find dressed-up Delta favorites, an Italian entrée or two, and even a selection of Sushi.

Shopping

McCormick Book Inn

662-332 5038
www.mccormickbookinn.com
825 S. Main St., Greenville, MS 38701

Mississippi's oldest independent bookstore, this cozy shop has been family owned since 1965. Located in a leafy residential area, the well-stocked store features a fantastic selection of work from the area's notably high concentration of writers, including Walker Percy and Shelby Foote, who called Greenville home. In fact, Percy, Foote, and six other Greenville writers published nearly one hundred books in the mid-20th century. As manager Hugh B. McCormick III is fond of saying, "Why does Greenville have so many writers? It's the brown water we drink." You can even purchase a novelty bottle of Greenville's ubiquitous brown water—yes, it's perfectly safe to drink. Beyond local luminaries, McCormick has an extensive knowledge of Mississippi writers, classic to contemporary, and is happy to provide insightful recommendations. Regional authors regularly stop by for book signings and other special events. The inventory isn't confined to regional work, however, and in addition to best-sellers, cookbooks, and children's titles, the Book Inn carries Crane stationery, local photography, and jewelry. A comfy seating area around the fireplace is a fine spot to settle in with your selections. A back museum room is dedicated to local history, including photos of the Great Flood of 1927, a display honoring James "Son" Thomas, and plenty of exhibits on local writers.

METCALFE

Culture

Eugene "Sonny Boy Nelson" Powell's Grave
Metcalfe, MS
Directions: From US 82, drive north on MS 1; veer right at Broadway Exit. Drive 1 mile, then fork right onto Deer Creek Drive. In 1 mile, turn left onto a dirt road that crosses a small bridge into the cemetery.

Born on December 23, 1908, in Utica, Mississippi, Eugene Powell, aka "Sonny Boy Nelson," who died on November 4, 1998, is buried here in the blink-and-you'll-miss-it Evergreen Cemetery. Married to blueswoman Mississippi Matilda, Powell was an adept multi-instrumentalist with a unique guitar style, in high demand in and around the Delta in the 1930s and '40s. Powell's only recordings from this era are a few sides he and his band cut for the New Orleans–based Bluebird label in 1936. In the 1940s, Powell and his family moved to Greenville, where he took up steady employment with the John Deere Company. During this period, music took a backseat, and Powell rarely played publicly. Like many blues musicians of his generation, Powell caught his second wind in 1970 when asked to perform at the Festival of American Folklife in Washington, D.C. The festival gig kick-started his career, and Powell continued performing—and occasionally recording— until his death. Powell's headstone bears three quotes, one of which reads, A GUITAR VIRTU-OSO, HIS MUSIC TOUCHED PEOPLE THE WORLD OVER. Between the quotes is an etching of Powell playing his guitar. The small, modest cemetery is located on a country road surrounded by fields, and sadly, when it hasn't been maintained in a while, it can be near impossible to locate Powell's flat headstone.

LELAND

Culture

Highway 61 Blues Museum
662-686-7646
www.highway61blues.com
307 N. Broad St., Leland, MS 38756
Open: Mon.–Sat.
Admission: $5

A veritable gold mine of Delta blues memorabilia, the Highway 61 Blues Museum in downtown Leland boasts a collection that covers well over half a century of blues history. With walls lined by photographs and regional folk art, and glass displays housing everything from rare acetates to old guitars, the museum exudes an atmosphere similar to a carefully curated personal collection—which is exactly what it is. In addition to putting on the

annual Highway 61 Blues Festival, the museum also occasionally hosts in-house performances and other events. Blues travelers can stock up on T-shirts, posters, music, books,
and more in the museum store.

James "Son" Thomas's Grave

St. Matthews Missionary Church Cemetery
Leland, MS
Directions: East of Leland on US 82 about a mile, turn south on Frazier Road. Turn left on
Tribbett Road; church is at the intersection with Mark Road.

Known for his bottle-neck blues style, James "Son" Thomas, a Delta-born blues musician,
grave digger, and sculptor, died in 1993 and was buried in his hometown of Leland in St.
Matthews Missionary Church Cemetery. His headstone—which is inscribed, GIVE ME BEEF-
STEAK WHEN I'M HUNGRY, WHISKEY WHEN I'M DRY, PRETTY WOMEN WHEN I'M LIVING, AND HEAVEN
WHEN I DIE—was paid for by fan and fellow musician John Fogerty of Creedence Clearwater
Revival notoriety. Laid to rest in the thick Mississippi clay that once formed the crux of his
folk art, Thomas's legacy lives on in both his music and the influence of his self-taught
sculpture.

The Jim Henson Delta Boyhood Exhibit

662-686-7383
www.lelandms.org/kermit.html
415 S. Deer Creek Dr. E., Leland, MS 38756
Open: Mon.–Sat.
Admission: Free

Ever dreamed of having your photograph taken while sitting on (a life-size) Kermit the
Frog's lap? If so, you most definitely need to stop at the Leland Chamber of Commerce,
where the Jim Henson exhibit is housed. Henson, who spent part of his childhood in
Leland, created both *Sesame Street* and *The Muppet Show,* and in the process revolutionized
the art of puppetry and children's programming. The inspiration for his first and most
famous creation, Kermit the Frog, is said to have been born here in Leland on the banks of
Deer Creek. The exhibit pays tribute to Henson's work with early family photographs,
videos, and most interestingly, the prototype Kermit the Frog doll sewn out of his mother's
old green coat. There is a Henson-centric gift shop, and the surrounding grounds overlooking Deer Creek provide a perfect picnic spot.

Leland Murals

Downtown Leland, MS

After a visit to the Highway 61 Blues Museum, stroll down sleepy Main Street to peruse a
handful of elaborate blues murals commissioned by the Leland Blues Project. The first
mural, located on the south wall of a building at Fourth and Main Street, depicts a slew of
bluesmen from Leland and the surrounding areas, including Willie Foster, Johnny Winter,
Jimmie Reed, Little Milton, and James "Son" Thomas. Several of the living musicians
depicted in the painting have autographed the bricks beneath a plaque to the left of the
mural (although some are fading)—including Johnny Winter, Pat Thomas, and Caleb
Emphrey Jr. Down the road on the west wall of a building at Third and Main, a second

Leland's fourth mural honors nearby Dunleith native Jimmy Reed, an electric bluesman who was inducted into the Rock and Roll Hall of Fame in 1991.

mural depicts a couple dancing at Lillo's Restaurant to music from Doc's Bees dance band, with "Doc" Booth on sax and the legendary Abie "Boogaloo" Ames on keys. Across Third Street (at Main) on the south side of the building, a mural dedicated to B. B. King spans five decades of the blues king's career. The fourth mural to go up is located on the south wall of Stovall's on the Creek framing and pottery store at Broad Street and South Deer Creek Drive East. Jimmy Reed, born in nearby Dunleith, is the subject here. Plans for additional murals are in the works.

Old Highways 10 and 61 Blues Trail Marker
www.msbluestrail.org
Leland, MS
Directions: Third Street between Main Street and Broad Street

Leland, Mississippi, is home to Highways 10 and 61, two thoroughfares that literally carried the blues from town to town. Whereas 61 has long been known as the Blues Highway, Highway 10 rivaled 61 in stature until the mid-1930s, when the completion of the more expeditious US 82 took its place. The Blues Trail marker sits on the corner where the two highways once intersected.

Seasonal Events

|UNE

Highway 61 Blues Festival
662-686-7646
www.highway61blues.com
Leland, MS

Presented and curated by Jimmy Johnson, who runs Leland's Highway 61 Blues Museum, this festival showcases the talents of local and regional Delta blues players. A two-stage setup, with performances by more than 20 artists, the festival is held at Railroad Park, west of Main Street in downtown Leland. The music gets going at noon and doesn't stop until around 10 PM. Past performers have included David "Honeyboy" Edwards, Mississippi Slim, Lil' Dave Thompson, and the John Horton Band.

Restaurants

Lillo's Family Restaurant
662-686-4401
1001 US 82 E., Leland, MS 38756
Open: Wed.–Sun.
Price: Moderate
Credit Cards: Yes
Cuisine: Italian
Serving: D
Handicap Access: Limited
Special Features: Full bar; live music; open Sun.

A local favorite since 1948, Lillo's offers Italian cuisine and weekly live music in a homey atmosphere just west of town on US 82. Italian menu standards include lasagna, cannelloni, spaghetti, chicken and veal Parmesan, and even a catfish Parmesan. Many of the recipes have been passed down through the family to the third generation, who now run the place. There are also steaks, seafood entrées, and homemade pizzas, plus a full bar. A keyboard player is a regular fixture on Wednesday, while a band cranks things up on Thursday nights. While blues tunes are not uncommon, the music runs the gamut from oldies to the occasional country song. Unlike many businesses in the Delta, the restaurant is open on Sunday nights. Lillo's also operates a tiny motel behind the restaurant with a handful of ultrabasic rooms for rock-bottom rates.

BOURBON

Restaurants

The Bourbon Mall
662-686-4389
105 Dean Rd., Leland, MS 38756
Open: Mon.–Sat.
Price: Moderate–Expensive
Credit Cards: Yes
Cuisine: American, regional
Serving: D
Handicap Access: Limited
Special Features: Full bar; live music

Located down a country road surrounded by corn and cotton fields in every direction, this rusted, tin-covered 1920s grocery store turned restaurant is a Delta landmark. While the address is Leland, you're technically in the tiny town of Bourbon, about 20 minutes southeast of Leland, a half hour southwest of Indianola, or 35 minutes from Greenville. The unique dining experience is well worth the trip. And if you don't want to make the drive, the Bourbon Mall offers limo service to and from the restaurant for a fee. Not a bad idea if you're planning a full night out at one of the Mall's two full bars, which feature live music several nights a week.

Beyond the original grocery store entrance, the Bourbon Mall opens up into a cavernous network of dining rooms. Wide-plank walls mounted with antique saws, black-and-white photos, and the occasional set of antlers give the dining rooms a rustic vibe, while tabletop candles keep things cozy. Like most restaurants around, the Bourbon Mall offers corn-shucked tamales to start with, but here you can try them deep fried and crispy with a side of creamy ranch dressing. Entrées include popular flame-broiled steaks, rich seafood dishes like catfish stuffed with Cajun sausage, and a few Italian standards thrown in for good measure. After dinner, drag your full belly to the bar. The smaller of the two is located in a cozy, narrow room with a few tables and a stage where live music (mainly acoustic covers) is frequently played during the dinner hour. The much larger back bar is only open on the weekends, when bands play rock or blues on the spacious stage.

DUNLEITH

Culture

Jimmy Reed Blues Trail Marker
www.msbluestrail.org
Dunleith, MS
Directions: From US 82, drive north on Dunleith Road and cross the railroad tracks where Dunleith becomes Collier Road. The marker will be on the west side of the street after the intersection with Longswitch Road.

Jimmy Reed, Mr. "Big Boss Man" himself, was born here, at the site of the marker honoring him, on the Shady Dell plantation in 1925. Reed's musical education began as a child singing gospel spirituals at the Pilgrim Rest Baptist Church in nearby Meltonia. After a tour in the Navy, Reed moved to Chicago, where he developed his own style of guitar and harmonica playing, eventually landing himself a home at Vee-Jay Records in 1953. With 19 hit singles to his name, Reed became the first blues artist to cross over to white audiences, ultimately paving the way for B. B. King, Muddy Waters, and a future generation of bluesmen. A man who transcended genre barriers, Reed was inducted into both the Blues and Rock 'n' Roll Hall of Fames.

HOLLY RIDGE

Culture

Charley Patton's Grave Site
Holly Ridge, MS
Directions: From US 82, turn north onto Holly Ridge Holmes Road. Drive for about a mile, and just over the railroad tracks, turn left on Holly Ridge Road. The graveyard is just past a cotton gin on the left.

Charley Patton's grave site can be found in Holly Ridge, Mississippi, about halfway between Leland and Indianola, Mississippi. The tiny cemetery, often overgrown, is located next to a cotton gin that acts as a de facto landmark. Guitar picks and empty bottles of beer and whiskey lie in front of the grave site, left by fellow blues travelers and local fans. The Mississippi Blues Commission placed the first Blues Trail marker here in honor of the Father of the Mississippi Delta Blues. One of two Blues Trail markers honoring Patton, the second is at the site of the Peavine Railroad. Also buried in the cemetery are blues musicians Willie Foster and Asie Payton.

INDIANOLA

B. B. King is clearly the biggest thing to ever happen to Indianola, and the town celebrates its hometown hero with great fanfare. Although he was actually born outside of Itta Bena, Riley B. King settled in Indianola around age 13 and has considered this his hometown since. In 2008, the 20,000-square-foot, $14 million B. B. King Museum and Interpretive Center opened with as much buzz as B. B.'s annual summertime homecoming concert. One of the Delta's biggest new attractions, the museum is breathing new life into once-sleepy Indianola. Beyond B. B., other famous bluesmen tied to the town include Albert King, who was born here, and Charley Patton, who died here. In addition to everything B. B., you can find a couple of great jukes in Indianola. To get to the small downtown area from US 82, turn south on Catchings Street, take a quick right on Percy Street, then an immediate left on Front Street. Be sure to drive east on Main Street, which follows along Indianola's picturesque bayou, where cypress trees emerge from the green-skimmed water. You'll eventually come to Fletcher Park on the right, site of B. B.'s homecoming concert.

Lodging

BED & BREAKFASTS

Bed on the Bayou
662-887-4606, 662-887-1129
114 Percy St., Indianola, MS 38751
One block from downtown Indianola
Price: Inexpensive
Credit Cards: No
Handicapped Access: No

Tucked away on a quiet corner of the bayou, this private, one-room shotgun shack offers a nice alternative to the highway motels. Located just across from the courthouse, it's centrally located within walking distance of downtown, unlike most of the motels. A private gravel road leads to the cozy accommodations, which consist of a bedroom with a full-size bed, full kitchen, private bathroom, and a screened-in back porch that overlooks the bayou. Antique accents complement the cypress walls and hardwood floors, but there are also modern amenities like a 32-inch flat-screen TV. The kitchen is generally stocked with snacks and a few beverages, like banana nut bread or brownies, juice, Coke, popcorn, and cereal. ·

MOTELS
Of the handful of highway motels in Indianola, the Best Western is generally the choice property, although it costs slightly more than the others. Still, Indianola's rooms are well

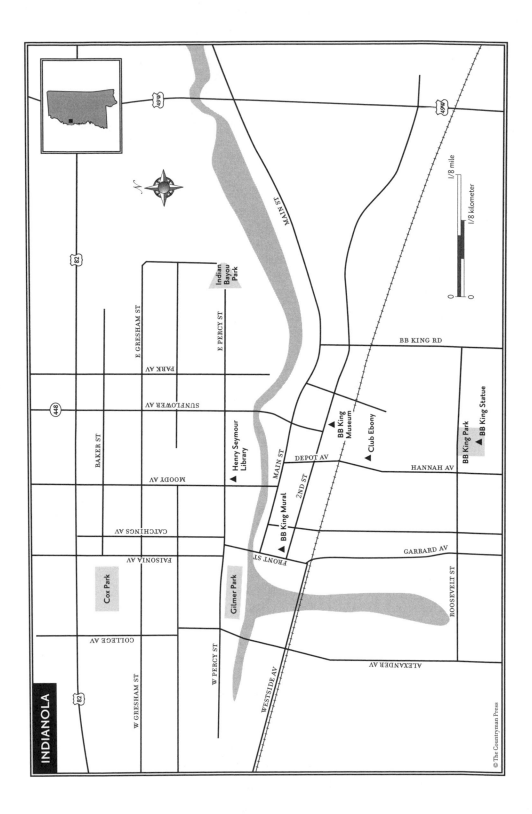

INDIANOLA

© The Countryman Press

1/8 mile
1/8 kilometer

82
449W
82
448
449W

Cox Park

COLLEGE AV

W GRESHAM ST

BAKER ST

E GRESHAM ST

FAISONIA AV

CATCHINGS AV

MOODY AV

SUNFLOWER AV

PARK AV

E PERCY ST

Gilmer Park

W PERCY ST

WESTSIDE AV

FRONT ST

MAIN ST

MAIN ST

Indian Bayou Park

Henry Seymour Library ▲

BB King Mural ▲

DEPOT AV

2ND ST

BB King Museum ▲

Club Ebony ▲

GARRARD AV

HANNAH AV

BB KING RD

ROOSEVELT ST

ALEXANDER AV

BB King Park
▲ BB King Statue

under $100 per night, with the majority hitting closer to $50 or $60, plus tax. All but the Travel Inn have Internet access, and the Best Western and Super 8 have outdoor pools. The accommodations listed below are all less than 2 miles from downtown.

Best Western Blues Traveler Inn
662-887-6611
www.bestwestern.com
910 US 82 E., Indianola, MS 38751

Days Inn
662-887-4242
www.daysinn.com
1015 US 82 E., Indianola, MS 38751

Economy Inn
662-887-6655
1112 US 82 E., Indianola, MS 38751

Super 8
662-887-7477
www.super8.com
601 US 82 W., Indianola, MS 38751

Travel Inn
662-887-2013
1110 US 82 E., Indianola, MS 38751

Culture

B. B. King Museum and Delta Interpretive Center
662-887-3009
www.bbkingmuseum.org
101 S. Sunflower Ave., Indianola, MS 38751
Open: Daily
Admission: Adults $10; seniors (over 65) and students $5; children (under 5) free

Truly the world's ambassador of the blues, and Indianola's favorite son, Riley B. King, aka B. B. King, is dutifully honored here in his adopted hometown at the B. B. King Museum and Delta Interpretive Center. From his humble beginnings in Itta Bena through his gradual rise to international fame, the museum tells King's life story, as well as that of the Delta itself. Opened in the fall of 2008, the museum is partly located in a historic brick cotton gin where King used to work. Visitors start off with an introductory video, then explore various exhibits that illustrate what life in the Delta was like for King and others regarding everything from race relations to the realities of sharecropping. Visitors will learn how B. B. became known as the Beale Street Boy, get a glimpse into what life on the road was like, interact with musical instruments and mixing stations in the museum's blues studio, and much more. The region's rich music, art, literature, and folklore are also given plenty of display space.

B. B. King Park
Roosevelt St., between Pershing and Hanna aves., Indianola, MS 38751

Located in a residential area south of the train tracks, B. B. King Park is home to a life-size statue of the King of the Blues. A nice brick walkway leads the way to B. B. in bronze, captured mid-riff with *Lucille* atop a platform overlooking a grassy area. Beyond the statue, a playground, basketball court, and a few benches complete the park. The park's sign and statue are good photo ops for fans of B. B., and also a good opportunity to drive down B. B. King Road; from the park, head east on Roosevelt, and B. B. King Road is just beyond Pershing.

B. B. King's Handprints, Footprints, and Mural
Corner of Second and Church sts., Indianola, MS 38751

This corner, just north of the railroad tracks, was hometown hero B. B. King's favorite busking spot when he was still an unknown teenager. While he started out singing gospel tunes, B. B. soon learned that blues music earned him more tips. The sidewalk is now marked with B. B.'s hand- and footprints—imprinted in 1980. There's also a sidewalk painting of B. B. King's guitar, *Lucille;* a historical marker; and a framed black-and-white photo of a young B. B. mounted on the brick wall above the sidewalk. After paying your respects at B. B.'s corner, head west on Second Street toward Front, where a mural of the King of the Blues wailing on *Lucille* is painted on the side of a building.

Located near B. B. King's hand- and footprints, this mural was painted by Mississippi artist Lawrence Quinn in 2001.

Church Street Blues Trail Marker
www.msbluestrail.org
Corner of Church and Mill sts., Indianola, MS 38751

The heart of Church Street is just south of the railroad tracks from B. B. King's old busking spot. In an era of segregation, this thoroughfare was central to the African American community, offering everything from doctors' offices and clothing stores to churches and late-night jukes. It was a place where African American businesses and culture thrived. Today, you can still find a few jukes along Church Street, but live music is a rarity. Thankfully, there are two great juke joints just around the corner.

Seasonal Events

|UNE

B. B. King Homecoming Festival
Fletcher Park and Club Ebony, Indianola, MS 38751

For the past three decades, B. B. King has returned to Mississippi to perform a concert in his hometown of Indianola, where, as a young man, he performed on Church Street for tips. Sponsored by the Indianola Chamber of Commerce, the event has grown over the years to become the B. B. King Homecoming Festival. Held at Fletcher Park, the festivities include a performance by B. B. King, plus live music by regional acts, food, fireworks, and more. The gates generally open around 4 PM, and the music gets going at 5. After the festival at Fletcher Park, King generally plays at Club Ebony, the celebrated Indianola juke joint that he now owns.

Nightlife

Club Ebony
Call Betty Fowler at 662-887-5436 or 662-207-5498
www.clubebony.biz
404 Hanna Ave., Indianola, MS 38751

In operation since 1945, this legendary juke joint has hosted big-name acts like James Brown, Ray Charles, Count Basie, Ike Turner, Howlin' Wolf, and, of course, B. B. King— who purchased the club in 2008 and regularly plays here following his annual homecoming concert in Fletcher Park. The spacious green structure is located in a residential area just south of the railroad tracks, and it is generally open Thursday through Sunday. There's usually live blues every Sunday night, and some Thursdays. When a band's not cranking, the jukebox provides the tunes, or occasionally, a DJ. Club Ebony also offers good eats like catfish, burgers, fried or grilled chicken, buffalo wings, and fried green tomatoes.

308 Blues Club and Café
662-887-7800
www.308bluesclubandcafe.com
308 Depot Ave., Indianola, MS 38751

Located just north of Club Ebony by the train tracks (where Hanna Avenue becomes Depot), this attractive brick-front club has been around since 2003. The dark, roomy venue hosts live music most weekends, including blues, rock, and beyond. This is a modern club, which means—for one thing—there's a full bar. You can also use a credit card here, and order up some soul food or a meat 'n three. In addition to two bars, 308 has a pair of pool tables, and the satellite radio generally stays tuned to the blues station.

Restaurants

The Crown Restaurant

662-887-4522
www.thecrownrestaurant.com
112 Front St., Indianola, MS 38751
Open: Tues.–Sat.
Price: Inexpensive–Moderate
Credit Cards: Yes
Cuisine: Luncheon, regional
Serving: L
Handicap Access: Yes
Special Features: Shop

You can't miss this coral-colored brick storefront in the heart of downtown Indianola. A local fixture since 1976 (although it used to be located in a rural area north of town), the Crown is divided into two sections: a cute dining room frequented by lunching ladies, and a shop stocked with gifts, books, art, and, most importantly, dessert mixes and award-winning catfish pâté—which you can taste, along with other goodies. Sample your way through the shop before settling into the cheery dining room, where coral walls are covered in vibrant local artwork—all for sale, of course, along with the antique furniture you're eating off. Expect friendly, helpful service in both the restaurant and the shop.

Lunch begins with piping hot, fresh-baked bread, sliced in wedges, that's served throughout the meal. Try a piece of both the regular beer bread and the sun-dried tomato basil version. Like what you taste? Pick up some bread mix on your way out. For the main course, light luncheon items include chicken salad, soup and salad, and a catfish salad plate. Heartier entrées, which are served with a salad and dessert, include the Crown's popular Catfish Allison, a rich poached catfish gratinéed with Parmesan cheese, butter, and green onion sauce. You can order a chicken breast cooked the same way, or try Catfish Florentine, made with a spinach cream sauce and Swiss cheese. Chances are, you'll be eying that dessert table at the back of the room throughout lunch. When it's finally time to splurge, serve yourself a taste of as many pies as you can handle. They taste as good as they sound, with names like Mississippi Delta Fudge Pie, Southern Praline Pie, Grand Old Chess Pie, and Magnolia Macaroon Pie. When you've had your fill, pick up some mix for the desserts you just devoured, and pay for lunch at the shop. Hint: Don't wait for the check to come to your table, or you'll be sitting there for a while. Simply tell them what you ordered at the shop's register, and you'll be on your way.

Nola

662-887-2990
112 Court Ave., Indianola, MS 38751
Open: Mon.–Sat.
Price: Inexpensive–Moderate

Credit Cards: Yes
Cuisine: American, regional
Serving: L (Mon.–Sat.), D (Wed.–Sat.)
Handicap Access: Yes

Breathing new life into Indianola's limited dining scene in 2008, this downtown restaurant is housed in what was once the Old Regent Theatre, a 1920s silent-movie house. In tribute to the old theater, exposed brick walls are covered in classic movie posters—many of them based in the South. The vibe is casual and artsy, and the menu features everything from down-home favorites to more exotic offerings. Start off with an order of the popular catfish sliders, and then choose from sandwich, steak, and seafood selections served with sides like sweet potato fries. Lunchtime favorites include the Ultimate BLT sandwich, made with fried green tomatoes and caramelized onions. Popular dinner entrées include shrimp and grits, catfish-based pasta dishes, and a grilled tuna steak.

Shopping

Gin Mill Galleries
662-887-3209
www.ginmillgalleries.com
109 Pershing Ave., Indianola, MS 38751

Located within an old cotton gin near the B. B. King Museum, this unique spot houses both a gallery and a restaurant—with live music and a great regional shop to boot. In fact, the Gin Mill claims to be the largest privately owned art gallery in Mississippi. In addition to paintings by Delta artists, the gallery offers photography, pottery, and glass art—plus shelves stocked with blues CDs, books, food seasonings, cookbooks, and plenty of blues-themed items. On the restaurant side of the building, corrugated tin walls and exposed beam ceilings are covered with guitars, artwork, and blues posters. The menu features regional favorites like tamales, a sausage and cheese plate, and pulled pork, plus all sorts of sandwiches, like a grilled pimento cheese, muffuletta, and the famous fried bologna sandwich. Thursday and Sunday nights, weather permitting, steak and salmon are served straight off the grill. For dessert, the Cool Moon consists of a Moon Pie topped with ice cream. Lunch and dinner are generally served Wednesday through Monday, and there's live music most weekends, including some blues.

Indianola Pecan House
662-887-5420
www.pecanhouse.com
1013 US 82 E., Indianola, MS 38751

Starting out as a simple pecan-cracking operation back in 1979, this family-owned business now boasts several retail locations, a thriving catalog and Internet business, and products in retail outlets across the country. And it all started here in Indianola at the original Pecan House. Stop by to sample some of more than 25 types of flavored pecans, including a Jack Daniel's Whiskey Praline variety. There are also cookies, candy, pecan pie mix, and all sorts of gourmet food items. Gift baskets, tins, and Delta gift items are also available.

MOORHEAD

Culture

Where the Southern Crosses the Dog
Moorhead, MS
Directions: From US 82, go south on Olive Street to Southern Avenue by the railroad tracks

Moorhead, Mississippi . . . "where the Southern crosses the Dog." As the story goes, while W. C. Handy was waiting on a train in Tutwiler, he heard an old bluesman scraping a knife's blade across the neck of a guitar, singing those words. This is what he was referring to: The Southern being the old Southern Railroad, and the Dog (or Yellow Dog) referring to the Yazoo Delta Railroad, whose tracks crossed here in Moorhead. While the tracks may no longer intersect (due to safety), both lines are still there and have been preserved for posterity. A couple of benches have been conveniently placed in front of the historic marker near a covered gazebo, and the grassy, tree-lined area surrounding the tracks is a pleasant place to take a load off.

The famed railroad track intersection "where the Southern crosses the Dog" has appeared in blues songs by W. C. Handy, Charley Patton, Bessie Smith, and many more.

BERCLAIR

Culture

B. B. King Birthplace Marker

www.msbluestrail.org

Berclair, MS

Directions: From US 82, turn south onto Berclair Road. Just across the railroad tracks, take the first right onto Blue Lake Road. The marker is located down a ways at the fork in the road.

Located at the site of his birth, this is one of two Blues Trail markers honoring famed Mississippi bluesman B. B. King, born Riley B. King on September 16, 1925. The Berclair marker pays tribute to B. B. in the town in which he was born. While it's often said that B. B. King was born in nearby Itta Bena, teeny Berclair is actually a few miles southwest. Born the son of sharecroppers, King was first exposed to the blues through work songs he heard while picking cotton on Delta plantations. This, coupled with the gospel music he heard in church, would take root in young Riley and color the music that would eventually be heard around the world.

GREENWOOD

Arguably the loveliest town in the Delta, verdant (and aptly named) Greenwood is home to several Blues Trail markers, including Robert Johnson's final resting place just north of town. Johnson frequently played for tips south of the tracks on Johnson Street (which is not named for him, however) along with other blues greats like Elmore James and Sonny Boy Williamson II. Robert Johnson lived his final days in Greenwood's Baptist Town neighborhood, east on Johnson Street where it turns into Carrollton Avenue. While some argue that he actually died in Baptist Town, it is now believed that the bluesman took his final breaths at a location outside of town. In more recent Robert Johnson history, it was in downtown's Leflore County Courthouse in 1998 that the dispute over his estate was settled 62 years after his death. While the blues legend never saw a penny of his royalties, includ- ing the significant revenues from Columbia Records's hit release of his complete record- ings in 1990, the sole ownership of the estate was awarded to Claud Johnson, the bluesman's son.

Sadly, there aren't too many places to hear live blues music in Greenwood these days, although the Blue Parrot features blues in its weekend rotation, and there's occasionally a blues artist at the Alluvian's happy hour, or playing at Webster's. Unlike many Delta towns, there's plenty to do here beyond visiting blues sites. Greenwood boasts a well-preserved historic downtown, three rivers (the Tallahatchie, Yalobusha, and Yazoo), gorgeous turn of-the-20th-century homes, and a handful of fantastic restaurants. In addition to the Mississippi Delta's most luxurious hotel, there are boutiques and antiques shops on quaint Howard Street, and stately homes to gawk at on both the oak-tree-lined Grand Boulevard and River Road bordering the Yazoo River. Known as the Cotton Capital of the World, Greenwood is also home to the second-largest cotton exchange in the United States (after Memphis), located on downtown's historic Cotton Row. Civil War buffs may also want to visit Fort Pemberton Park to see where *The Star of the West* rests at the bottom of the Tallahatchie River. The shots fired upon this Union steamship at Fort Sumter signaled the start the Civil War.

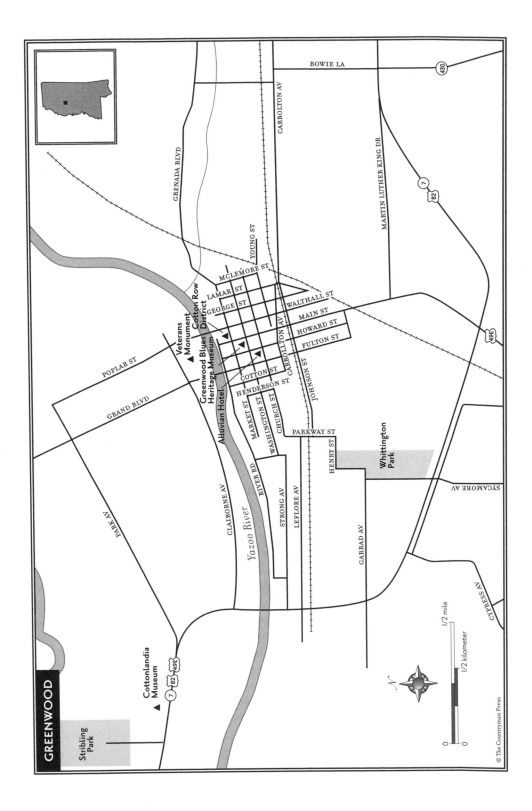

Lodging

One of the few Delta cities to offer a range of lodging options, Greenwood's handful of unique accommodations include a pair of bed & breakfasts, converted sharecropper shacks, and the finest accommodations in the Mississippi Delta. There are also plenty of chains just beyond downtown on US 82.

INNS AND BED & BREAKFASTS

The Alluvian

662-453-2114, 1-866-600-5201
www.thealluvian.com
318 Howard St., Greenwood, MS 38930
Downtown Greenwood
Price: Expensive–Very Expensive
Credit Cards: Yes
Handicap Access: Yes
Special Features: Free wireless, breakfast; on-site restaurant and bar

Luxurious, boutique-style accommodations in the heart of the Delta? Yes, indeed. A welcome relief from the region's endless motels, this posh property in the heart of lovely downtown Greenwood gives Memphis's finest hotels a run for their money. Owned by Viking Range Corporation founder and CEO, Fred Carl Jr., the Alluvian has breathed new life into downtown Greenwood—not to mention Carl's aggressive restoration of downtown's historic buildings. Hands down the nicest place to stay in the Mississippi Delta, the Alluvian manages to exude chic, urban style without losing a warm sense of Southern hospitality. Inside the lobby, sleek marble floors and contemporary design elements blend seamlessly with local artwork and fine-art photography. The property features 45 rooms, 5 suites, and 4 extended-stay lofts, all of which feature roomy bathrooms with marble floors and showers, flat-screen TVs, and quite possibly the Delta's most comfortable bed. Bonus: You can purchase the heavenly linens across the street at the Viking retail store. Suites are equipped with whirlpool tubs, while all accommodations boast luxurious extras like cushy robes, wireless Internet, electric safes, and a well-stocked honor bar. There's plenty of room to spread out, with a work nook and a comfy purple armchair with a large round ottoman to kick back in.

The hotel's common areas provide plenty of places to bask in the luxury. A full, Southern-style breakfast buffet (included with the room rate) is served every morning in the fourth-floor terrace room, a stylish but cozy area with a stainless-steel and green tile fireplace, several tables and seating areas, a shelf of books, and a lovely outdoor terrace overlooking downtown Greenwood. Downstairs, a contemporary lounge area with plenty of Delta soul features leather chairs, striking local artwork, a grand piano, and a nice selection of coffee table books on the area. Across the way, Giardina's cozy bar area connecting the lobby to the restaurant is a sharp spot for cocktails, with rich wood accents, marble tables, and a mosaic tile floor. If it's not too hot, the small courtyard with a trickling fountain behind the hotel is another pleasant spot to settle in for a while. Every Thursday and Friday night from 5 to 8, the bar and patio fill up for the Alluvian's popular happy hour, which features live music.

Greenwood's Bridgewater Inn is located a few doors down from the Rivers' Inn Bed & Breakfast.

Bridgewater Inn Bed & Breakfast

662-453-9265, 1-877-793-7473
www.bbonline.com/ms/bridgewater
501 River Rd., Greenwood, MS 38930
Just outside downtown Greenwood
Price: Inexpensive–Moderate
Credit Cards: Yes
Handicap Access: No
Special Features: Wireless Internet; corporate discount during the week; senior citizen discount

This grand 1910 Greek Revival house perched on genteel River Road feels like it's straight out of a Tennessee Williams play. The white-columned property features expansive patios on both levels with rocking chairs and fantastic views of the Yazoo River. Inside, formal living and dining rooms are adorned with antique furnishings, intricate chandeliers, and stained-glass window accents. Two rooms with king beds share a bathroom and have direct access to the upstairs porch, while one of these rooms also features a fireplace. A third room with a queen bed has a sitting area and a private bathroom with a claw-foot tub. The inn also offers one suite with a queen and a day bed, separate sitting area, private sun porch, and a private bathroom with a claw-foot tub. Guests have access to a computer with

Internet as well as a fax machine. Continental breakfast is served during the week, while weekend mornings start off with a full meal that may be an omelet, French toast, pancakes, or similar. A few additional rooms are also available at the property next door, including a suite with a whirlpool tub.

The Rivers' Inn Bed & Breakfast

662-453-5432
1109 River Rd., Greenwood, MS 38930
Less than a mile northwest of downtown
Price: Inexpensive
Credit Cards: Yes
Handicap Access: Yes
Special Features: Free wireless; long-term rates available

Located along historic River Road, this comfortable brick home was built in 1912. Outside, the front of the house is lined with white New Orleans–style ironwork, and in the backyard, there's a pool (call ahead to find out if it's open). While the inn is usually home to working professionals during the week, leisure travelers are welcome anytime. Three spacious bedrooms downstairs feature private bathrooms, antique furniture, and unique accents like deep pink walls, floral window treatments, and hardwood floors. Two more rooms on the second level share a bathroom. Ample well-appointed common areas include a formal dining room and a glassed-in garden patio, where a full Southern-style breakfast is served every morning.

Tallahatchie Flats

662-453-1854, 1-877-453-1854
www.tallahatchieflats.com
58458 County Rd. 518, Greenwood, MS 38930
North of downtown Greenwood
Price: Inexpensive
Credit Cards: Yes
Handicap Access: No

Heading north on Grand Boulevard, approximately 3 miles north of Greenwood, you'll come upon a row of six sharecropper shacks that are reminiscent of (and inspired by) the Shack Up Inn in Clarksdale. These would be the Tallahatchie Flats: re-created Delta farmhouses, located along the Tallahatchie River on a working cotton plantation, that have been reengineered to provide an authentic experience without the sacrifice of oh, say, modern plumbing and heating. The three- or four-room shacks are part authentic sharecropper digs—wood-plank floors, tin roofs, period antique decor—and part modern accommodations with full kitchens and even a flat-screen satellite TV (in the Red House). Each shack is equipped with front and back porches, the latter of which overlook the river. Adding to the area's Robert Johnson lore, it is hinted that one of the shacks may be the home where the bluesman died after his fatal poisoning in 1938. Johnson's grave site is located less than a mile up the road in the cemetery at Little Zion Church. Rentable by the day, week, or month, the shacks (or "tenant houses," as they're locally known) accommodate two to four people, depending upon the unit. The owners have plans to add several more shacks to the

"Mr. Bubba's Place" at Tallahatchie Flats is where guests pick up their keys before settling into their own personal shack.

grounds, as well as the Tallahatchie Tavern commissary. The grounds are the main site of the Rhythm on the River Festival held on Labor Day weekend, which includes live blues, jazz, country, and gospel music, plus food, beer, and more.

MOTELS
Greenwood has several chain hotels in all price ranges, from basic accommodations for rock-bottom rates (under $50) to pricier properties with expanded amenities (more than $100). The accommodations in this section are all less than 3 miles (five minutes) from downtown. The Best Western, Ramada Inn, and Travel Inn feature outdoor pools, while the Hampton Inn has an indoor-outdoor version. The Holiday Inn Express, new in 2007, features 27-inch flat-screen TVs.

America's Best Inn & Suites
662-453-4364
www.americasbestinngreenwood.com
335 US 82 W., Greenwood, MS 38930

Best Western Greenwood
662-455-5777
www.bestwestern.com
635 US 82 W., Greenwood, MS 38930

Econo Lodge Inn & Suites
662-453-5974
www.econolodge.com
401 US 82 W., Greenwood, MS 38930

Golden Coach Inn
662-453-5561
1900 Strong Ave., Greenwood, MS 38930

Hampton Inn
662-455-7985
www.hamptoninn.com
1815 US 82 W., Greenwood, MS 38930

Holiday Inn Express
662-455-1885
www.hiexpress.com
401 Clements St., Greenwood, MS 38930

Ramada Inn
662-455-2321
www.ramada.com
900 W. Park Ave., Greenwood, MS 38930

The Regency Inn & Suites
662-453-8101
620 US 82 W., Greenwood, MS 38930

Relax Inn
662-455-8008
1705 Garrard Ave., Greenwood, MS 38930

Travel Inn
662-453-8810
623 US 82 W., Greenwood, MS 38930

Culture

Cottonlandia Museum
662-453-0925
www.cottonlandia.org
1608 US 82 W., Greenwood, MS 38930
Open: Daily
Admission: Adults $5; seniors and college students $3.50; children (4–18) $2

Don't let the name fool you. Greenwood's Cottonlandia Museum strives to present the Delta's history and heritage using the self-described five A's: art, archaeology, agriculture, antiques, and animals. Strolling through the museum, you'll experience the five A's, and much more, with exhibits that include regional folk art; a life-size, walk-in diorama depicting Mississippi swamp life; and enough prehistoric fossils to make the Flintstones jealous. Those interested in the region's military history will want to be sure to follow the battle timeline of the area's various exploits and campaigns, from the battlefields of the Civil War to the impact of World War II.

Elks Lodge Blues Trail Marker
www.msbluestrail.org
Ave. F and Scott St., Greenwood, MS 38930

Not just an ordinary Elks Lodge, this location (Lodge #640) on the south side of the tracks regularly played host to blues, R&B, and soul artists—including B. B. King, Etta James, T-Bone Walker, Ike and Tina Turner, James Brown, and many more—from the 1940s through the 1970s. During the segregation era, the "Black Elks," as they were known, were established under the IBPOEW: the Improved Benevolent Protective Order of the Elks of the World. Throughout the South, these lodges became important gathering places where African Americans held political and social events.

Greenwood Blues Heritage Museum & Gallery
662-451-7800
222 Howard St., Greenwood, MS 38930
Open: Mon.–Sat.
Admission: Free

Owned and operated by local blues collector and historian Stephen LaVere, the Greenwood Blues Heritage Museum & Gallery opened its doors in downtown Greenwood in 2001. The museum has an impressive collection by even the most stringent of standards, and LaVere regularly switches out displays to keep the museum fresh—warranting repeat visits. The museum is located above the Blue Parrot Café in the historic Three Deuces building, for-mer home of WGRM radio, where B. B. King was first broadcast live with the St. John's Gospel Singers. The collection's second-story home provides a warm, cozy atmosphere with rich woods, and chock-full-o-blues display cases house everything from blues LPs to aged, yellowing photographs of the Delta greats. The museum's crown jewel is a staggering assortment of extremely rare Robert Johnson 78s—reportedly the world's most complete collection. Not surprisingly, rock 'n' roll is also represented, with records, autographs, prints, and posters that would make even the Hard Rock Café envious.

Greenwood Heritage Tours
662-451-7800
www.threedeuces.net
222 Howard St., Greenwood, MS 38930

Tour the stomping grounds of Robert Johnson and Mississippi John Hurt (from nearby Avalon) on a three-hour Delta Blues Tour. Operated by the Greenwood Blues Museum, the van or bus tours stick to the back roads for an authentic Delta experience, during which guides sing work songs, field hollers, and spirituals. See the fields that gave birth to these plantation songs and learn how they morphed into blues standards. The tour will take you to all three of Robert Johnson's grave markers, the town of Avalon, and beyond.

Greenwood Heritage Tours also offers Civil War, literary, civil rights, cotton plantation, and Native American tours that last from one to three hours.

Hubert Sumlin Blues Trail Marker
www.msbluestrail.org
Greenwood, MS
Directions: From US 82 (Frontage Road), turn west onto Strong Avenue just south of the Yazoo River Bridge (by the hospital). At the dead end (one block), turn right; the marker is on the right.

Hubert Sumlin is honored with a Blues Trail marker just west of the Pillow plantation, where he was born on November 16, 1931. Cited by *Rolling Stone* magazine in 2003 as one of "the 100 greatest guitarists of all time," Sumlin made a name for himself on the Chicago blues scene backing his longtime mentor, Howlin' Wolf, both live and on records cut for the legendary Chess label. In addition to Wolf, Sumlin lent his guitar talents (in the studio and on the stage) to various music legends, including Chuck Berry, Muddy Waters, Willie Dixon, Sonny Boy Williamson, Eric Clapton, and the Rolling Stones, among many others. In 2008, Sumlin was inducted into the Blues Hall of Fame.

Robert Johnson's Grave—Greenwood
Little Zion Missionary Baptist Church, Greenwood, MS
Directions: From downtown Greenwood, drive north over the Yazoo River on Grand Boulevard (becomes Money Road). The church will be on the left.

While there are headstones for Robert Johnson in both Quito and Morgan City, Greenwood's grave site is thought to be his true final resting place, thanks to an eyewitness.

One of three grave sites in Mississippi said to be the final resting place of famed bluesman Robert Johnson, this location, it seems, may be the actual site of his burial. While the Little Zion M.B. Church cemetery was the last of the grave sites to receive a marker, it's the only site with an eyewitness. Rosie Eskridge has gone on record stating that she witnessed her husband, Tom, bury Johnson here in this cemetery. Although she's not certain of the exact spot, Eskridge recalls the casket lying next to a large tree where the hole was being dug. As if to make it official, this is the only one of Johnson's grave sites with a Blues Trail marker. It also happens to be the most picturesque of the three sites, situated north of town next to a pine-tree-shaded church on a country road surrounded by endless fields. It's a lovely drive from downtown Greenwood, heading north on the oak-tree-lined Grand Avenue and over the Yazoo River, where the town abruptly ends and the cotton fields begin. Johnson's headstone is located near the middle of the cemetery beneath a large pecan tree. It's likely to be adorned with guitar picks, empty bottles of bourbon, and weathered photos of Johnson, left by fellow blues travelers.

WGRM Radio Blues Trail Marker
www.msbluestrail.org
222 Howard St., Greenwood, MS 38930

The historic Three Deuces building, which now houses the Blue Parrot Café and the Blues Heritage Museum, was the former home to WGRM radio, which began broadcasting from this location in 1939. Whereas most radio shied away from integrated programming during that time, gospel music was an exception to the rule, and WGRM regularly broadcast the famous St. John's Gospel Singers. The popular gospel group included one Riley King on guitar, who would later change his name to B. B. and go on to become the world's ambassador to the blues. This was the first time B. B. King was broadcast live on the radio.

Restaurants

Crystal Grill
662-453-6530
423 Carrollton Ave., Greenwood, MS 38930
Open: Tues.–Sun.
Price: Inexpensive–Moderate
Credit Cards: Yes
Cuisine: Regional
Serving: L, D
Handicap Access: Yes

The old brick building by the railroad tracks at the corner of Lamar and Carrollton has been serving food of some sort for nearly a century. Owned by the same family since 1932, the small 60-seat café gradually expanded into a sprawling neighborhood institution that now seats around 250. Throughout the maze of dining rooms, paper place mats encourage diners of all faiths to give thanks before their meal. Grab a seat in the cozy back dining room and settle in among the friendly locals. The varied menu features steaks, seafood, and pasta, but the Southern delicacies on the special Sunday menu can't be beat. Supper starts with warm yeast rolls followed by regional specialties like addictive fried pickles, hot tamales, extra-crispy fried chicken, shrimp Creole, and maybe even fried frog's legs.

Whatever you decide upon, save room for dessert. The Crystal Grill is famous throughout the Delta for its mile-high coconut and chocolate meringue pies, although the lemon icebox pie is equally fantastic.

Delta Bistro

662-455-9575
www.deltabistro.com
117 Main St., Greenwood, MS 38930
Open: Mon.–Sat.
Price: Moderate–Expensive
Credit Cards: Yes
Cuisine: Upscale regional
Serving: L, D
Handicap Access: Yes
Special Features: Bring your own wine ($2 corkage fee) or liquor; take-out window

Located in the heart of downtown Greenwood in the historic Nored Cotton Company building, this charming, eclectic bistro remains rooted in the past. Large skylights originally used for cotton classifying let in plenty of light, while the original exposed-brick walls are now covered in artwork by co-owner/chef Taylor Ricketts and her husband (available for purchase). The seasonally updated menu includes globe-spanning small-plate selections, tasty sandwiches, and dressed-up regional entrées. Lunch may include a fried green tomato and bacon sandwich, barbecue shrimp po' boy, or a toasted pimento cheese sandwich with a side of crispy sweet potato fries. Dinner items include shrimp over cheese grits, pan-roasted artichoke and sun-dried tomato stuffed chicken, and Cajun andouille pasta. You can also get a nicely prepared filet mignon or rib eye. Lunch and dinner specials change daily, and Wednesday night is sushi night.

Giardina's Restaurant

662-455-4227
www.thealluvian.com/giardinas.html
314 Howard St., Greenwood, MS 38930
Open: Daily
Price: Moderate–Expensive
Credit Cards: Yes
Cuisine: Italian, steaks, seafood
Serving: D
Handicap Access: Yes
Special Features: Full bar

A sleeker, shinier version of its humble original location established outside of town on Park Avenue in 1936, Giardina's (pronounced Gardina's) is now located within the posh Alluvian Hotel. A handsome bar connecting the hotel to the waiting area sets a sophisticated tone without being stuffy. Inside the restaurant, the main dining room features well-worn hardwood floors, white tablecloths, and vibrant local artwork. The choice tables, however, are located in private booths with heavy green curtains and a buzzer to call the waiter (much like Lusco's). The dinner menu is heavy on steak, seafood, and Italian entrées, with a few Delta and Creole selections thrown in for good measure. Start with one of many seafood appetizers, including crawfish bisque, seafood gumbo, or oysters offered five different ways. In addition to steaks, there are a slew of Italian entrées to choose from, like spaghetti with meatballs, beef ravioli, lasagna, various pastas, and veal prepared three ways. As for seafood options, there are broiled fish fillets (catfish, grouper, or red snapper), fried or broiled shrimp, and fried soft-shell crab. Giardina's also offers a whole broiled pompano and flounder. For dessert, Italian specialties like gelato, tiramisu, panna cotta, and cannoli are the highlight. Giardina's also boasts a wine list that's impressive by any standards (even beyond the Delta), with more than 300 bottles from across the globe, around 20 half-bottle selections, and nearly 30 wines offered by the glass.

Lusco's
662-453-5365
722 Carrollton Ave., Greenwood, MS 38930
Open: Tues.–Sat.
Price: Moderate–Expensive
Credit Cards: Yes
Cuisine: Steak, seafood
Serving: D
Handicap Access: No
Special Features: Bring your own wine and liquor; sauces and dressings available for purchase

A local institution since 1933, this storied restaurant started out as a grocery store with a limited menu. It wasn't until the owners added private, curtained booths in the back (where guests could enjoy Lusco's homemade wine and beer in private) that the restaurant gained notoriety. Of course, there are plenty of rumors that those curtained booths were also appreciated by many a cotton mogul and his mistress. Today, the restaurant is run by the family's fourth generation—and yes, the booths are still there. Lusco's may be on the rough side of the tracks, but inside, the atmosphere is warm, friendly, and rich with well-worn character. Don't miss the framed tablecloth scrawled with a poem by local literary legend Willie Morris, who wrote *My Dog Skip*, among other titles. Beneath the lofty tin ceiling, mossy green booths boast individual coat racks, spinning fans overhead, and buzzers to summon the waiter.

Even without the unique atmosphere, Lusco's menu is a Delta standout, anchored by steaks and seafood with influences from Italy to New Orleans. Start with a cup of seafood or crawfish gumbo, oysters on the half shell (in season), or crispy homemade onion rings. Don't bypass the salads; this is one of the very few places in the Delta where you'll find mixed greens on the menu. Selections include Lusco's Special Salad, topped with capers, olives, and anchovies; a Mediterranean salad; and the knockout crabmeat salad. For the main event, Lusco's is well known for its steaks, from a T-bone for two to the filet mignon, all cut on-site and priced according to weight. Seafood standouts include shrimp broiled in Lusco's famous shrimp sauce, a deliciously tangy combination of butter, Worcestershire, and lemon that's served hot or mild. You can also try crabmeat broiled in either the fish or shrimp sauce. Broiled fish selections include a popular whole pompano (in season). Sides range from homemade french fries to a fantastic spinach soufflé.

Veronica's Custom Bakery/Blue Parrot Café

662-451-9425, 662-451-9430

www.threedeuces.net

222 Howard St., Greenwood, MS 38930

Open: Tues.–Sat.

Price: Inexpensive–Moderate

Credit Cards: Yes

Cuisine: Bakery, American, Latin

Serving: L (Tues.–Sat.), D (Fri.–Sat.)

Handicap Access: Yes

Special Features: Wireless Internet; Blue Parrot is closed Jan.–mid-Mar. and Sept.–late Nov.

Located downstairs from the Greenwood Blues Museum in the historic Three Deuces building, this popular spot is a lunch café, dinner restaurant, and live-music venue. Inside, exposed-brick walls, rich hardwood floors, antique furniture, and lofty ceilings create a charming ambience. The main room is anchored by a bakery display case stocked with tempting goodies like coconut macaroons, turtle cookies, Cuban pastries, and scones. Veronica's also offers fresh-brewed coffee and made-to-order bread, pies, and cakes. To the right of the bakery counter, a staircase lined with blues posters and records leads to the museum above. To the left, a narrow dining area opens up to a slightly larger room with several tables and a stage in the corner. By day, the café offers a lunch menu with eclectic salads, croissant sandwiches, and daily specials. On weekend evenings, the Blue Parrot serves Latin cuisine and dishes from Cuba, Puerto Rico, Mexico, and Italy. Entrées include *ropa vieja* (shredded beef with onions), Italian meatballs, carne asada, and pan-roasted fish of the day. The restaurant also serves specialty Latin cocktails, martinis, and tropical concoctions that you won't find many other places in the Delta. One night each weekend, there's live music during dinner, which may be blues, jazz, or a local singer-songwriter.

Webster's Food and Drink

662-455-1215

www.webstersfoodanddrink.com

216 W. Claiborne Ave., Greenwood, MS 38930

Open: Mon.–Sat.

Price: Moderate

Credit Cards: Yes

Cuisine: American, regional

Serving: D

Handicap Access: Limited

Special Features: Live music; full bar; happy hour

A local Greenwood hangout since 1975, Webster's can easily be summed up by its unofficial motto: "good food, good friends, good times!" Not surprisingly, the establishment takes great pride in creating an environment where regulars can come in and unwind with a few drinks and some good food. Regional comfort food rules the menu (shrimp po' boys, burgers, salads, pizzas, steaks, and seafood), with the option of dining in the homey main dining room or outside on the expansive patio. After the dinner hour, Webster's becomes a bar scene with live music and a full bar. Live music is featured two or three times a week (call ahead), with genres ranging from blues to classic rock.

Recreation

The Alluvian Spa
662-451-6700, 1-866-728-6700
www.thealluvian.com/alluvian_spa.html
325D Howard St., Greenwood, MS 38930

Located above the Viking Cooking School across the street from the Alluvian Hotel, this downtown oasis offers first-rate pampering with a splash of Delta flavor. In addition to standard spa offerings, the extensive service menu includes therapeutic baths, waxing, salon services, and couples treatments. While the spa would be at home in any cosmopolitan city, treatments give a nod to the Delta, in both name and process. Sweet tea makes several appearances, from the signature Sweet Tea Manicure to an exfoliating Sweet Tea Refresher body scrub and a therapeutic bath called the Sweet Tea Soul Soak. Even grits get into the mix as part of the Three Rivers body scrub. Among the menu of hydrotherapy baths, there's the Muddy Waters option for purification or the relaxing Blues Bath. Enjoy a sweet tea sorbet and cold or hot tea during an aromatic bath that's followed by a 30-minute massage using—you guessed it—a sweet tea massage cream. Sweet tea has never sounded so good.

Viking Cooking School
662-451-6750, 1-866-451-6750
www.thealluvian.com/cooking_school.html
325C Howard St., Greenwood, MS 38930

With the headquarters of the Viking Corporation occupying an entire block on historic Cotton Row, and offices spread through more than 10 restored historic buildings, a cooking school in the heart of downtown Greenwood was a natural extension for the Viking Range Corporation. A variety of classes are offered in the handsome test kitchen nearly every day of the week. Options range from hour-long demonstrations with appetizers and drinks to hands-on instruction that lasts five hours. Overseas culinary excursions and weekends with visiting chefs are also offered. The subject matter runs the gamut, from cooking Delta-style tamales, catfish, fried dill pickles, and mile-high coconut meringue pie at a Delta Dinner and Blues class to a session where participants learn to roll their own sushi. Of course, there's also instruction on the basics (soups and sauces, roasting and baking, soufflés) and specialized classes on topics like cakes, pies, and tarts.

Shopping

The Mississippi Gift Company
662-455-6961
www.themississippigiftcompany.com
300 Howard St., Greenwood, MS 38930

This cheery shop on Howard Street's main drag is a must-stop for locally produced art, food, books, jewelry, pottery, baskets, stationery, and more. Vibrant lime, orange, and chocolate walls contrast with the cement floors to create an artsy vibe that suits the shop's

Turnrow Books hosted its first annual Mississippi Delta Lay-By Literary & Music Festival in July 2008.

varied selection of goods. In the food section, stock up on sauces, spices, and dressings from famed Delta restaurants, including Lusco's fish and shrimp sauce, Lillo's steak marinade, and Giardina's house salad dressing. There are also cheese straws, preserves, and flavored pecans. Upstairs, a loft overlooking the store is stocked with a nice selection of local artwork that ranges from blues paintings to fine-art photography depicting Delta landscapes. If you're jonesing for more Mississippi-made goods after you leave the Delta, you can always order from the Mississippi Gift Company's catalog or Web site.

Turnrow Book Company

1-888-453-5995
www.turnrowbooks.com
304 Howard St., Greenwood, MS 38930

This inviting independent bookstore is the kind of place where you can easily, and quite happily, lose an hour or two. The shop is set up in a two-level shotgun configuration, with a narrow upper balcony running the length of the perimeter. Sturdy columns, an intricate ceiling, black chandeliers, and hardwood floors create the perfect environment for browsing an impressive regional section that includes fiction, nonfiction, and cookbooks. Book signings by local luminaries are frequent, and you can often find an autographed copy of titles by the likes of John Grisham and Daniel Wallace on the shelves. Upstairs, there are more books, plus local artwork and a small café for coffee, cookies, and a few breakfast items.

Viking Retail Store
662-451-6750
www.thealluvian.com/kitchen_center.html
325C Howard St., Greenwood, MS 38930

Located adjacent to the Viking Cooking School, this kitchen shop is a must-stop for culinary kings and queens. Browse an impressive selection of Viking's professional-quality cookware, cutlery, kitchen appliances, Viking logo gear, and much more. This is also the place to purchase the Alluvian's coveted bedding linens.

Avalon Area

Culture

Mississippi John Hurt Blues Trail Marker
www.msbluestrail.org
Valley, MS
Directions: Located southwest of the museum site on MS 41, just east the intersection with MS 254 (Hoffman Road)

Mississippi John Hurt was born on July 3, 1893, in Teoc, several miles from Avalon, where a Blues Trail marker was erected in his honor in 2008. The marker is located in front of the Valley Store, where Hurt once regularly played. Beginning his musical journey at the age of nine, Hurt would go on to record with the Okeh record label in the late 1920s, cutting songs that would become an intricate thread in the collective blues narrative, including "Stack 'O Lee," "Candy Man Blues," and "Frankie." Hurt would lead a fairly quiet life, playing for friends and family in Mississippi until the early 1960s, when, during the so-called blues revival, he became the toast of the Newport Folk Festival in Rhode Island. Hurt played the festival for the next few years until he died in 1966. He is buried in the St. James Cemetery in Avalon.

Mississippi John Hurt Museum/Blues & Gospel Festival
662-455-3958
www.msjohnhurtmuseum.com
1951 County Rd. 109, Carrollton, MS 38917
Open: By appointment
Admission: Adults $10; children (under 12) $5

Located off a dirt road southeast of Avalon, the Mississippi John Hurt Museum is housed in the very home where Hurt resided until his death. The structure allegedly only survived because it was used to store hay after the Hurts moved on. The museum now provides a look into the bluesman's life and career, through photographs, memorabilia, and original furnishings from the modest home. Blues travelers will want to spend some time exploring the surrounding area with a visit to Hurt's Blues Trail marker, grave site, and the Valley Store, where he regularly played for locals. Every July 4th weekend, the museum grounds host the Mississippi John Hurt Blues & Gospel Festival. Admission to the daylong event is $10, and festivities include live blues and gospel music, barbecue, and more.

Sharecropper shacks like this one, near Robert Johnson's Quito grave, are scattered along country roads across the Delta.

QUITO

Culture

Robert Johnson's Grave—Quito

32830 County Rd. 167, Quito, MS 38941

Directions: From US 82, follow MS 7 south past Itta Bena. Cross a bridge, then turn right (west) onto Leflore County 167 across from the Hardwicke Etter Ginning Systems cotton gin. The church will be on the right.

One of three grave sites in Mississippi said to be the final resting place of famed bluesman Robert Johnson, the Quito location in the Payne Chapel Missionary Baptist Church cemetery is aesthetically the least impressive of the three. It was one of Johnson's girlfriends who identified this as the bluesman's final resting place, although there's more evidence that he's buried in the Little Zion Church north of Greenwood. It is also said that Johnson was poisoned at the Three Forks Store just north of this grave site on the night of his final gig, although the exact location of the poisoning is also disputed, and the Three Forks Store is no longer there. The Payne Chapel is located down a lonely rural road dotted with rusted tin-roof shacks perched on cinderblocks. The actual gravestone, a small, flat, granite number adorned with an acoustic guitar and a treble clef, is positioned near the tree line. The simple stone reads: ROBERT JOHNSON / MAY 8, 1911—AUGUST 16, 1938 / RESTING IN THE BLUES. The stone was reportedly paid for by the Georgia-based rock 'n' roll band the Tombstones. How appropriate.

One of three grave sites for Robert Johnson is located in the cemetery of Morgan City's quaint Mount Zion Church.

MORGAN CITY

Culture

Robert Johnson's Grave—Morgan City

Morgan City, MS

Directions: Around 4 miles south of Quito on MS 7, look for a sign on the west side of the highway for a wildlife refuge. At the sign, turn left (east); church will be on the left.

Yet another Robert Johnson grave site in the Mississippi Delta. This one, located on the grounds of Mount Zion Missionary Baptist Church, boasts the most impressive headstone of the three. Funded by Sony Records, the carefully crafted obelisk pays tribute to Johnson with various inscriptions on all four sides, including the famous photograph of Johnson with a cigarette dangling from his mouth just above the oft-quoted inscription, KING OF THE DELTA BLUES SINGERS. While it was once believed that Johnson was indeed laid to rest here, the exact location of the plot was unknown, prompting the marker to be placed close to the road—per the lyrics, "you may bury my body down by the highway side" from Johnson's "Me and the Devil Blues." In the tiny, well-maintained cemetery, the plot is situated to the left of the small church and is predictably strewn with tokens of affection (beer cans, guitar picks, and so on) from fellow blues travelers paying their respects.

7

Southern Delta and Jackson

From the Catfish Capital to the State Capital

While the majority of Mississippi's blues sites are north of this area, the southern Delta boasts its share of blues heritage. In tiny Bentonia, the Blue Front Café is a can't-miss spot for blues travelers. The iconic juke boasts its own Blues Trail marker and hosts the annual Bentonia Blues Festival. Jackson may be slightly outside of the region, but the state capital has an especially rich blues history, from Farish Street to the site of the sadly demolished Subway Lounge. You'll also find some of Mississippi's top museums in Jackson and plenty of big-city amenities. Located at the southern tip of the Delta, Vicksburg is more well known for gorgeous antebellum bed & breakfasts and Civil War battlefields than blues sites, but the home of Willie Dixon is slowly beginning to embrace its blues heritage as well.

The price codes used in this chapter are as follows:

	Lodging	Dining
Inexpensive	Up to $90	Up to $15
Moderate	$90–130	$15–30
Expensive	$130–225	$30–65
Very Expensive	More than $225	More than $65

The following abbreviations are used for restaurants to identify what meals are served:

B—Breakfast
L—Lunch
D—Dinner
SB—Sunday brunch

BELZONI

Culture

Pinetop Perkins Blues Trail Marker

www.msbluestrail.org
US 49 W., east of the highway, just north of the intersection with MS 12/7, Belzoni, MS 39038

Directions: Northwest of Belzoni on US 49 W.; marker is on the northeast side of the highway

In May 2008, Joe Willie "Pinetop" Perkins was honored with a Blues Trail marker in his hometown of Belzoni, where he was born on July 7, 1913, on the Honey Island Plantation. An elder statesman of blues piano, Perkins was a seminal figure in the early Delta blues scene of the 1940s and '50s, playing with everyone from Muddy Waters to Sonny Boy Williamson II. With a career spanning six decades, Perkins was awarded the Grammy Lifetime Achievement Award in 2005, and in 2008—at age 95—he won the Grammy for Best Traditional Blues Album for his work on the live LP *Last of the Great Mississippi Delta Bluesmen.*

Seasonal Events

April

World Catfish Festival
1-800-408-4838
www.catfishcapitalonline.com
Belzoni, MS

With 30,000 of Humphreys County's acres under water, it's no surprise that in 1976 the state's governor proclaimed the county the Catfish Capital of the World. In the same year, the World Catfish Festival was established. Festivities include live blues and soul music, arts and crafts, and all manner of events related to catfish, including a catfish-eating contest, a catfish fry, and the Miss Catfish pageant. (In the past, the African-American Heritage Buffalo Fish Festival—which as of 2006 has been called the Denise LaSalle Homecoming Weekend—was held on the same weekend, with plenty of fantastic live blues, jazz, gospel, and other festivities. Although this festival has been on hiatus for the past couple of years, be sure to check www.deniselasallehomecoming.com for news of its revival.)

BENTONIA

This tiny farming town boasts its own style of blues music, founded by Henry Stuckey and his protégés Skip James and Jack Owens—who used to play regularly at the Blue Front Café. The distinct sound of Bentonia-style blues has to do with the way the guitar is tuned, and it's usually of the acoustic variety.

Culture

Blue Front Café
662-528-1900, 662-755-2278
108 E. Railroad Ave., Bentonia, MS 39040

This iconic juke joint has been a local fixture in Bentonia since 1948. It's a narrow, one-room operation with painted cinderblock walls and a rusted tin roof on a quiet country road. In other words, about as authentic as it gets. Inside, a counter topped with jars of pickles, eggs, and pickled pigs' feet dominates one side of the room, with a few tables filling the rest of the space. A Blues Trail marker was erected out front in 2007. Now run by the original owners' son, Jimmy "Duck" Holmes, the juke is open most days from the late afternoon on, but live music is somewhat of a rarity. While there aren't regular bookings, Holmes (a bluesman himself) will sometimes arrange live music if he knows a group is coming in, but impromptu performances are more the norm. Otherwise, you can catch live music at the Blue Front during the Bentonia Blues Festival.

Jack Owens's Grave

Bentonia, MS
Directions: From US 49, turn east on MS 433 (Cannon Road); follow MS 433 beyond town (around 4 miles). Turn right on Scotland Road and continue for around 3 miles. Pass the Old Liberty M.B. Church and turn right at the Day Cemetery sign.

Farmer, musician, and juke joint proprietor Jack Owens (born in 1904) lived a varied and colorful life. Heralded for his Bentonia-style blues, Owens was one of the early Delta blues musicians profiled by American folklorist and musicologist Alan Lomax for the Library of Congress in the 1940s. Like many of his contemporaries, Owens fell out of the blues scene for decades prior to his rediscovery in the 1980s, prompting tours throughout America and Europe. It was also around this time that Owens starred in a Levi's jeans commercial with harp player Bud Spires that was filmed at the Blue Front Café. Owens died in 1997 and is buried in Day Cemetery with a double headstone marking his and his wife's graves. A bluesman until the end, Owens's grave site is adorned with a stone vase that's etched with a guitar.

Skip James Blues Trail Marker

www.msbluestrail.org
Bentonia, MS
Directions: From US 49, turn east onto MS 433; marker is near the intersection on the right

Born in Bentonia in 1902, Nehemiah Curtis "Skip" James was a Delta blues guitarist, singer-songwriter, and pianist. Seeing minor success in the 1930s while recording for Paramount, James was sidetracked by the Great Depression and shelved his muse for the next few decades. During America's 1960s blues revival, James and his music were rediscovered, prompting his appearance at the 1964 Newport Folk Festival. Skip James's catalog

Beyond the Delta: Yazoo City Side Trip

Located between Belzoni and Bentonia, Yazoo City (www.yazoo.org) is home to a mystery that makes for a fun—and creepy—side trip. Legend has it that in the 1800s, the city had a notorious resident witch who lured fishermen to her house on the edge of the river only to poison them. When locals chased her to her death in a pool of quicksand, the witch vowed to return from the dead to burn down the city on the morning of May 25, 1904. The witch's body was buried in Yazoo's Glenwood Cemetery, where the grave was surrounded by a thick iron chain. On the morning of May 25, 1904, the witch's threat was realized when downtown Yazoo City went up in flames. At the witch's grave, a link was broken in the massive chain. The legend of Yazoo's witch was immortalized by famed local author Willie Morris in his book *Good Old Boy*. Today, you can see the Witch of Yazoo's grave in Glenwood Cemetery, where the broken chain remains. You can also pay your respects to Willie Morris, who is buried just 13 paces from the witch.

The legendary Blue Front Café is the main site of Bentonia's Blues Festival, held every June.

would go on to influence future generations of bluesmen as well as rock 'n' roll musicians. James, who died in 1969, was one of the principal players of a highly distinctive style of blues guitar that has become known as Bentonia School.

Seasonal Events

JUNE

Bentonia Blues Festival

Call Jimmy Holmes at 662-528-1900 or 662-755-2278
www.bentoniablues.com/BentoniaBluesFestival.shtml

Your best bet to hear fantastic live blues in Bentonia is this annual one-day festival. Music starts cranking inside the Blue Front around noon, along with gospel music from a stage in front of City Hall. At around 2 PM, the main stage outside the Blue Front gets going, with performances by local bluesmen like T-Model Ford, Bill "Howlin' Mad" Perry, Terry "Harmonica" Bean, and Jimmy "Duck" Holmes—who also owns the Blue Front and organizes the festival. In addition to the music, there are stalls with arts and crafts, down-home Southern cooking, and plenty of dancing.

HOLLANDALE

Culture

Sam Chatman's Grave

Hollandale, MS

Directions: From Highway 61, turn west on MS 12 into town; turn right onto East Avenue S. Turn left onto E. Washington Street, then right onto N. Morgan Avenue. The cemetery will be on the right.

A noted blues guitar, banjo, and harmonica player, Sam Chatman was born on January 10, 1897, and died February 2, 1983. He is buried in Hollandale at the Sanders Memorial Garden Cemetery. A half brother of famed Delta bluesman Charlie Patton, Chatman was born in Bolton, Mississippi, and played throughout the Delta in the 1930s before moving to Hollandale in the early '40s in search of work on plantations. In the 1960s Chatman was rediscovered, and he consistently toured throughout the 1970s both in the United States and internationally. His grave marker was paid for by fellow musician and blues enthusiast Bonnie Raitt.

ROLLING FORK

Culture

Muddy Waters's Birthplace

Rolling Fork, MS

Directions: From Highway 61, turn west on Walnut Street. Turn left on Hicks Avenue, then right on China Street

The father of the Chicago blues, McKinley Morganfield, better known as Muddy Waters, was born in Rolling Fork on April 4, 1915. While he moved to the Clarksdale area when he was just a few years old, Rolling Fork is proud to claim him as its own. Downtown, a gazebo and marker outside of the Sharkey County Courthouse in the center of town stands in the bluesman's honor. Across the street, a storefront window is painted with the bluesman's image, while another declares, "Rolling Fork, Home of Muddy Waters." A nearby Blues Trail marker, located north of Walnut Street between Sidney Alexander and Hoyt streets, went up in 2008. Raised by his grandmother, Waters initially picked up the harmonica before switching to the guitar in his late teens. A quick study, Waters was a great fan of local blues legends Robert Johnson and Son House, whose music and style he incorporated into his own technique. After being recorded by American folklorist and musicologist Alan Lomax for the Library of Congress in the early 1940s, Waters headed north for Chicago. It was there that Waters put down the acoustic guitar in favor of an electric, and in doing so revolutionized the blues.

VICKSBURG

Vicksburg sits on the mighty Mississippi River on the southern edge of the Delta. As author and historian David Cohn writes, "The Mississippi Delta begins in the lobby of the Peabody Hotel and ends on Catfish Row in Vicksburg." Here at the tip of the Delta, Civil

War history and antebellum homes overshadow the blues, but the charming town is home to world-renowned historic sites like the Vicksburg National Military Park. In historic downtown Vicksburg, quaint Washington Street is lined with galleries, boutiques, cafés, and museums. The downtown strip is a good place for live music, although it's rarely blues. There are, however, a couple of spots where blues travelers are more likely to catch a blues act. Vicksburg is home to a pair of Blues Trail markers, one of which honors hometown hero Willie Dixon. In 2008, the city held a successful weekend of blues music that included live shows at several downtown venues, and B. B. King was the headliner. Since then, ongoing efforts have been under way to promote Vicksburg's blues scene.

Lodging

BED & BREAKFAST INNS

Vicksburg is home to several antebellum mansions and historic homes that have been converted to gracious bed & breakfast inns. While the inns provide lovely accommodations, they're also attractions in and of themselves. Homes are filled with antiques, period decor, and original details, and most offer tours (included with an overnight stay). If you're not staying at the inn, tours generally cost around $6 and last 30 minutes. Overnight stays start around $100 per night and may be more than double that for suites and cottages. Full breakfasts are included with room rates, and credit cards are accepted. A few properties also feature on-site shops and restaurants.

Ahern's Belle of the Bends

601-634-0737, 1-800-844-2308
www.belleofthebends.com
508 Klein St, Vicksburg, MS 39183
Historic Garden District of Vicksburg
Handicap Access: No
Special Features: Free wireless Internet

This 1876 Italianate home offers four guest rooms and double wraparound verandas with porch swings, rocking chairs, and lovely views. Details throughout the elegant property include 13-foot ceilings with gold leaf crown moldings and hand-carved mill-work on the windows and doors. Rooms and spacious suites may feature an antique four-poster or canopy bed, original crystal chandelier, handwoven Oriental rug, decorative fireplace, Jacuzzi tub, and river views. All rooms are equipped with private bathrooms with marble floors. Guests have access to movies, books and games in the parlor, and the property's century-old gardens. An on-site shop offers a selection of antiques, handmade quilts, and Victorian gifts.

Anchuca Historic Mansion & Inn

601-661-0111, 1-888-686-0111
www.anchuca.com
1010 First East St., Vicksburg, MS 39183
Old Town neighborhood of Vicksburg
Handicap Access: No
Special Features: Free wireless Internet; all-inclusive packages available

Dating back to 1830, Anchuca (which means "happy home" in Choctaw) claims to be Mississippi's first bed & breakfast and Vicksburg's first columned mansion. The Greek Revival property not only survived the Civil War, but provided shelter for the wounded during the Siege of Vicksburg. Jefferson Davis addressed local townspeople from Anchuca's porch after the war finally ended. While the main structure has been expanded upon, several original details remain, including cypress and heart pine floors, ceiling medallions, fireplace mantles, and crown moldings. The property features ornate period furnishings and decor throughout, including common areas like the ladies' and gentlemen's parlors. Three guest rooms in the main house include two well-appointed master suites and the mansion's original servant quarters with a full kitchen. Four more rooms in the adjacent carriage house feature lofty ceil-

ings, gas fireplaces, and private bathrooms. Guests also have access to a lovely court-yard, swimming pool, and hot tub. The Anchuca Café serves upscale Southern cuisine in the garden room for lunch and dinner, Thursday through Sunday, when the Library Bar is also open.

Annabelle
601-638-2000, 1-800-791-2000
www.annabellebnb.com

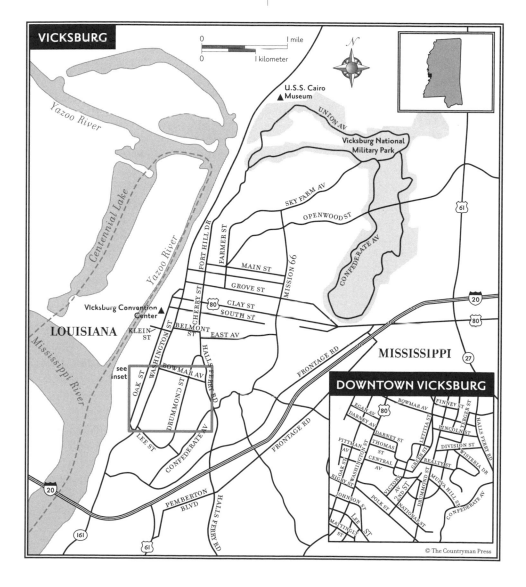

501 Speed St., Vicksburg, MS 39183
Historic Garden District of Vicksburg
Handicap Access: No
Special Features: Free wireless Internet

This stately brick Victorian-Italianate home
built around 1868 consists of three rooms
in the main house, and four more in a guest
house dating back to 1881. Rooms feature
13-foot ceilings, chandeliers, and private
baths. Guests have access to a Victorian
parlor and formal dining room in the main
house, where a Southern-style breakfast is
served every morning. Accommodations in
the slightly more modern guest house
include a spacious suite with a parlor and
access to a kitchen (for an extra fee). The
guest house also boasts a patio overlooking
the swimming pool. A New Orleans–style
brick courtyard on the grounds is home to a
fountain and lovely magnolia and crepe
myrtle trees.

Baer House Inn

601-883-1525, 1-866-510-1525
www.baerhouseinn.ms
1117 Grove St., Vicksburg, MS 39183
Historic downtown Vicksburg
Handicap Access: No
Special Features: Free wireless Internet;
elevator to second floor

This charming Eastlake Victorian property,
built around 1870, includes original details
like intricate woodwork and chestnut,
heartwood pine, and oak floors. All seven
rooms are located in the main house, five
with private bathrooms and two with
shared facilities. Accommodations include
the spacious Bonnie Blue room, with a
sunny sitting area surrounded by bay windows; the Leona Suite, with Eastlake
Victorian furnishings; and the Melanie
Suite, featuring Chinese antiques and art.
On the front of the house, the double-
gallery porch affords views of downtown

Vicksburg, the Old Courthouse Museum,
and the river. Behind the house, guests
have access to the property's lovely gardens,
where weddings and events are sometimes
held. In addition to breakfast, guests are
treated to a social hour with wine and
snacks in the parlor.

Cedar Grove Mansion Inn

601-636-1000, 1-800-862-1300
www.cedargroveinn.com
2200 Oak St., Vicksburg, MS 39183
Historic Garden District of Vicksburg
Handicap Access: No
Special Features: Free wireless Internet;
specials and packages are available

The crown jewel among Vicksburg's antebellum homes, the Cedar Grove estate sprawls
over 5 beautiful acres. Built in 1840, the
Greek Revival mansion was a gift for General
Sherman's cousin from her husband-to-be.
During the Civil War, the home served as
Union headquarters and was also used as a
military hospital. You can sleep in the canopy
bed where General Grant once spent the
night and see a Civil War cannonball that
remains lodged in the parlor wall. Rooms in
the main house are the most opulent,
including a two-story suite with a library,
private patio, and spiral staircase. The rest of
the inn's 33 rooms are located in a handful of
buildings, including shotgun-style accommodations in the carriage house, poolside
garden rooms, and cute cottages across the
street from the main house. Ample common
areas include the formal gardens, courtyards, and several porches and patios,
including a rooftop patio with views of the
river. In addition to a full breakfast, guests
enjoy wine and cheese in the evening, sherry
turndown service, and early-morning
muffins. Cedar Grove also boasts a romantic
fine-dining restaurant and a quaint bar area
overlooking the gardens.

The Corners Mansion Bed & Breakfast Inn

601-636-7421, 1-800-444-7421
www.thecorners.com
601 Klein St., Vicksburg, MS 39180
Across the side street from Cedar Grove
Handicap Access: Yes
Special Features: All-inclusive packages available

This blufftop inn, built in 1873, is blessed with expansive porches that offer nice sunset views over the river. Breakfast is served in the formal dining room, while guests enjoy afternoon cookies in a spacious double parlor with floor-to-ceiling windows, two fireplaces, and a baby grand piano. A glassed-in veranda overlooks a back garden with crepe myrtle trees and brick walkways, and guests can also stroll through the original parterre gardens. In addition to eight bedrooms in the main house, the inn offers accommodations in the original guest quarters adjacent to the house and in an additional building designed as a smaller replica of the main house, with rooms that feature period furnishings and whirlpool tubs. The Corners also offers accommodations across the street in a cute cottage equipped with living, dining, and kitchen areas. All 15 rooms have private baths and Internet access, and some feature fireplaces.

The Duff Green Mansion

601-636-6968, 601-638-6662, 1-800-992-0037
1114 First St., Vicksburg, MS 39183
Historic downtown Vicksburg
Handicap Access: Yes
Special Features: Free wireless Internet

Constructed by skilled slave labor around 1856, this three-story Palladian-style home features four rooms and one suite. In order to save their home from cannonball fire during the Civil War (after it was hit a few times), Mr. and Mrs. Green volunteered their property for use as a hospital.

Wounded troops from both the Union and Confederate armies were treated at the mansion—on different floors, of course—with the kitchen serving as an operating room. Later, in the 20th century, the house was used as Salvation Army headquarters for several years. Today, rooms with private bathrooms and working fireplaces feature both antique and contemporary furnishings. Guests enjoy breakfast as well as complimentary beverages during happy hour. Common areas include bilevel porches with intricate wrought-iron railings, and a swimming pool.

Motels and Hotels

Vicksburg has ample chain accommodations off I-20 and near the National Military Park, plus four casino hotels by the river. If you're looking for something a little different, try the Battlefield Inn for an inexpensive motel with a little something extra (breakfast buffet and evening cocktails), or the Ware House for unique upscale accommodations in the heart of historic downtown Vicksburg. Below is just a sampling of available lodging options. For a complete list, visit www.visitvicksburg.com/accommodations.

Ameristar Casino Hotel

601-638-1000, 1-800-700-7770
www.ameristarcasinos.com
4155 Washington St., Vicksburg, MS 39183

Battlefield Inn

601-638-5811, 1-800-359-9363
www.battlefieldinn.org
4137 I-20 N. Frontage Rd., Vicksburg, MS 39183

Best Western Vicksburg Inn

601-636-5800, 1-800-362-2345
www.bestwestern.com/Vicksburg
2445 I-20 N. Frontage Rd., Vicksburg, MS 39183

Comfort Inn
601-634-8438
www.choicehotels.com
3959 E. Clay St., Vicksburg, MS 39183

Days Inn
601-638-5750, 1-800-531-5900
www.daysinn.com
90 Warrenton Rd., Vicksburg, MS 39183

DiamondJacks Casino Hotel
601-636-5700, 1-877-711-0677
www.diamondjacks.com
3990 Washington St., Vicksburg, MS 39183

Fairfield Inn by Marriott
601-636-1811, 1-800-228-2800
www.marriott.com
20 Orme Dr., Vicksburg, MS 39183

Hampton Inn & Suites
601-636-6100, 1-800-426-7866
www.vicksburghamptoninn.com
3330 Clay St., Vicksburg, MS 39183

Holiday Inn Express
601-634-8777
www.ichotelsgroup.com
4330 S. Frontage Rd., Vicksburg, MS 39183

Horizon Casino Hotel Vicksburg
601-636-3423, 1-800-843-2343
www.horizonvicksburg.com
1310 Mulberry St., Vicksburg, MS 39183

Motel 6
601-638-5077, 1-800-466-8356
www.motel6.com

4127 I-20 N. Frontage Rd., Vicksburg, MS
39183

Rainbow Hotel Casino
601-638-7111
www.rainbowhotelcasino.com
1350 Warrenton Rd., Vicksburg, MS 39183

Rodeway Inn
601-634-1622
www.rodewayinn.com
2 Pemberton Pl., Vicksburg, MS 39183

The Ware House
601-634-1000
www.thewarehouse.ms
1412 Washington St., Vicksburg, MS 39183

CAMPING

Chotard Landing Resort
601-279-4282
www.chotardlandingresort.net
350 Chotard Lake Rd., Vicksburg, MS 39183

Magnolia RV Park
601-631-0388
www.magnoliarvparkresort.com
211 Miller St., Vicksburg, MS 39183

River Town Campground
601-630-9995, 1-866-442-2267
www.rivertown-campground.com
5900 Hwy. 61 S., Vicksburg, MS 39183

Vicksburg Battlefield Campground
601-636-2025
4407 I-20 Frontage Rd., Vicksburg, MS
39183

Culture

Biedenharn Museum of Coca-Cola Memorabilia

601-638-6514

www.biedenharncoca-colamuseum.com

1107 Washington St., Vicksburg, MS 39183

The history of Coca-Cola is honored at the site where the very first Coke beverage was bottled in 1894. There's also a soda fountain where you can sip a Coke float.

Catfish Row Landing

Downtown on Levee St., between Clay St. and Grove St.

The park area adjacent to the flood wall by the boat landing features outdoor history exhibits, a steamboat-shaped playground, history murals along the levee, and more.

Margaret's Grocery

601-638-1163

4535 N. Washington St. (Old Hwy. 61), Vicksburg, MS 39183

This eccentric roadside site is part shrine, part church, and part folk art collection. Built by the Reverend H. D. Dennis, who promised to turn Margaret's store into a palace if she'd marry him, the sprawling structure is hard to miss with its with pink, white, and yellow brick towers, and larger-than-life messages of faith.

Old Court House Museum

601-636-0741

www.oldcourthouse.org

1008 Cherry St., Vicksburg, MS 39183

This grand antebellum courthouse is chock-full of interesting artifacts, including Jefferson Davis's tie, thousands of Civil War relics, and a minié ball said to impregnate a woman after passing through a soldier's private parts and then her own.

The Red Tops Blues Trail Marker

www.msbluestrail.org

721 Clay St., Vicksburg, MS 39183

The Harlem Globetrotters of blues, jazz, and pop, the Red Tops, who formed during World War II under the name the Rebops, were known as much for their showmanship as their music. For two decades, beginning in 1953, the Red Tops traveled in and around the Delta decked out in their custom red performance jackets, consistently winning over audiences and building a devoted fan base. Led by drummer and manager Walter Osborne, Red Tops shows consisted of live music, dancing, and crowd interaction. They famously acted out many of their lyrics onstage, much to the crowd's delight. Based in Vicksburg, the group recorded only one single, and because most of the members had day jobs, they rarely performed outside of weekends. While the Red Tops ceased performing in the mid-1970s, they've reunited several times over the years for special engagements. The Blues Trail marker stands in front of downtown's BB Club, where they regularly performed.

Vicksburg Battlefield Museum

601-638-6500
www.vicksburgbattlefieldmuseum.net
4139 I-20 Frontage Rd., Vicksburg, MS 39183

Housed in a building designed to resemble a gunboat, this museum features an extensive collection of ship models, an intricate diorama of the Siege of Vicksburg, and a 30-minute widescreen film presentation.

Vicksburg National Military Park

601-636-0583
www.nps.gov/vick
3201 Clay St., Vicksburg, MS 39183
Open: Daily
Admission: $8 per vehicle or $4 per individual
Special Features: Educational tours are available

During the Civil War, Vicksburg was under siege from Union troops under the command of Ulysses S. Grant from May 18th through July 4th, 1863. Established in 1899, the Vicksburg National Military Park, at 1,728 acres, pays tribute to those fallen on both sides of the campaign. The tour begins in the visitor's center with a brief film documenting the events leading up the siege, the momentous battle, and its aftermath. From there, you begin the 16-mile driving tour throughout the expansive park that includes 1,330 historic monuments and memorials, two restored antebellum homes, the gunboat USS *Cairo*, 144 emplaced cannons, historic battle trenches, the Vicksburg National Cemetery, and Grant's Canal. The USS *Cairo* Gunboat and Museum is impressive in its own right—a must-see for Civil War history buffs. Confederate forces sank the Union gunboat on December 12, 1862, using two underwater torpedoes. Preserved by the river's natural mud and silt, the boat sat at the bottom of the Yazoo for more than a century until its excavation, and eventual restoration, in 1964.

Willie Dixon Blues Trail Marker

www.msbluestrail.org
Vicksburg, MS
Directions: Willie Dixon Way, downtown Vicksburg; located between (and parallel to) Mulberry Street and Washington Street, connecting Veto Street and South Street.

Willie Dixon was born on July 1, 1915, at 1631 Crawford Street, less than a mile east of the marker honoring him on Willie Dixon Way. Known to blues enthusiasts as "the poet laureate of the blues," Dixon left the Delta in 1936 for Chicago, where (after a short-lived boxing career) he would later make a name for himself as a musician—as well as a songwriter, arranger, and producer. Along with his contemporaries, Dixon was instrumental in shaping the sound of Chicago's electric blues with such compositions as "Little Red Rooster," "Wang Dang Doodle," and "Hoochie Coochie Man"—many of which would transcend the blues and inspire an entire generation of rock 'n' roll bands, from the Rolling Stones to Led Zeppelin. Dixon, who was inducted into both the Blues Hall of Fame and the Rock 'n' Roll Hall of Fame, died in 1992. He is buried in Alsip, Illinois.

Yesterday's Children Antique Doll and Toy Museum
601-638-0650
www.yesterdayschildrenmuseum.com
1104 Washington St., Vicksburg, MS 39183

Located in historic downtown Vicksburg across from the Coca-Cola Museum, this collection includes more than a thousand antique dolls, some dating back to the mid-1800s, plus a variety of antique toys.

Nightlife

While Vicksburg's live music scene is still struggling to get off the ground, there are a few spots where you're likely to catch some music, and a couple of places where you can sometimes hear the blues. Every second and fourth Tuesday of the month, the Central Mississippi Blues Society presents live blues at **LD's Restaurant and Lounge** downtown at Catfish Row Landing (1111 Mulberry St.; 601-636-9838). Located in the Ameristar Casino, the **Bottleneck Blues Bar** (4,146 Washington St.; 601-638-1000) is a medium-size venue that sometimes hosts blues acts ranging from Jonny Lang to Ruby Wilson. You can't escape the gaming machines—there are several throughout the bar—but the space is designed to resemble an old theater, and judging by the folk art and blues posters plastering the walls, the theme is most definitely Delta blues.

Historic downtown's Washington Street is home to several spots with live music, although it's usually not the blues. The sleek and swanky **Ware House Lounge** (1412 Washington St.; 601-634-1000) hosts music once or twice a week, generally of the smooth jazz variety. Down the street, **The Loft** (1306A Washington St.; 601-629-6188) is a sprawling sports bar/club that features New Orleans artists on the weekends. Located below the Attic Gallery, the **Highway 61 Coffeehouse** (1101 Washington St.; 601-638-9221) offers live music of various genres on Thursday evenings, including occasional blues.

Restaurants

Goldie's Trail Bar-B-Que
601-636-9839
2430 S. Frontage Rd., Vicksburg, MS 39180
Open: Mon.–Sat.
Price: Inexpensive–Moderate
Credit Cards: Yes
Cuisine: Barbecue
Serving: L, D
Handicap Access: Yes

Locals love this modest barbecue spot for its slow-cooked pit barbecue. Red booths line the walls, and painted wood-paneled walls are adorned with a few Civil War relics and framed drawings, but otherwise, the space is simple and spare. The menu features barbecue plates, sandwiches, and simple sides like onion rings and baked beans. Pork shoulders, Boston butts, chicken, beef brisket, pork ribs, and sausage are slow cooked over hickory wood. If you're not in the mood for barbecue, you can get a country fried steak or a grilled chicken breast. While the barbecue may not be on par with Memphis 'cue, this friendly spot has remained a local fixture since 1960.

Rowdy's Family Catfish Shack

601-638-2375
60 US 27, Vicksburg, MS 39183
Open: Daily
Price: Inexpensive–Moderate
Credit Cards: Yes
Cuisine: Seafood, regional
Serving: L, D
Handicap Access: Limited

This longtime local favorite specializes in Mississippi pond-raised catfish served in a casual, family-friendly atmosphere. The Rowdy family, which has been in the catfish business since 1933, serves up their specialty fried, grilled, or blackened, including an extra-crispy, thin-sliced version. In addition to catfish plates, Rowdy's offers a blackened catfish pasta. Other favorites include country fried steak, po' boys, fried shrimp, and fried oysters. There are also sandwiches, salads, five types of burgers, and daily blue plate lunch specials. Sides include a cast-iron skillet of corn bread, buttermilk hush puppies, battered french fries, black-eyed peas, and turnip greens. If you can manage it, top off a meal with a homemade cobbler, Mississippi mud pie, or lemon icebox pie.

Walnut Hills Restaurant

601-638-4910
www.walnuthillsms.net
1214 Adams St., Vicksburg, MS 39183
Open: Mon.–Fri., Sun.
Price: Inexpensive–Moderate
Credit Cards: Yes
Cuisine: Regional
Serving: L (Mon.–Fri., Sun.), D (Mon.–Fri.)
Handicap Access: Limited
Special Features: Family-style dining

Located on a leafy residential street in a gracious home that dates back to 1880, this popular round-table restaurant offers fantastic Southern food and a unique, friendly dining experience. Peruse a collection of Civil War artifacts before settling in at one of the large round tables for the ultimate midday meal. Your fellow diners may be halfway through their lunch, but no matter—diners are welcome to come and go at the communal tables that seat around 10. Chatting with your tablemates about that extra-crispy fried chicken or those mind-blowing biscuits is part of the fun. Around a dozen down-home dishes are served on a large lazy Susan, and the food just keeps on coming from polite and friendly servers. Offerings may include country fried steak, creamy chicken and artichoke or seafood casserole, fried catfish, and a slew of veggies like snap beans, purple hull peas, okra, mustard greens, and creamed corn. Desserts like blackberry cobbler or bread pudding top off the gigantic meal. Chances are, you're going to overeat, but you can always rest for a while in a rocking chair on the lovely front porch. If you're not up for the round table, you can always sit at a regular ol' table and opt for a blue plate lunch or a po' boy. For dinner, à la carte items include many dishes served in the round-table feast, plus boiled shrimp, fried pork chops, and a pork loin cooked with molasses, apple cider, and sage. *Oooo weeee!* Pass the biscuits.

Beyond the Delta: Side Trip to Hazlehurst and Crystal Springs

Head south of Jackson on I-55 to pay your respects to Robert Johnson in the town where he was born, and later married Calletta Craft. Johnson's Blues Trail marker is located off US 51 on North Ragsdale Avenue by the railroad tracks. A few minutes north, Crystal Springs is home to the Robert Johnson Blues Foundation (601-892-7883), which runs a museum room and organizes an annual Blues Jam in May. Crystal Springs was also the home of bluesman Tommy Johnson, who is honored with a Blues Trail marker in a grassy area by the tracks off West Railroad Avenue North.

JACKSON

Mississippi's capital is technically outside of the Delta (it's about 45 miles east of Vicksburg), but there's some outstanding blues history here, not to mention big-city amenities and attractions. Jackson's once-bustling Farish Street, a center for African American businesses, culture, and blues, is poised for renewal, but the historic street's transformation into an entertainment district seems to be slow going. You can find live blues music around town, and the *Jackson Free Press* Web site (www.jacksonfreepress.com) does a good job of keeping track of what's going on. If you happen to be in town on a Sunday, don't miss the opportunity to hear some of the city's outstanding gospel music at a local church. For blues on the radio, tune in to 1400 AM.

Lodging

INNS

Fairview Inn
601-948-3429, 1-888-948-1908
www.fairviewinn.com
734 Fairview St., Jackson, MS 39202
North of downtown
Price: Expensive–Very Expensive
Credit Cards: Yes
Handicap Access: Yes
Special Features: On-site restaurant, spa

Tucked away in the historic Belhaven neighborhood, this 1908 Colonial Revival mansion features 7 rooms and 11 suites. Located less than five minutes north of downtown, the property is near Millsaps and Belhaven colleges. Uniquely decorated rooms are adorned with antique reproductions, while some accommodations feature separate sitting areas, gas fireplaces, and Jacuzzi tubs. Common areas include the grand foyer, with original oak woodwork and an antique Louis XV marble mantel; a study featuring quarter-sawn oak paneling, Tiffany lamps, and a Herschede grandfather clock; and a formal hedge garden. Site of many special events, the inn is also home to Sophia's fine-dining restaurant, serving dinner and Sunday brunch. An on-site spa offers massage, facials, body wraps, reflexology, hair removal, and nail care.

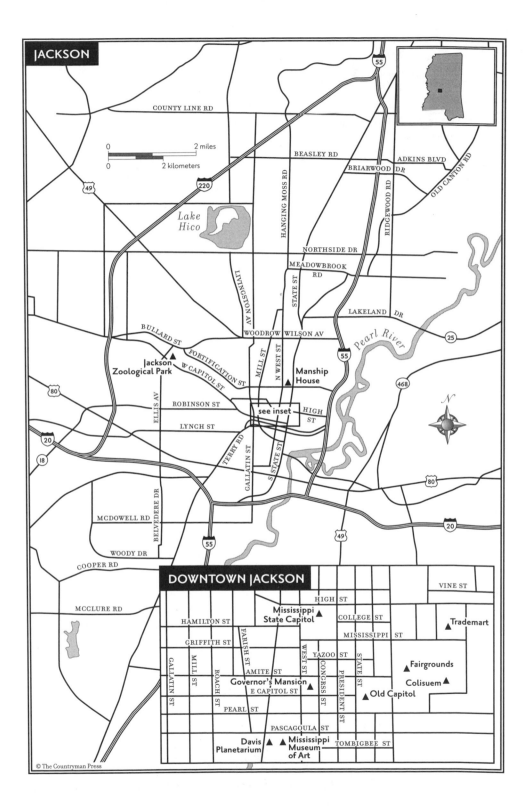

JACKSON

COUNTY LINE RD

BEASLEY RD

BRIARWOOD DR

ADKINS BLVD
OLD CANTON RD

Lake
Hico

HANGING MOSS RD

NORTHSIDE DR

MEADOWBROOK
RD

RIDGEWOOD RD

LIVINGSTON AV

STATE ST

LAKELAND DR

WOODROW WILSON AV

Pearl River

BULLARD ST

FORTIFICATION ST

MILL ST

N WEST ST

Jackson
Zoological Park

W CAPITOL ST

Manship
House

ELLIS AV

ROBINSON ST

LYNCH ST

see inset

HIGH
ST

TERRY RD

GALLATIN ST

S STATE ST

BELVEDERE DR

MCDOWELL RD

WOODY DR

COOPER RD

N

MCCLURE RD

DOWNTOWN JACKSON

VINE ST

HIGH ST

HAMILTON ST

Mississippi
State Capitol

COLLEGE ST

Trademart

GRIFFITH ST

MISSISSIPPI ST

FARISH ST

GALLATIN ST

MILL ST

ROACH ST

WEST ST

YAZOO ST

CONGRESS ST

STATE ST

PRESIDENT ST

Fairgrounds

Coliseum

AMITE ST

Governor's Mansion

E CAPITOL ST

Old Capitol

PEARL ST

PASCAGOULA ST

TOMBIGBEE ST

Davis
Planetarium

Mississippi
Museum
of Art

0   2 miles
0   2 kilometers

© The Countryman Press

Old Capitol Inn

601-359-9000, 1-888-359-9001
www.oldcapitolinn.com
226 N. State St., Jackson, MS 39201
Downtown Jackson
Price: Expensive
Credit Cards: Yes
Handicap Access: Yes
Special Features: Wireless Internet; free gated parking

This genteel redbrick inn offers unique accommodations in the heart of downtown Jackson. Twenty-four rooms and suites with downtown or garden views are tastefully decorated in traditional decor, with nice extras like robes, desks, and Aveda bath products. There's also an Elvis-themed room, and Faulkner's Flat for literary buffs. Suites boast spacious roomy seating areas and bathrooms with Jacuzzi tubs. Popular for meetings and private events, the inn features ample event space, plus a pool, garden area, and a rooftop hot tub with downtown views. Guests are pampered with a full Southern breakfast and evening wine and cheese, and have access to an off-site fitness center next door to the inn.

Poindexter Park Inn

601-944-1392
803 Deer Park St., Jackson, MS 39203
Just west of downtown
Price: Inexpensive–Moderate
Credit Cards: Yes

The majority of guests at the Poindexter Park Inn are European blues travelers looking for an authentic Delta experience.

Handicap Access: No
Special Features: Dial-up Internet

This adorable inn, located in a self-proclaimed "blues neighborhood" near downtown Jackson, caters to blues travelers. Owner Marcia Weaver is one of Jackson's foremost blues experts, and she is more than happy to point guests to live gigs, historic blues sites, self-guided tours, and more. A wealth of knowledge when it comes to the area's blues history and current live music scene, Weaver also happens to manage local blueswoman Dorothy Moore of "Misty Blue" fame. While the neighborhood may be a little rough around the edges, the inn itself is safe, tidy, and pretty darn cool if you're a fan of the blues. A cute yellow two-story with white trim and fantastic porches, the inn's walls are plastered with records, vintage signs, blues posters, instruments, folk art, washboards, and a large section devoted to Dorothy Moore. The five rooms are cozy, clean, and simple, if not exactly luxurious, with private bathrooms (one of which has a claw-foot tub), brass beds, vintage furniture, and folk art decor. Two rooms are singles, and three are doubles. Continental breakfast with blueberry muffins is offered in the mornings.

MOTELS AND HOTELS

The capital of Mississippi is home to ample accommodations covering all price ranges. Many of these properties can be found just off I-55 near the Coliseum on the edge of downtown Jackson. Of the accommodations listed in this section, the Edison Walthall Hotel and Jackson Marriott are among the most centrally located downtown properties. Downtown Jackson's iconic King Edward Hotel, vacant for nearly 40 years, is currently being renovated. More than $80 million is being invested to convert the property into a Hilton, which will likely be called the King Edward Hilton or something similar. Started in 2007, the renovations are slated to be complete in 2009. The new property will include hotel accommodations as well as a few floors of apartment living. For a complete listing of Jackson accommodations, go to www.visitjackson.com.

America's Best Suites
601-899-9000
www.americasbestinn.com
5411 I-55 N. Frontage Rd., Jackson, MS 39206

Cabot Lodge Millsaps
601-948-8650
www.cabotlodgemillsaps.com
2375 N. State St., Jackson, MS 39202

Edison Walthall Hotel
601-948-6161
www.edisonwalthallhotel.com
225 E. Capitol St., Jackson, MS 39201

Hampton Inn & Suites Coliseum
601-352-1700
www.hamptoninn.com
320 Greymont Ave., Jackson, MS 39202

Once a thriving hub for African American culture, downtown's historic Farish Street is poised for renewal.

Holiday Inn Express Hotel & Suites
1-877-863-4780
www.ichotelsgroup.com
310 Greymont Ave., Jackson, MS 39202

Jackson Marriott
601-969-5100
www.marriott.com
200 E. Amite St., Jackson, MS 39201

Quality Inn & Suites
601-969-2230
www.jacksonqualityinn.com
400 Greymont Ave., Jackson, MS 39202

Red Roof Inn
601-969-5006
www.redroof.com
700 Larson St., Jackson, MS 39202

Regency Hotel & Conference Center
601-969-2141
www.regencyjackson.com
400 Greymont Ave., Jackson, MS 39202

Residence Inn Jackson
601-355-3599
www.marriott.com
881 E. River Pl., Jackson, MS 39202

Culture

Bobby Rush Blues Trail Marker
www.msbluestrail.org
Jackson, MS
Directions: Southwest of downtown Jackson at the intersection of J. R. Lynch and Valley streets.

If James Brown was the hardest-working man in show business, then Bobby Rush is surely a close second. Reigning king of the hybrid genre known as soul blues, Rush is honored with a Blues Trail marker in his adopted hometown of Jackson, Mississippi. Born on November 10, 1940, in Louisiana, Rush has been steadily touring, and releasing albums for decades. The artist recently gained a newfound notoriety after being profiled in Martin Scorsese's 2003 documentary *The Blues*.

Eudora Welty House

601-353-7762
www.eudorawelty.org
1119 Pinehurst St., Jackson, MS 39296

Take a guided tour of the home and gardens in historic Belhaven where Pulitzer prize–winning writer Eudora Welty lived and wrote for 76 years.

Farish Street

Downtown Jackson, between Capitol St. and Monument St.

In the early 20th century, downtown's Farish Street was the thriving hub for Jackson's African American business, culture, and blues music, much like Beale Street in Memphis and Nelson Street in Greenville. For the past few decades, however, Farish has suffered from desertion and decline, with a few longtime businesses breathing a little life into the historic district. Today, plans are in the works to restore the area as a Beale Street–style entertainment district. Progress can be seen in the form of a few restored storefronts, new vintage-style street lamps, and handsome redbrick sidewalks with freshly planted trees, but progress appears to be slow going. Still, a daytime stroll down Farish will take you past several historic landmarks, a pair of which have received Blues Trail markers.

During the 1920s and '30s, record store owner H. C. Speir, who ran **Speir Phonograph Company** (225 N. Farish St.), scouted blues artists throughout the Southern states for various record companies—in part, to boost his own record sales. Speir discovered a great deal of blues talent, including Charlie Patton, Skip James, Willie Brown, the Mississippi Sheiks, and none other than Robert Johnson, whom he hooked up with American Record Co.

Just down the street, **Ace Records** (241 N. Farish St.) was founded by producer Johnny Vincent in 1955. He recorded Earl King, Huey "Piano" Smith, Bobby Marchand, Willie Clayton, Johnny Littlejohn, and many more. Perhaps more famously, Farish Street is home to **Trumpet Records** (309 N. Farish St.), a label launched out of the Record Mart store once located here. While gospel records marked Trumpet's foray into the recording industry, Lillian McMurry (who owned Record Mart along with her husband, Willard) soon began recording blues records in house by the likes of Sonny Boy Williamson II, Elmore James, Willie Love, and Big Joe Williams. Trumpet Records is recognized with one of two Blues Trail markers on Farish Street.

The second Blues Trail marker belongs to the **Alamo Theater** (333 N. Farish St.; 601-352-3365), here since 1949 and restored in 1996. It its heyday, the Alamo was a movie house and also hosted jazz and blues concerts, vaudeville shows, and the regular Apollo talent contest where many artists got their first big break, including Jackson native Dorothy Moore. Moore was on hand for the unveiling of the Alamo's Blues Trail marker (on which she's also honored) in 2008.

Beyond the Alamo Theater, on the opposite side of the street near the Big Apple Inn, the brick two-story that's now home to a bar called **Birdland** (538 Farish St.) was once the location of the Crystal Palace, a popular venue for jazz and R&B acts where Louis Armstrong and Duke Ellington once played. Today, the bar draws more of a young hip-hop crowd.

Malaco Records
601-982-4522
www.malaco.com
3023 W. Northside Dr., Jackson, MS 39286

The Malaco Records Blues Trail marker stands just in front of the company's longtime headquarters, which are still in operation today. The label's story begins in 1968 with the release of a single 45 record from Hattiesburg native Cozy Corley. Over the next four decades, Malaco Records would leave its mark on Southern soul, blues, R&B, and gospel. Working with various label partners like STAX, Atlantic, and Capitol, Malaco spawned many a hit you probably know by heart, à la "Groove Me" and "Mr. Big Stuff." Based just outside of downtown Jackson, Malaco was Mississippi's first modern state-of-the-art recording facility, and it continues to flourish today. Studio tours are available by request and are led by legendary sound engineer (FAME Studios, Muscle Shoals) Jerry Lee Masters. The studio exudes an atmosphere of the days when everything was done in house, from the recording to the marketing and PR. Malaco recording artists include Bobby "Blue" Bland, Little Milton, Johnnie Taylor, and Dorothy Moore.

Mississippi Museum of Art
601-960-1515
www.msmuseumart.org
380 S. Lamar St., Jackson, MS 39201

In addition to hosting traveling exhibitions, the state's largest art museum is home to a permanent collection of more than four thousand works, as well as the Palette Café by Viking.

Mississippi Museum of Natural Science
601-354-7303
www.msnaturalscience.org
From I-55, take exit 98B (Lakeland Dr.)

Located in LeFleur's Bluff State Park, this 73,000-square-foot museum complex overlooks 300 acres of natural landscape that includes 2.5 miles of nature trails and an outdoor amphitheater. Inside, exhibits include a 100,000-gallon aquarium and a 1,700-square-foot greenhouse.

Mississippi Sports Hall of Fame and Museum
601-982-8264
www.msfame.com
1152 Lakeland Dr., Jackson, MS 39216

Interactive exhibits featuring archival footage, artifacts, and interviews pay tribute to famous Mississippi athletes like Walter Payton, Jerry Rice, and Archie Manning.

Old Capitol Museum/Museum of Mississippi History
601-576-6920
www.mdah.state.ms.us
100 S. State St., Jackson, MS 39201

Formerly the home of the Museum of Mississippi History, the grand Greek Revival capitol building downtown was closed for restoration due to damage by Hurricane Katrina. Scheduled to reopen in 2009, the new museum will focus on the building's history, which served as Mississippi's statehouse from 1839 to 1903. A new Museum of Mississippi History is slated for construction downtown.

Subway Lounge
619 W. Pearl St., Jackson, MS 39296

Pearl Street was the site of the now-defunct Summers Hotel—one of the two prominent African American hotels in Jackson during the years of segregation. The hotel was a virtual home away from home for countless musicians traveling though the deep South. In 1966, bandleader Jimmy King was brought in to manage the hotel's new basement club, appropriately dubbed the Subway Lounge, which primarily featured local and touring jazz acts. The club continued to thrive after the civil rights movement, and in the mid-1980s, under King's watchful eye, it was transformed into a blues joint, with the music starting at midnight. Over the years, the legendary dark, smoky club welcomed performers like Bobby Rush, Jackie Bell, Fingers Taylor, Taj Mahal, and many more. Sadly, with the hotel in a dilapidated state, the Subway closed in 2003, and the building was demolished in 2004, despite efforts to save it. Today, all there is to see is the Blues Trail marker on an empty lot, although longtime Subway regulars the House Rockers can still be seen most weekends at Schimmel's. There's also talk of a new Subway Lounge opening on Farish Street.

Seasonal Events

JUNE

Jubilee Jam
www.jubileejam.com
Capital St., Jackson, MS 39202

This two-day downtown music and arts festival features more than 20 bands playing on three stages. The diverse lineup includes everything from blues to rock, including well-known national touring acts. Past performers have included ZZ Top, the Black Crowes, Bobby Rush, Blind Melon, Pat Green, and Willie Nelson. There's also a booth that hosts various DJs, and a roots and gospel stage. A Children's Village keeps the kids entertained, while the Mississippi Arts Village showcases works of art in various mediums, from photography to metal. There are also plenty of food and drink vendors.

SEPTEMBER

Farish Street Heritage Festival
601-948-5667
Farish Street Historic District, Jackson, MS 39202

Held on historic Farish Street, this daylong street festival features live blues, soul, and gospel music, plus arts and crafts, soul food, and a Kiddie Cottage set up for the youngsters. An annual event for more than 30 years, Farish Street Fest is Mississippi's second-longest-running African American festival. Tickets can generally be purchased at Bebop Records locations, Bully's Soul Food Restaurant, and BIP Records. Buy tickets in advance to save a few bucks.

Nightlife

Until Farish Street is reinvented as an entertainment district, the live blues scene in Jackson remains a little patchy, although you can generally catch some live blues on weekends. To find out who's playing, visit the *Jackson Free Press* Web site at www.jacksonfree press.com and click on Music. Among the most reliable places to hear some blues, the **930 Blues Café** (930 N. Congress St.; 601-948-3345) is a cute two-story house that usually hosts blues acts on Friday and Saturday ($10 cover), and sometimes other nights as well. As far as real-deal juke joints, **Queen of Hearts** (2243 Martin Luther King Jr. Dr.; 601-352-5730) is a local favorite. You'll know it's open if the door on the right is open. There's live blues some weekends, plus good fish sandwiches.

Several Jackson bars and restaurants feature occasional live blues, including **Hal & Mal's** (see the Restaurants section), which presents blues acts every Monday. While the sleek, sophisticated **Schimmel's** (2615 N. State St.; 601-981-7077) may seem an unlikely spot for some down-home blues, the upscale restaurant and lounge hosts the Subway Lounge Revisited every Saturday night with one-time Subway Lounge regulars the House Rockers. An Irish pub favored by the college crowd, **Fenian's Pub** (901 E. Fortification St.; 601-948-0055) sometimes hosts blues acts, along with Celtic music, funk, and acoustic singer-songwriters, depending upon the night. **Martin's** (214 S. State St.; 601-354-9712), an old-school lounge that's been around since the 1950s, also occasionally hosts live blues music.

Restaurants

Big Apple Inn

601-354-9371
509 N. Farish St., Jackson, MS 39202
Open: Tues.–Sat.
Price: Inexpensive
Credit Cards: Yes
Cuisine: Regional
Serving: B, L, D
Handicap Access: Limited
Special Features: Take-out

Located on the first floor of a brick-front building on Farish Street, this landmark spot known by locals as Big John's is famous for serving pig's ear sandwiches. It may look a little rough around the edges from the outside thanks to a few missing window panes in the second-story apartments, but those upstairs accommodations have been home and host to bluesman Sonny Boy Williamson II, Elmore James, and Willie Love. The same apartment also served as NAACP headquarters, where civil rights activist Medgar Evers worked before his tragic assassination. Downstairs, the Big Apple Inn is a modest, narrow spot with wood-paneled walls, a few tables in back, and a counter where you order. Folks come from all over for a sack of spicy pig's ear sandwiches, served on a small white bun with coleslaw and mustard. Pig's ear devotees reportedly include B. B. King and Bobby "Blue" Bland, who refers to them as "listener sandwiches." You can also get a sack of "Smokes," which consist of minced sausage topped with the coleslaw-mustard mix and pressed between a small white bun. The sandwiches are about the same size as a Krystal or White Castle burger— with a heck of a lot more soul. Sandwiches only cost around a buck, and you can order them mild or hot, but even mild has a kick. The small menu also includes tamales, hot dogs, burgers, bologna sandwiches, and large, inexpensive beers.

Hal & Mal's

601-948-0888
www.halandmals.com
200 S. Commerce St., Jackson, MS 39202
Open: Mon.–Sat.
Price: Inexpensive–Moderate
Credit Cards: Yes
Cuisine: American, Creole, Southern, seafood
Serving: L (Mon.–Fri.), D (Tues.–Sat.)
Handicap Access: Limited
Special Features: Live music; trivia

This popular restaurant and bar is housed in an old train depot dating back to the 1920s. The vibe here is casual and festive, as much a bar scene as it is a restaurant. The main dining area features exposed brick walls covered in blues posters and photos, while the adjacent bar area has black-and-white checkered floors and a lengthy bar backed by glowing neon lights. A cozy separate room dubbed the Oyster Bar features a vague nautical theme and walls plastered with ubiquitous black-and-white photos and framed newspaper clippings. A section of wall space is also dedicated to Elvis Presley. Down the narrow hallway, a back room is stocked with a couple of pool tables. Hal & Mal's features live music just about every night, trivia on Tuesday, and live blues every Monday. On the menu, you'll find lots of New Orleans flavor, including gumbo, a muffuletta, po' boys, red beans and rice, and seafood gumbo. There are also several salads, burgers, blue plate lunch specials, and fried seafood platters.

Mayflower Café

601-355-4122
123 W. Capitol St., Jackson, MS 39202
Open: Mon.–Sat.
Price: Inexpensive–Moderate
Credit Cards: Yes
Cuisine: Southern, seafood
Serving: L (Mon.–Fri.), D
Handicap Access: Limited
Special Features: Bring your own wine, liquor ($2 corkage fee)

By day, this longtime downtown favorite serves politicos Southern-style plate lunches in an old-school diner atmosphere. By night, however, the Greek-owned eatery moonlights as one of Jackson's favorite seafood restaurants. The retro neon sign and art deco entrance have been a downtown fixture since 1935. Inside, the narrow space is lined with three rows of tables—brown vinyl booths (with individual coat racks) on the outer walls, with a row of white-tablecloth-topped four-tops in between. The floors are black and white mosaic tiles, and the walls are lined with old photos and a few mounted fish. Lunch here suits the retro-diner atmosphere, with daily plate lunch specials like country fried steak and gravy, beef tips, fried catfish, and chicken and dumplings with black-eyed peas, candied yams, turnip greens, and butter beans. Dinner is all about ultrafresh seafood like broiled lemon fish, flounder, speckled trout, and the ever-popular redfish. There are also soft-shell crabs (in season), creamy crab bisque, and broiled oysters. A few Greek accents find their way onto the menu in the form of a feta burger for lunch and fish prepared in a Greek-style sauce for dinner. Regulars swear by the "comeback dressing," which is creamy with a bit of spice. For dessert, finish off with the coconut cream pie.

Peaches Café

601-354-9267
327 N. Farish St., Jackson, MS 39202
Open: Mon.–Sat.
Price: Inexpensive
Credit Cards: No
Cuisine: Soul food
Serving: B, L
Handicap Access: Limited

Located in the heart of historic Farish Street next to the landmark Alamo Theater, Peaches has been serving up hearty soul food favorites since 1961. Inside the well-worn diner, regulars settle onto mismatched stools at the long counter or opt for a booth on the opposite wall of the shotgun-style space. Images of African American icons like Martin Luther King Jr., Mohammed Ali, Bob Marley, and Jackie Robinson cover the walls. Breakfast at Peaches consists of salty meats like sausage, ham, and bacon, plus grits, pancakes, and salmon croquettes—if you're looking to branch out. Lunch plates are generally anchored with a soul food staple like fried chicken, smothered pork chops, meat loaf, fried catfish, beef liver, or pig's feet, ears, or tails. You can also get soups like beef stew and oxtail, depending upon what's cooking that day. Southern-style veggies include yams, turnip greens, black-eyed peas, mac 'n cheese, and the like. Dessert may include sweet potato pie, bread pudding, or a cobbler. The best way to wash down a meal at Peaches is with an ice-cold glass of red Kool-Aid. On occasion, the café hosts live blues music during lunch or weekend nights. Otherwise, the tunes are provided by one of the best blues jukeboxes in the city.

Two Sisters Kitchen

601-353-1180
707 N. Congress St., Jackson, MS 39202
Open: Sun.–Fri.
Price: Moderate
Credit Cards: Yes
Cuisine: Southern
Serving: L
Handicap Access: Limited
Special Features: Patio seating; buffet

This charming house turned restaurant is one of Jackson's best, and most popular, lunch spots. Tucked away on a pleasant leafy street, the eatery doesn't feel like it's only a block or two from the capitol building in the heart of downtown Jackson. Beyond the quaint columned front porch (complete with rocking chairs) you'll find cozy dining rooms with well-worn hardwood floors. There are also a couple of prime tables on an upstairs patio, as well as a large covered patio to the side of the house. But the main attraction is downstairs just to the right of the entrance: the buffet. Everyone from capitol workers on their lunch break to the Sunday after-church crowd pack the place for overflowing plates of down-home Southern cooking. Voted the best in the city by the *Jackson Free Press,* the extra-crispy fried chicken has a little secret—it's skinless, which is pretty hard to believe considering the outstanding taste. You also won't believe that the flavor-packed veggies are cooked without animal fat. Did we mention that most dishes are low sodium, as well? Trust us, you won't miss it. In addition to the fried chicken, buffet items include creamy chicken and dumplings, crunchy fried okra, black-eyed peas, cabbage, corn, collard greens, grits, rice and gravy, lima beans, biscuits, corn bread, and—stop the press—a salad bar with mixed greens! Save a tiny corner of your stomach for dessert, which may include banana pudding, bread pudding, or chocolate cake.

Recreation

PARKS, NATURE, AND WILDLIFE

The Jackson Zoo

601-352-2581

www.jacksonzoo.org

2918 W. Capitol St., Jackson, MS 39209

Located on 11 acres of land, the Jackson Zoo is home to nearly 800 animals representing 120 species, 14 of them endangered.

Tutwiler Murals

8

INFORMATION

Essentials, Media, and Event Listings

AMBULANCE, FIRE, POLICE, AND EMERGENCIES

MEMPHIS
All emergencies: 911
Police, nonemergency: 901-545-2677
Memphis Fire Department: 901-458-8281
Crisis Intervention: 901-274-7477
Poison Control: 1-800-222-1222
Sexual Assault Resource Center: 901-272-2020
Health Department: 901-544-7600
Red Cross: 901-726-1690

THE DELTA
All emergencies: 911
Clarksdale Police, nonemergency: 662-621-8151
Clarksdale Fire Department: 662-627-8487
Cleveland Police, nonemergency: 662-843-3611
Cleveland Fire Department: 662-843-2711
Greenville Police, nonemergency: 662-378-1515
Greenville Fire Department: 662-378-1616
Helena–West Helena Police, nonemergency: 870-572-3441
Helena–West Helena Fire Department: 870-338-9047

Indianola Police, nonemergency: 662-887-1811
Indianola Fire Department: 662-887-4955
Jackson Police, nonemergency: 601-960-1217
Jackson Fire Department: 601-960-2093
Vicksburg Police, nonemergency: 601-636-2511
Vicksburg Fire Department: 601-636-1603

AREA CODES, CITY HALLS, AND ZIP CODES

	Area Code	City Hall Phone Number	Zip Code
Memphis	901	901-576-6500	38103
Clarksdale	662	662-621-8164	38614
Cleveland	662	662-846-1471	38732
Greenville	662	662-378-1500	38701
Helena–West Helena	870	870-572-2528	72342
Indianola	662	662-887-4454	38751
Jackson	601	601-960-1084	39202
Vicksburg	601	601-634-4553	39183

BANKS

Bank of America: Memphis
901-320-5510; 2731 Union Ext., Memphis, TN 38112
901-725-8000; 945 S. Cooper St., Memphis, TN 38104
901-348-5700; 4350 Elvis Presley Blvd., Memphis, TN 38116

Regions Bank: Memphis
901-524-5700; 158 Madison Ave., Memphis, TN 38103
901-579-2790; 50 N. Front St., Ste. 100, Memphis, TN 38103
901-762-5970; 1415 Union Ave., Memphis, TN 38104

Regions Bank: Delta
662-627-3281; 211 E. Second St., Clarksdale, MS 38614
662-843-4001; 129 S. Sharp Ave., Cleveland, MS 38732
662-378-3902; 540 Main St., Greenville, MS 38701
662-686-4034; 104 N. Broad St., Leland, MS 38756
662-453-2894; 112 Howard St., Greenwood, MS 38930
601-631-3030; 825 Crawford St., Vicksburg, MS 39180
1-800-734-4667; 210 E. Capitol St., Jackson, MS 39201

Planters Bank: Delta
662-843-3300; 428 N. Davis, Cleveland, MS 38732
662-335-5258; 424 Washington Ave., Greenville, MS 38701
662-453-1770; 110 W. Park Ave., Greenwood, MS 38930
662-887-3363; 212 Catchings Ave., Indianola, MS 38751 (ATM: 521 US 82)
662-686-2002; 1002 US 82 E., Leland, MS 38756

BOOKS

Beifuss, Joan Turner. *At the River I Stand: Memphis, the 1968 Strike, and Martin Luther King, Jr.* Orlando: Carlson Publishing, 1989.

Bowman, Rob. *Soulsville U.S.A.: The Story of Stax Records.* New York: Schirmer Trade Books, 2003.

Cheseborough, Steve. *Blues Traveling: The Holy Sites of the Delta Blues.* Jackson: University Press of Mississippi, 2004.

Davis, Francis. *The History of the Blues: The Roots, the Music, the People.* New York: Da Capo Press, 2003.

Edwards, David "Honeyboy." *The World Don't Owe Me Nothin'.* Chicago: Chicago Review Press, 2000.

Escott, Colin. *Good Rockin' Tonight: Sun Records and the Birth of Rock 'N' Roll.* New York: St. Martin's Griffin, 1992.

Ferris, William. *Blues from the Delta.* New York: Doubleday, 1978.

Gordon, Robert. *Can't Be Satisfied: The Life and Times of Muddy Waters.* Boston: Back Bay Books, 2003.

Gordon, Robert. *It Came from Memphis.* New York: Atria, 2001.

Guralnick, Peter. *Last Train to Memphis: The Rise of Elvis Presley.* Boston: Back Bay Books, 1995.

——. *Sweet Soul Music: Rhythm and Blues and the Southern Dream of Freedom.* Boston: Back Bay Books, 1999.

——. *Careless Love: The Unmaking of Elvis Presley.* Boston: Back Bay Books, 2000.

Handy, W. C. *Father of the Blues: An Autobiography.* New York: Da Capo Press, 1991.

King, B. B., and David Ritz. *Blues All Around Me: The Autobiography of B. B. King.* New York: Harper Paperbacks, 1999.

Lomax, Alan. *The Land Where Blues Began.* New York: Pantheon, 1993.

McKee, Margaret, and Fred Chisenhall. *Beale Black & Blue: Life and Music on Black America's Main Street.* Baton Rouge: Louisiana State University Press, 1993.

Moore, Scotty, with James Dickerson. *That's Alright, Elvis.* New York: Schirmer Trade Books, 2005.

Norris, Randall. *Highway 61 Heart of the Delta.* Knoxville: University of Tennessee Press, 2008.

Palmer, Robert. *Deep Blues: A Musical and Cultural History of the Mississippi Delta.* New York: Viking Press, 1981.

Petrusich, Amanda. *It Still Moves: Lost Songs, Lost Highways, and the Search for the Next American Music.* New York: Faber and Faber, 2008.

Wardlow, Gayle Dean. *Chasin' That Devil Music: Searching for the Blues.* San Francisco: Backbeat Books, 1998.

CLIMATE AND WEATHER REPORT

MEMPHIS

Rising above the Mississippi River in the southwest corner of Tennessee, Memphis is known for hot, humid summers that stretch from May through late September. Always drink plenty of water and pack a hat, sunglasses, and sunscreen, as the intense Memphis sun can be unforgiving. Summer temperatures frequently climb into the upper 90s, especially in July and August. If you're planning on traveling to the city in the spring or summer, be sure to pack a small umbrella, as 30- to 45-minute bursts of rain are common. Those unaccustomed to mosquitoes should be advised that spending 30 seconds to apply insect repellent can prevent a week's worth of scratching. In the fall, expect mild weather, rich foliage, and a relatively dry season. The Bluff City's winters, while not extreme, do see snowfall, with an average of 5.7 inches annually. Depending on Punxsutawney Phil, spring usually begins in late February or early March. For current weather information in the Memphis area, call the **National Weather Service's Memphis branch** at 901-544-0399, ext. 1, or visit their Web site at www.srh.noaa.gov/meg.

THE DELTA

The weather in the Mississippi Delta is similar to that of Memphis, although the flat, rural landscape marks the passage of the seasons in a more dramatic way. Down in the Delta, sweltering summers marked by endless fields of soybeans give way to temperate springs when the rice fields are a vibrant green contrast to endless blues skies. In the cool days of fall, the cotton fields are plump with puffy white cotton bolls, ready for the picking. After the November harvest, the winter winds whip through the barren fields, and the Delta turns a cold and desolate gray.

CONVENTION & VISITORS BUREAUS

Cleveland Tourism Council: 662-843-2712 or 1-800-295-7473; www.visitclevelandms .com; 600 Third St., Cleveland, MS 38732

Clarksdale & Coahoma County Tourism Commission: 662-627-7337 or 1-800-626-3764; www.clarksdaletourism.com; P.O. Box 160, Clarksdale, MS 39614

Greenville Convention & Visitors Bureau: 662-334-2711 or 1-800-467-3582; www.visit greenville.org; 216 S. Walnut St., Greenville, MS 38701

Greenwood Convention & Visitors Bureau: 662-453-9197 or 1-800-748-9064; www .greenwoodms.org; P.O. Drawer 739, Greenwood, MS 38935

Indianola Chamber of Commerce: 662-887-3009 or 1-877-816-7581; www.indianolams .org; P.O. Box 151, Indianola, MS 38751

Jackson Convention & Visitors Bureau: 601-960-1891 or 1-800-354-7695; www.visit jackson.com; 111 E. Capitol St., Ste. 102, Jackson, MS 39201

Memphis Convention & Visitors Bureau: 901-543-5300; www.memphistravel.com; 47 Union Ave., Memphis, TN 38103

Mississippi Delta Tourism Association: 1-877-DELTA-MS; www.visitthedelta.com; P.O. Box 68, Greenville, MS 38701

Tunica Convention & Visitors Bureau: 1-888-488-6422; www.tunicamiss.com; P.O. Box 2739, Tunica, MS 38676

Vicksburg Convention & Visitors Bureau: 601-636-9421 or 1-800-221-3536; www.visit vicksburg.com; 3300 Clay St., Vicksburg, MS 39183

CRIME AND SAFETY

Be aware that crime is a problem in Memphis, and always use common sense. Avoid walking alone at night, especially in less-populated areas. Always park in well-lit places (garages rather than the street, when possible), and don't leave anything of value in your car—that includes keeping CDs, change, sunglasses, coats, and small items out of sight. The city of Memphis also encourages individuals to say no to panhandling. If you want to help, donate money to charities for the homeless instead.

DOCUMENTARIES

Blues Masters—The Essential History of the Blues. Rhino, 2002.
Blues Story. Dir. Jay Levey. Shout Factory, 2003.
Can't You Hear the Wind Howl? The Life and Music of Robert Johnson. Dir. Peter Meyer. Winstar, 1997.
Deep Blues: A Musical Pilgrimage to the Crossroads. Dir. Robert Mugge. Fox Lorber, 2000.
The Fingerpicking Blues of Mississippi John Hurt. Dir. John Sebastian. Homespun Tapes, 2004.
Hard Times: Big George Brock. Dir. Damien Blaylock. Cat Head Presents, 2006.
The Howlin' Wolf Story: The Secret History of Rock & Roll. Dir. Don McGlynn. BMG, 2003.
John Lee Hooker: That's My Story. Dir. Jörg Bundschuh. New Video Group, 2003.
Juke. Dir. Mary Flannery. Yellow Cat Productions, 2007.
Last of the Mississippi Jukes. Dir. Robert Mugge. Starz! Encore Entertainment, 2003.
M for Mississippi: A Road Trip through the Birthplace of the Blues. Dirs. Jeff Konkel and Roger Stolle. Broke & Hungry Records/Cat Head, 2008.
Martin Scorsese Presents the Blues—A Musical Journey. Various directors. PBS, 2003.
Muddy Waters: Can't Be Satisfied. Dirs. Morgan Neville and Robert Gordon. Winstar, 2003.
Muddy Waters: Got My Mojo Working. Rare Performances 1968–1978. Yazoo, 2000.
The Search for Robert Johnson. Dir. Chris Hunt. Sony, 2000.
Son House & Bukka White: Masters of the Country Blues. Dir. Jirí Sequens. Yazoo, 2000.

HOSPITALS

MEMPHIS
Baptist Memorial Hospital—Memphis: 901-226-5000; 6019 Walnut Grove Rd., Memphis, TN 38120
Methodist University Hospital: 901-516-7000; 1265 Union Ave., Memphis, TN 38104

THE DELTA
Delta Regional Medical Center: 662-378-3783; 1400 E. Union St., Greenville, MS 38703
Greenwood Leflore Hospital: 662-459-7000; 1401 River Rd., Greenwood, MS 38930
Mississippi Baptist Medical Center: 1-800-948-6262; 1225 N. State St., Jackson, MS 39202
Northwest Mississippi Regional Medical Center: 662-627-3211; 1970 Hospital Dr., Clarksdale, MS 38614

MAGAZINES AND NEWSPAPERS

The Bolivar Commercial (662-843-4241; www.bolivarcom.com; 821 N. Chrisman Ave., P.O. Box 1050, Cleveland, MS 38732) Cleveland's evening-edition newspaper serves Bolivar and Sunflower Counties in the Mississippi Delta.

The Clarksdale Press Register (662-627-2201; www.pressregister.com; 123 E. Second St., P.O. Box 1119, Clarksdale, MS 38614) This daily newspaper serves Clarksdale and Coahoma County, Mississippi.

The Clarion-Ledger (601-961-7240; www.clarionledger.com; P.O. Box 40, Jackson, MS 39205) This Jackson-based newspaper is Mississippi's second-oldest company and circulates statewide.

The Commercial Appeal (901-529-2345 or 1-800-444-6397; www.commercialappeal .com; 495 Union Ave., Memphis, TN, 38103) Memphis's daily newspaper serves the metro area as well as surrounding counties in Mississippi and Arkansas.

Delta Democrat Times (662-335-1155; www.ddtonline.com; 988 N. Broadway, P.O. Box 1618, Greenville, MS 38701) Based in Greenville, this daily newspaper has been delivering the news since 1868.

Delta Magazine (662-843-2700; www.deltamagazine.com; P.O. Box 117, Cleveland, MS 38732) Launched in 2003, this glossy lifestyle magazine published six times a year focuses on the food, people, and culture of the Mississippi Delta.

The Greenwood Commonwealth (662-453-5312 or 1-800-898-0730; www.gwcommon wealth.com; P.O. Box 8050, Greenwood, MS 38935) Local news for the Greenwood area since 1896.

Jackson Free Press (601-362-6121; www.jacksonfreepress.com; P.O. Box 5067, Jackson, MS 39296) Jackson's alternative paper covers news, arts, events, and music, including frequently updated live-music listings.

Memphis Flyer (901-521-9000; www.memphisflyer.com; 460 Tennessee St., Memphis, TN 38103) Memphis's largest alternative weekly covers news, opinion, and entertainment, and offers the city's most comprehensive event listings.

Memphis Magazine (901-521-9000; www.memphismagazine.com; 460 Tennessee St., Ste. 200, Memphis, TN 38103) This glossy city magazine covers arts, entertainment, dining, news, shopping, and more.

The Vicksburg Post (601-636-4545; www.vicksburgpost.com; 1601-F N. Frontage Rd., P.O. Box 821668, Vicksburg, MS 39182) Vicksburg's daily newspaper since 1883.

WHEN TO GO: SEASONAL EVENTS AND FESTIVALS

Festivals and events in Memphis, and especially the Delta, can often be unpredictable. Some of the smaller festivals may drop off for a year, only to come back at a new location. Dates shift to neighboring months, and new festivals constantly pop up. Bottom line: Always check up-to-date listings before making your plans. For events in Memphis, check the CVB's Web site at www.memphistravel.com/visitors/events. For the Delta, check www.msblues trail.org/festivals.html or www.cathead.biz/livemusic.html. As we've mentioned before, if you're planning on going to the bigger blues fests, like Clarksdale's Juke Joint or Sunflower Fest, or the Arkansas Blues & Heritage Fest in Helena, book a room well in advance, as limited accommodations fill up fast. For more detailed information on most of the events listed in this section, check the Seasonal Events listings within each town's content section.

January
Dr. Martin Luther King Jr.'s Birthday (Memphis). Every year, the National Civil Rights Museum celebrates Dr. King's birthday with educational programs and a special event at the museum on Martin Luther King Jr. day.

Elvis Presley Birthday Celebration (Memphis). Elvis fans descend upon Graceland every January for a slew of events honoring the King's birthday.

February

Beale Street Zydeco Festival (Memphis). Blues gives way to fantastic zydeco music and Creole culture during this weekend festival on Beale.

International Blues Challenge (Memphis). This competition for unsigned blues bands and artists features live performances at various clubs on Beale Street, and the finals at the Orpheum Theatre.

Regions Morgan Keenan Championships and Cellular South Cup (Memphis). Held on the indoor courts at the Racquet Club of Memphis, this annual tournament draws top names in tennis.

March

Memphis International Film Festival (Memphis). Four days of independent film, workshops, and events featuring nearly 100 films from around 20 different countries.

April

Africa in April Cultural Awareness Festival (Memphis). Held at downtown's Robert R. Church Park off Beale Street, this four-day festival celebrates African culture through music, food, performances, arts and crafts, and more.

Dr. Martin Luther King Jr. Memorial (Memphis). The National Civil Rights Museum commemorates the assassination of Dr. Martin Luther King Jr. annually with an event like a march or candlelight vigil.

Juke Joint Festival (Clarksdale). Live blues music on several downtown stages by day, and at Clarksdale's many juke joints by night, plus fair-style fun including pig races and crawfish boils.

Wild Hog Musicfest & Motorcycle Rally (Helena). Motorcycle enthusiasts flock to Helena for three days of live music and bike-centric events.

World Catfish Festival (Belzoni). The Catfish Capital of the World celebrates the town's favorite fish with live blues, jazz, and gospel music, plus a catfish-eating contest, a catfish fry, and the Miss Catfish pageant.

May

Arkansas Delta Family Gospel Family (Helena). Free gospel performances in downtown Helena from regional and national groups.

Blues Music Awards (Memphis). Formerly known as the W. C. Handy Awards, the Blues Foundation's awards are the highest form of recognition within the genre, honoring recordings and performances from the previous year.

Caravan Music Festival (Clarksdale). Held the Saturday after the Blues Music Awards in Memphis, this relatively new festival run by Theo Dasbach (of Theo's Rock 'n' Roll & Blues Heritage Museum) features live blues, rock, pop, and country.

Crossroads Blues Festival (Rosedale). Held the second Saturday of May, this festival features live blues music, plus food, craft vendors, and after-fest music at the Blue Levee.

Memphis In May (Memphis). A fantastic monthlong celebration that includes the three-day Beale Street Music Festival with live music next to the Mississippi River, plus the World Championship Barbecue Cooking Contest and the Sunset Symphony.

June
B. B. King Homecoming Festival (Indianola). For the past three decades, B. B. King has returned to Mississippi to perform a concert in his hometown at Fletcher Park, followed by a nighttime set at Club Ebony.

Bentonia Blues Festival (Bentonia). Held the third Saturday of June outside the Blue Front Café, this festival features live blues, plus arts and crafts, Southern cooking, and a gospel stage in front of City Hall.

Highway 61 Blues Festival (Leland). More than 20 musicians perform on two stages throughout the day at this festival that showcases the talents of local and regional Delta blues players.

Jubilee Jam (Jackson). Downtown Jackson's street festival features three stages where more than 20 acts perform over two days, including national touring acts in a range of genres.

Mother's Best Music Fest (Helena). Presented by the Delta Cultural Center, this free, day-long event held at downtown's Cherry Street Pavilion features live music from various genres, including plenty of blues.

Stanford St. Jude Classic (Memphis). Held at the Tournament Players Club at Southwind, this popular PGA Tour event features top names in golf.

July
Blues On The Bluff (Memphis). WEVL radio (89.9 FM) hosts a day of live blues music overlooking the Mississippi River on the grounds of the Metal Museum.

Mississippi John Hurt Blues and Gospel Festival (Avalon). Held on the grounds of Mississippi John Hurt's former home (now a museum), this small, daylong event features live blues and gospel music, barbecue, and more.

August
Elvis Week (Memphis). A candlelight vigil at the King's final resting place caps off a week of Elvis events that commemorate the anniversary of his death, drawing thousands of Elvis faithful from all over the world.

Memphis Music & Heritage Festival (Memphis). Presented by the Center for Southern Folklore over Labor Day weekend, this two-day festival on downtown's Main Street features live music of various genres on indoor and outdoor stages, plus workshops, cooking demonstrations, and more.

Rhythm on the River Festival (Greenwood). Held on Labor Day weekend at Tallahatchie Flats, this festival (new in 2008) features live blues, jazz, country, and gospel music, plus food, beer, and more.

Sunflower River Blues & Gospel Festival (Clarksdale). One of Mississippi's biggest blues festivals, this free, weekend-long festival draws more than twenty-five thousand fans every year.

September

Farish Street Heritage Festival (Jackson). Held in the Farish Street Historic District, this annual festival features live blues, soul, and gospel music, plus soul food, arts and crafts, and more.

Little Wynn Nelson Street Festival (Greenville). Held the day before the Mississippi Delta Blues & Heritage Festival, this event is a great time to hear live blues music on historic Nelson Street.

Mid-South Fair (Tunica). A local tradition since 1856, this nonprofit fair featuring carnival rides, entertainment, exhibits, contests, fair food, and more moved from Memphis to Tunica County in 2009.

Mississippi Delta Blues & Heritage Festival (Greenville). The second-oldest continuously operating blues festival in the country, this daylong fest features three stages and national acts that have included B. B. King, John Lee Hooker, Bobby Rush, and Stevie Ray Vaughn.

Mississippi Delta Tennessee Williams Festival (Clarksdale). Fifteen-minute front porch plays performed in the historic Tennessee Williams District, plus lectures, plays, dinners, and receptions in honor of Clarksdale's one-time resident.

October

Arkansas Blues & Heritage Festival (Helena). Formerly known as the King Biscuit Blues Festival, this huge, three-day event held on Columbus Day weekend has been drawing more than one hundred thousand blues enthusiasts since 1986.

Delta Day (Tunica). Daylong family festival on Tunica's quaint Main Street includes food, fair-style activities, arts and crafts, a classic-car show, and live music (sometimes blues) at Rivergate Park. Held annually on the last weekend in October.

Hambone Festival (Clarksdale). In celebration of artist-musician Stan Street's birthday, this Halloween weekend festival features live blues music, soul food, and more at Hambone Art Gallery and venues throughout downtown Clarksdale.

Indie Memphis Film Festival (Memphis). Showcasing films that celebrate Southern stories and storytelling, this festival brings together regional filmmakers and nationally known talent.

Pinetop Perkins Annual Homecoming (Clarksdale). Held every year on the Sunday after the Arkansas Blues & Heritage Festival, this one-day event honoring Pinetop Perkins's birthday is a full afternoon of live blues music on Hopson Plantation.

November

Freedom Awards (Memphis). The National Civil Rights Museum presents this award to pay tribute to individuals whose actions depict the spirit of the civil rights movement. Festivities include a public forum and the award celebration; past honorees include Al Gore, Oprah Winfrey, Bill Clinton, and Nelson Mandela.

December

Beale Street New Year's Eve Celebration (Memphis). One of the Memphis's biggest New Year's Eve parties takes place every year on Beale Street.

If Time Is Short

If you have limited time to spend in Memphis, your best bet is to stay downtown, where most of the city's attractions are concentrated. If you only have time to visit one town in the Delta, make it Clarksdale. This Delta hub offers the most consistent opportunities to hear authentic live blues and is home to several historic blues sites and attractions. If catching live blues is number one on your agenda, try to visit during one of the Delta's numerous blues festivals, which include Clarksdale's Juke Joint and Sunflower River Blues and Gospel Festivals. In addition to the lineups on event stages, most juke joints come to life with live music during festival time. The following are a few of our favorite picks in Memphis and throughout the Delta. These blues-centric spots are well worth a visit, even when time is short.

Lodging

Memphis

Madison Hotel (901-333-1200; 79 Madison Ave.) This luxury boutique property brings modern style to downtown Memphis, plus a fantastic rooftop with unbeatable river and city views.

The Peabody Hotel (901-529-4000; 149 Union Ave.) The grand dame of downtown Memphis, this historic hotel's lobby is a bustling social hub where you can catch a glimpse of the world-famous Peabody ducks.

Sleep Inn at Court Square (901-522-9700; 40 N. Front St.) This central downtown hotel on the Main Street trolley line is one of the city's most popular value-minded properties.

Talbot Heirs Guesthouse (901-527-9772; 99 S. Second St.) This unique lodging option offers artsy, apartment-style rooms and personal service in the heart of downtown Memphis.

The Delta

The Alluvian (662-453-2114; 318 Howard St., Greenwood) The Mississippi Delta's most luxurious lodging option, this cosmopolitan boutique hotel in lovely Greenwood is well worth the splurge.

Magnolia Hill Bed and Breakfast (870-338-6874; 608 Perry St., Helena–West Helena) One of several historic B&Bs in Helena, this gorgeous Queen Anne Victorian is located in the heart of the city's quaint historic district.

Poindexter Park Inn (601-944-1392; 803 Deer Park St., Jackson) The owner of this funky inn (who manages local blues chanteuse Dorothy Moore) caters to blues travelers, giving visitors the inside scoop on Jackson's historic blues sites and current live music scene.

The Shack Up Inn (662-624-8329; 001 Commissary Circle, Clarksdale) Blues enthusiasts flock here to stay in an authentic sharecropper shack on historic Hopson Plantation.

Cultural Attractions

MEMPHIS

Beale Street (downtown Memphis) A trip to Memphis wouldn't be complete without experiencing historic Beale Street, where live blues pours out of endless clubs and partiers pack the street.

Graceland (1-800-238-2000; 3734 Elvis Presley Blvd.) Tour the home of Elvis Presley, where you can gawk at the "jungle room," step aboard the King's private jet, and pay your respects at his grave site.

Memphis Rock 'n' Soul Museum (901-205-2533; 191 Beale St.) This fantastic Smithsonian Institute museum takes an in-depth look at the city's rich musical heritage, from the cotton fields to the birth of rock 'n' roll, and beyond.

Stax Museum of American Soul Music (901-946-2535; 926 E. McLemore Ave.) Head down to Soulsville, USA to learn about the story of legendary Stax Records and see Isaac Hayes's tricked-out Superfly Cadillac El Dorado.

Sun Studio (901-521-0664; 706 Union Ave.) See where rock 'n' roll was born and legends like Elvis, Johnny Cash, Carl Perkins, Roy Orbison, and many more recorded.

THE DELTA

The Delta Blues Museum (662-627-6820; 1 Blues Alley, Clarksdale) Housed in Clarksdale's old train depot, this blues collection is home to everything from Muddy Waters's cabin to the sign from the Three Forks Store, where Robert Johnson was allegedly poisoned.

Ground Zero (662-621-9009, 0 Blues Alley, Clarksdale) Morgan Freeman's blues club in downtown Clarksdale is one of the Delta's most reliable spots to hear live blues.

Po' Monkey's Lounge (Merigold) While live music may be a rarity here, this authentic juke joint gem throws a heck of a Thursday-night party in a shack on a rural country road.

Red's Lounge (395 Sunflower Ave., Clarksdale) Located down the street from the historic Riverside Hotel (where legendary blueswoman Bessie Smith took her final breath), Clarksdale's real-deal juke joint packs 'em in for authentic Delta blues most weekends.

Robert Johnson's Grave (Little Zion Missionary Baptist Church, Greenwood) Of Robert Johnson's three grave sites in the Mississippi Delta, this one is widely regarded as the bluesman's true resting place. It's also the most picturesque of the three sites.

Restaurants

MEMPHIS

The Arcade Restaurant (901-526-5757; 540 S. Main St.) Stroll around the historic South Main Arts District, then grab lunch at this retro gem dating back to 1919 that's appeared in numerous films.

Four Way Restaurant (901-507-1519; 998 Mississippi Blvd.) Located near the Stax Museum, this longtime soul food favorite was once frequented by luminaries like Martin Luther King Jr.

Gus's Fried Chicken (901-527-4877; 310 S. Front St.) This beloved downtown chicken shack serves up the city's favorite spicy fried chicken in a no-frills space with juke-joint style.

The Rendezvous (901-523-2746; 52 S. Second St.) In a city with a slew of legendary barbecue restaurants, this downtown spot remains a favorite for its dry ribs and festive atmosphere.

THE DELTA

Doe's Eat Place (662-334-3315; 502 Nelson St., Greenville) The neighborhood is rough around the edges, and the funky atmosphere is as no-frills as it gets, but if you're looking for one of the best steaks in America, Doe's is well worth a trip to Greenville.

Lusco's (662-453-5365; 722 Carrollton Ave., Greenwood) A local institution since 1933, this old-school spot features fantastic steaks and seafood prepared in Lusco's famous sauce, plus curtained dining booths that date back to Prohibition.

Madidi (662-627-7770; 164 Delta Ave., Clarksdale) Co-owned by Morgan Freeman, this upscale dining gem in downtown Clarksdale is one of the Delta's few fine-dining establishments.

White Front Café (662-759-3842; 902 Main St., Rosedale) You can't leave the Delta without trying a hot tamale, and this modest spot serves up some of Mississippi's best.

General Index

Lodging by Price

Inexpensive: Up to $90
Moderate: $90 to $130
Expensive: $130 to $225
Very Expensive:$225 and up

Memphis

Inexpensive

Best Western West Memphis Inn, 39
Clarion Hotel Airport/Graceland Area, 41
Comfort Suites I-240 East-Airport, 44
Courtyard by Marriott Memphis Airport, 42
Days Inn West Memphis, 39
Econo Lodge West Memphis, 39
Fairfield Inn & Suites Memphis—I-240 & Perkins, 44
Hampton Inn Memphis—I-240 at Thousand Oaks, 44
Homestead Studio Suites, 42
Howard Johnson, 39
Kings Court Motel, 38
Memphis Marriott—East, 44
Motel 6 (Midtown), 40
Motel 6 (West Memphis), 39
Quality Inn (West Memphis), 39
Quality Inn Airport/Graceland Area, 42
Radisson Hotel Memphis Airport, 42
Ramada Plaza—Mt. Moriah Rd. & I-240, 44
Red Roof Inn, 40
Relax Inn, 39
Sleep Inn—American Way, 44
Super 8 Memphis, 38

Moderate

Courtyard by Marriott—Park Avenue, 42
Days Inn at Graceland, 40–41
Doubletree Hotel Memphis, 42
Embassy Suites Memphis, 42–43
Extended Stay America—Quail Hollow, 43
Gen X Inn, 39
Hampton Inn & Suites Memphis—Shady Grove, 43
Hampton Inn—Poplar, 43
Hilton Memphis, 43
Holiday Inn Express Memphis Medical Center
  Midtown, 39–40
Holiday Inn Select (East Memphis), 43
Holiday Inn Select Memphis Airport, 42
Homewood Suites by Hilton, 43
La Quinta Inn & Suites, 43
Park Place Hotel, 44
Residence Inn—Memphis East, 44
Staybridge Suites, 44

Moderate-Expensive

Sleep Inn at Court Square, 37
Talbot Heirs Guesthouse, 37–38

Moderate-Very Expensive

Elvis Presley's Heartbreak Hotel at Graceland, 41

Expensive

Comfort Inn Downtown, 30
Crowne Plaza Hotel Memphis, 31
Doubletree Hotel Memphis Downtown, 31
Holiday Inn University of Memphis, 40
Memphis Marriott Downtown, 34–35
Westin Memphis Beale Street, 38

Expensive-Very Expensive

Hampton Inn & Suites at Peabody Place, 31–32
Holiday Inn Select Downtown Memphis, 32
Residence Inn Memphis Downtown, 35–36
Springhill Suites by Marriott, 37

Very Expensive

Inn at Hunt Phelan, 32–33
Lauderdale Courts, 33
Madison Hotel, 33–34
The Peabody, 35
River Inn of Harbor Town, 36–37

Clarksdale

Inexpensive

Budget Inn, 138
Comfort Inn, 138
Econo Lodge, 138
Executive Inn, 138
Riverside Hotel, 134–36
Royal Inn, 138
Shack Up Inn and Cotton Gin Inn, 136, 138
Southern Inn, 138
Uptown Motor Inn, 139

Moderate-Expensive

Blues Hound Flat, 132–33
Delta Cotton Company Apartments, 133–34
Loft at Hopson Plantation, 134

Expensive

Big Pink Guesthouse, 131–32

Northern Delta

Inexpensive

Best Western Inn (Helena), 180
Crown Inn Motel, 180
Holiday Star Motel, 181
Isle of Capri Casino, 181
Motel 6 (Helena), 181
Sands Motel, 181
Super 7 (Helena), 181

Dining by Price

Inexpensive: Up to $15
Moderate: $15 to $30
Expensive: $30 to $65
Very Expensive:$65 and up

Memphis

Inexpensive
Alcenia's, 79–80
Arcade Restaurant, 80–81
Barksdale Restaurant, 95
Blue Plate Café, 107
Brother Junipers, 96–97
Cozy Corner, 99
Cupboard Restaurant, 100
Dyer's Burgers, 84–85
Four Way Restaurant, 105–6
Gus's Fried Chicken, 87
Huey's, 101–2
Jim Neely's Interstate Bar-B-Que, 106
The Little Tea Shop, 88–89

Inexpensive-Moderate
The Bar-B-Q Shop, 94–95
Café Ole, 97–98
Central BBQ, 98–99
Corky's, 107–8
Flying Fish, 86
Germantown Commissary, 108
Harry's Detour, 101
Neely's BBQ, 102
Soul Fish, 104

Moderate
Big Foot Lodge, 82
Café 1912, 97
Dish, 100
Do Sushi, 100–101
Marlowe's Ribs & Restaurant, 106–7
Pearl's Oyster House, 91
The Rendezvous, 91–92
Sekisui, 102–3

Moderate-Expensive
Beauty Shop, 95–96
Blue Fish, 96
Bluefin Edge Cuisine and Sushi Bar, 82
Café 61, 83
Circa, 84
Majestic Grille, 89
McEwen's on Monroe, 90
Spindini, 92–93
Tsunami, 104–5

Moderate-Very Expensive
Stella, 93

Expensive
Automatic Slim's Tonga Club, 81
Butcher Shop, 83
Encore, 85
Itta Bena, 88
Texas de Brazil, 93–94

Expensive-Very Expensive
Felicia Suzanne's, 85–86
Grill 83, 86–87
Inn at Hunt Phelan Restaurant & Veranda Grill, 87–88
Mesquite Chophouse, 90–91

Clarksdale

Inexpensive
Abe's Bar-B-Q, 158–59
Delta Amusement Café, 159–60
Dutch Oven, 160
Hick's World Famous Hot Tamales & More, 161

Inexpensive-Moderate
Chamoun's Rest Haven, 159

Moderate
Ramon's, 162
The Ranchero, 163

Expensive
Rust Restaurant, 163

Expensive-Very Expensive
Madidi, 162

Northern Delta

Inexpensive
Blue and White, 174
Granny Dee's Homestyle Cooking, 186–87
Pasquale's Tamales, 187–88
Uncle Henry's Place Inn & Restaurant, 190

Inexpensive-Moderate
Hollywood Café, 174–75
Olivers' Restaurant, 187

Inexpensive-Expensive
River Road, 188–89

Expensive
Kathryn's on Moon Lake, 189–90
Uncle Henry's Place Inn & Restaurant, 190

Dining by Cuisine